Product Data Interfaces in CAD/CAM Applications

Design, Implementation and Experiences

Edited by
J. Encarnação R. Schuster E. Vöge

With 147 Figures

Springer-Verlag
Berlin Heidelberg New York Tokyo

Prof. Dr.-Ing. José Encarnação
Institut für Informationsverwaltung
und Interaktive Systeme
FB 20 – TH Darmstadt
Alexanderstraße 24
D-6100 Darmstadt

Dr.-Ing. Richard Schuster
BMW AG
CAD/CAM-Systeme (FS-30)
Postfach 400240
D-8000 München 40

Dr.-Ing. Ernst Vöge
BMW AG
FS-3
Postfach 400240
D-8000 München 40

ISBN-13: 978-3-642-82428-9 e-ISBN-13: 978-3-642-82426-5
DOI: 10.1007/978-3-642-82426-5

Library of Congress Cataloging in Publication Data.
Product data interfaces in CAD/CAM applications.
(Symbolic computation. Computer graphics)
"Papers presented in a seminar of the ZGDV (Zentrum für Graphische Datenverarbeitung) . . . held at the Technical University Darmstadt from December 1984 to February 1985" –
Includes bibliographies.
1. CAD/CAM systems – Congresses. I. Encarnação, José Luis. II. Schuster, R. (Richard), 1944 –. III. Vöge, E. IV. Zentrum für Graphische Datenverarbeitung (Germany) V. Series. TS155.6.P758 1986 670'.28'5 86-11920

Softcover reprint of the hardcover 1st edition 1986

Typesetting, printing and binding: Konrad Triltsch, Graphischer Betrieb, 8700 Würzburg

2145/3140-5 4 3 2 1 0

Preface

Interest in product data exchange and interfaces in the CAD/CAM area is steadily growing. The rapidly increasing graphics applications in engineering and science has led to a great variety of heterogeneous hardware and software products. This has become a major obstacle in the progress of systems integration. To improve this situation CAD/CAM users have called for specification and implementation of standardized product data interfaces.

These needs resulted in the definition of preliminary standards in this area. Since 1975 activities have been concentrated on developing standards for three major areas:

- computer graphics,
- sculptured surfaces, and
- data exchange for engineering drawings.

The Graphical Kernel System (GKS) has been accepted as an international standard for graphics programming in 1984, Y14.26M (IGES) was adopted as an American Standard in 1981 and the VDA Surface Interface (VDAFS) has been accepted by the German National Standardization Institute (DIN NAM 96.4).

Although considerable progress has been achieved, the complexity of the subject and the dynamics of the CAD/CAM-development still calls for more generality and compatibility of the interfaces. This has resulted in an international discussion on further improvements of the standards.

The major goal of this book is to bring together the different views and experiences in industry and university in the area of Product Data Interfaces, thereby contributing to the ongoing work in improving the state of the art.

The book contains papers presented in a seminar of the ZGDV (Zentrum für Graphische Datenverarbeitung) in cooperation with industry held at the Technical University Darmstadt from December 1984 to February 1985.

Chapter 1 focuses on the necessity of product data interfaces within the applications framework and on the basic methods of computer graphics. The entire scope of applications, especially in the automotive industry, is shown.

Design, implementation and experience of specific interfaces for graphic systems (GKS), product definition data, drawings and sculptured surfaces (IGES, VDAFS) are presented in Chaps. 2, 3 and 4. Special consideration has been given to VDAFS since a lot of work has been done in industry in this area.

The growing importance of specification and validation of software products supporting the interfacing process has to be acknowledged. Three contributions in Chap. 5 concentrate on this matter.

Chapter 6 contains an outlook on further developments in the area of product data interfaces.

The editors thank the authors for their valuable contributions which stem from their expertise and experience. Thanks also to the Technical University Darmstadt and to the Zentrum für Graphische Datenverarbeitung for their support, and especially to the manager of the ZGDV for the organization of the seminar from which this book resulted.

Darmstadt/München, May 1986

J. Encarnação
R. Schuster
E. Vöge

Contents

Chapter 1

Introduction

Reference Models, Interfaces, Integration Issues

1.1 Goals in the Application of CAD Interfaces

E. Vöge

1.1.1 Global Objectives

1.1.1.1 Introduction

Within a few years of the Massachusetts Institute of Technology (MIT) introducing the concept CAD – Computer Aided Design – in the 1950s, a considerable range of diverse applications were being developed. These include not only applications in the representation and analysis of geometrical contexts (CAD), but also systems for calculation processes (CAE, mainly using the finite element method – FEM), systems for test automation (data acquisition of test systems in real time operation), and systems for computer aided manufacturing (CAM, e.g., automatically programmed tool – APT).

The main goals were the elaboration of basic concepts in the form of solutions to principles as well as the demonstration of technical feasibility. The application of computer assisted processes for the entire range of engineering problems was not the primary goal, although the significance of the integration of various systems for a complete computer assisted application was recognized very early.

If a resume of the work during the first ten years (1960–1970) is made, it may be said that the technical concepts developed at that time have proved operable for immediate application, and have laid the foundations for subsequent research work. At the same time, however, the tasks of

- systems integration,
- economy, and
- integration in management organisation

have still proven to be key problem areas to be rethought and solved. In this context, CAD interfaces assume a major significance in systems integration.

1.1.1.2 Ranges of Application for the CAD Interfaces

Figure 1.1.1 summarizes the tasks in engineering from the initial idea of a product to the commencement of its manufacture. Figure 1.1.2 shows a rough sketch of the more traditional course of development.

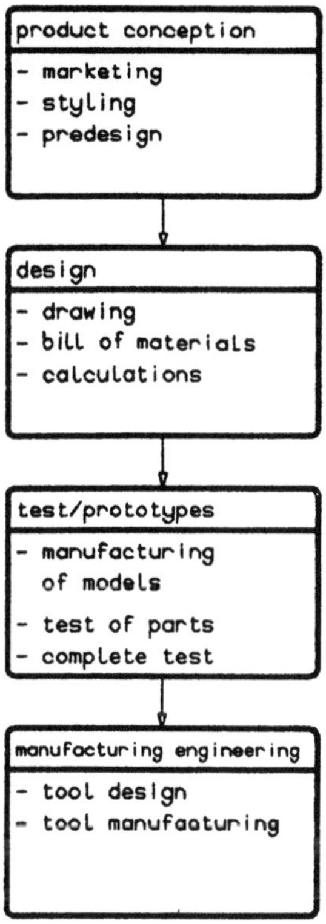

Fig. 1.1.1. Engineering tasks (without manufacturing and quality control)

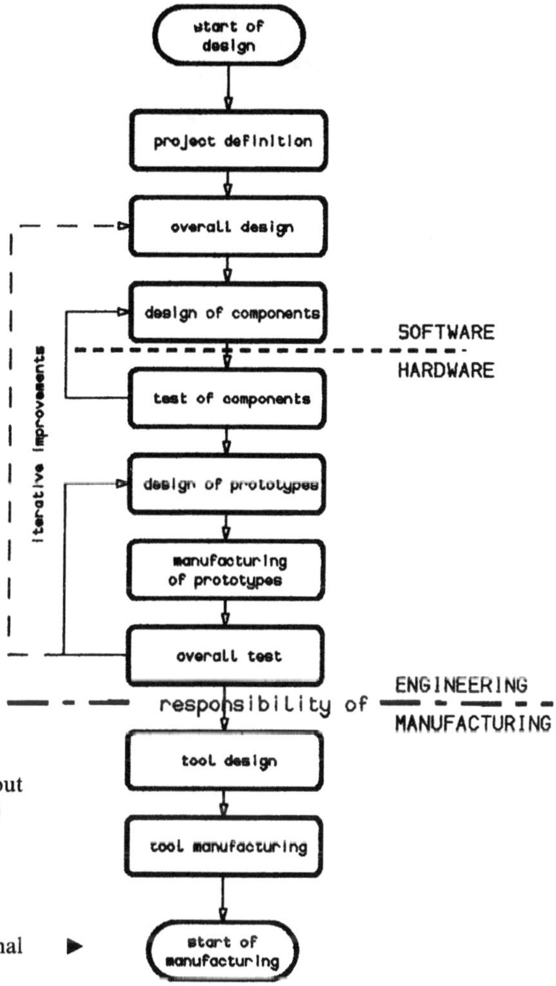

Fig. 1.1.2. Schema of the conventional design process ▶

1.1.1.3 Global Objectives for the Application of Computer Assisted Systems and of CAD Interfaces

Figure 1.1.2 illustrates that, when verifying design decisions using test results, the development quality of the product can only be improved at the end of the scheduled development time in order to meet the original design goals. This correlation is shown qualitatively in Fig. 1.1.3 (lower line). If on the other hand, the fixed product properties resulting from design decisions are shown as a function of time (upper line), there is rather the opposite tendency.

First, many decisions are based on assumptions and experience which in the course of product development can turn out to be wrong, thereby negatively affecting the:

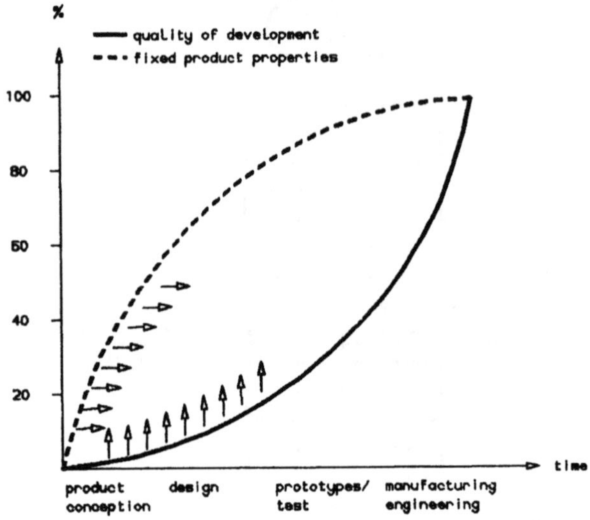

Fig. 1.1.3. Quality of development versus product features fixed

- quality of the product,
- scheduled development time,
- budget caused by unplanned tests and engineering changes.

It is in the interest of the company to reduce this discrepancy between development quality and fixed product properties. In view of this situation computer assisted processes (Computer Aided Engineering (CAE) systems) can reduce the above mentioned effects by being employed in early phases to verify design decisions (cf. Fig. 1.1.3). This is possible since their application requires no test hardware (e.g. calculation processes as a supplement to test processes, [1]). The application of computer assisted systems increases the flexibility of development in response to engineering changes. The determination of a product's properties can be deferred, thereby diminishing the discrepancy between development quality and fixed product properties. The advantages of the employment of computer assisted processes are (cf. Fig. 1.1.4):

- product improvement,
- reduced development time, and
- cost reduction caused by engineering changes.

These factors justify the high costs of computer assisted systems.

A quantification of these advantages is in most cases only partially possible, and only after having gained experience with the application of these systems.

The primary objective is therefore to clarify the above-mentioned decisive advantages and to establish an implementation strategy while simultaneously considering the integration problem within a complete chain of tasks (cf. Fig. 1.1.4).

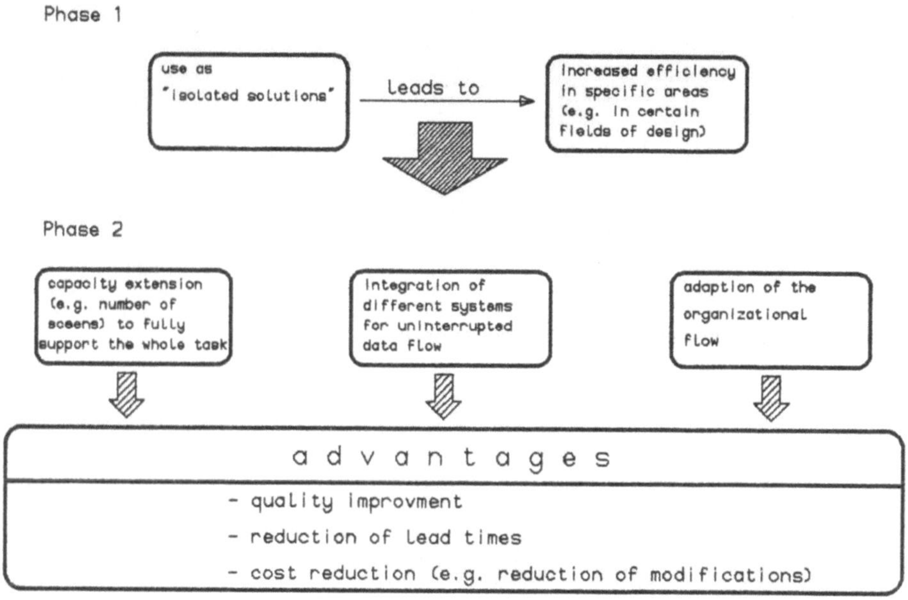

Fig. 1.1.4. Targets for the use of computer aided systems

The availability of CAD interfaces is an important prerequisite for the integration of computer assisted processes.

1.1.2 Application of CAD Interfaces in Computer Assisted Processes

1.1.2.1 Product Concept

The tasks of the early stage of product development are not well suited to the establishment of formalisms with respect to computer applications. They are dependent on experience with corresponding earlier product developments and hence are difficult to computerize. However, there is considerable potential for a successful application of computers, provided that

- the above-mentioned limitations can be overcome,
- the subsequent extensive development phase (e.g. construction/test) can be reduced, and
- the continuity of data flow is given.

In general, this is not the situation today and hence applications in this project phase should predominantly be viewed as research projects.

The present technical level of computer assisted processes in the phase of product conception can be illustrated with the following applications:

- Analysis of automotive concepts using simulation and optimization processes on the basis of mathematical parameter models [2].

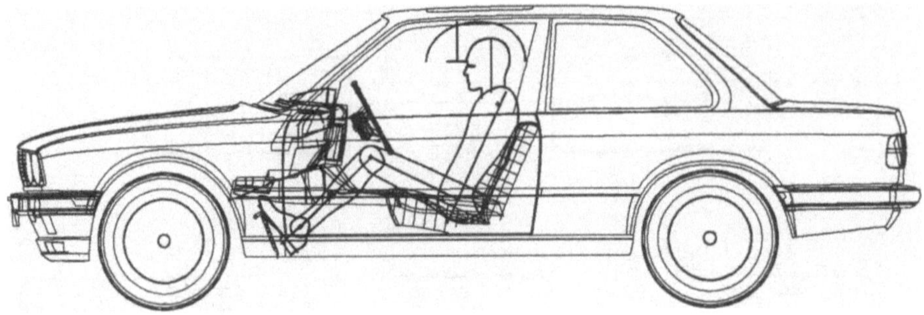

Fig. 1.1.5. Ergonomic model of car interior geometry

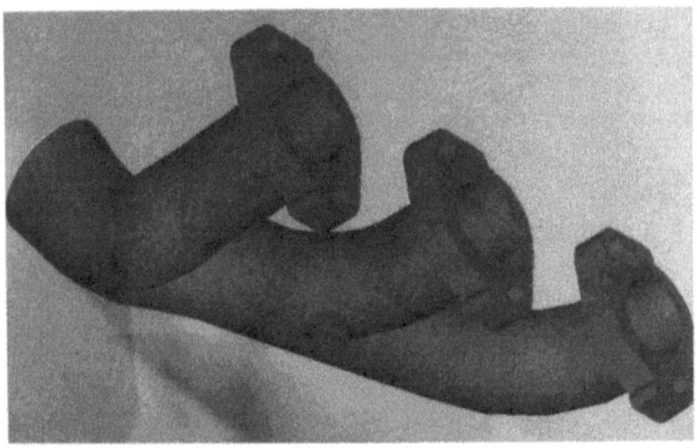

Fig. 1.1.6. Visualization of an exhaust manifold in raster technology

- Determination of car interior geometry under consideration of ergonomic requirements (CAD models of the human body [3]) (cf. Fig. 1.1.5).
- Support of subjective design assessments by means of visualization techniques (raster technology) [4] (cf. Fig. 1.1.6).

The transfer of computer data gained in this early stage of product development to systems in subsequent development stages is not generally practiced today. The data from preceding models are currently being used but not via a standardized interface.

1.1.2.2 Construction, Calculation, Testing

During this stage of product development the geometrical properties of the product have to be determined in such detail that the subsequent production planning and manufacturing can commence.

In the past, the elaboration of two-dimensional drawings was the major field of application of CAD systems. Today, the internal three-dimensional representation is the key requirement for integrated computer assistance.

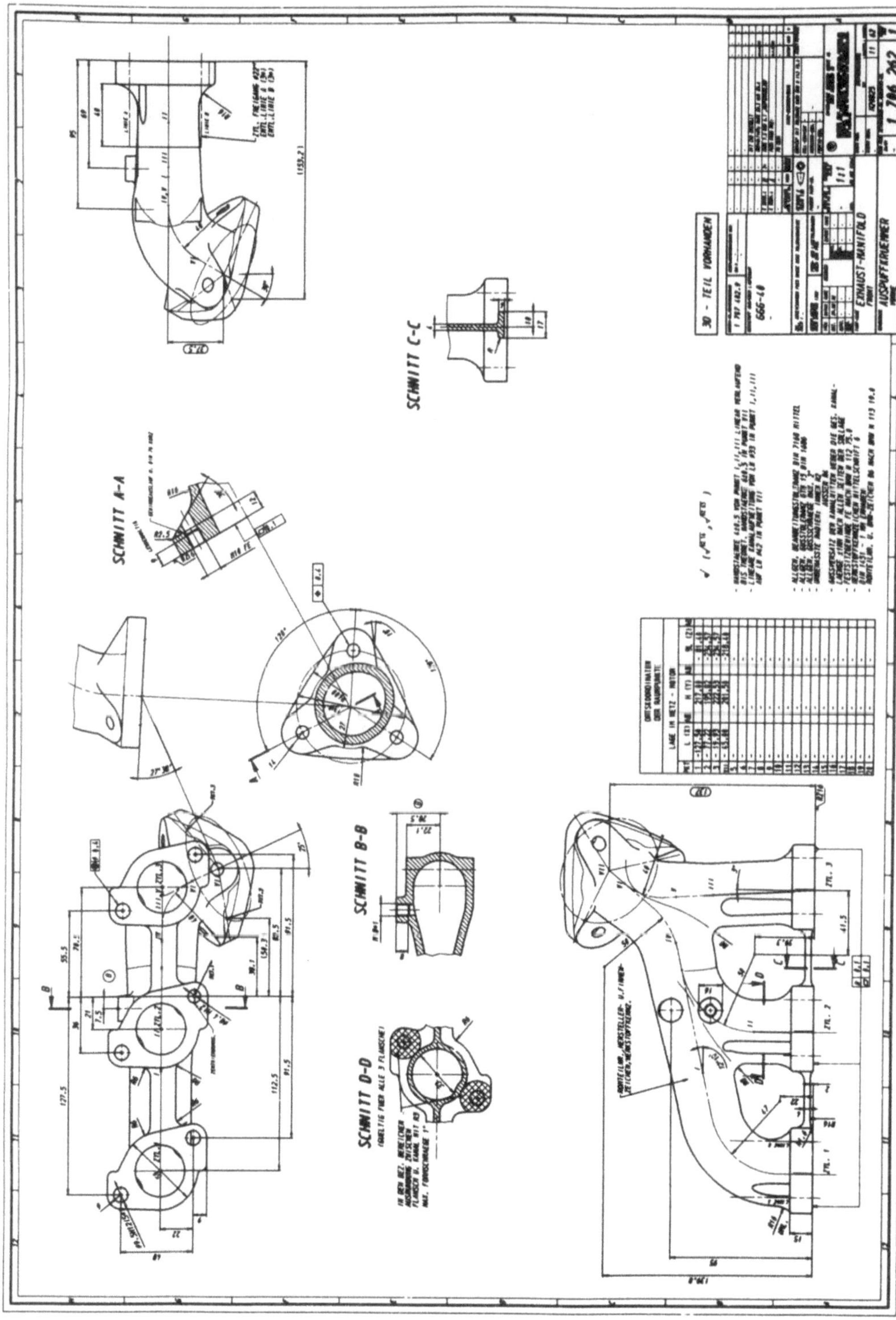

Fig. 1.1.7. Technical drawing of an exhaust manifold

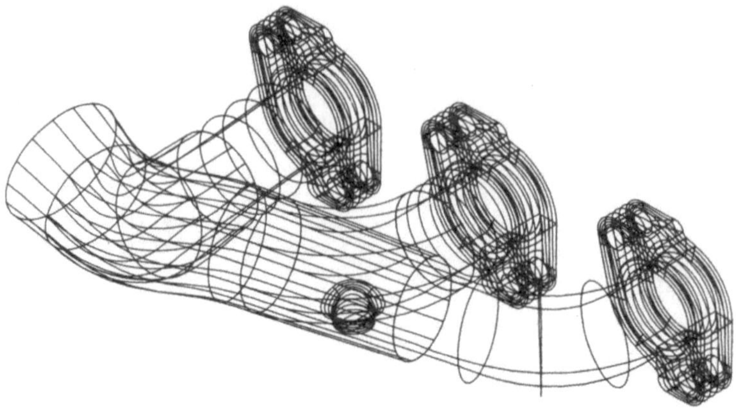

Fig. 1.1.8. Three-dimensional surface model of an exhaust manifold

The three-dimensional geometric model can be used for the following tasks:

- determination of geometrical forms,
- proof of geometrical compatibility (installation examination),
- determination of physical properties,
- elaboration of workshop drawings for manufacturing,
- NC-manufacturing, and
- representation of the model with special visualization techniques (e.g. for spare parts catalogues).

An example of an integrated CAD procedure is shown below. Using the centre lines as base lines and a given cross-sectional form, a three-dimensional wireframe and a surface model of an exhaust manifold is produced (Fig. 1.1.8). This is done by moving the cross-sectional contours along the base lines (piping).

The geometrical model can not only be used for installation examinations and for the elaboration of technical drawings (cf. Fig. 1.1.7), but also as a basis for calculation processes in conjunction with other CAE systems. This, however, requires the existence of a suitable interface.

The determination of the first eigenvalues and -forms of a given structure can be made on the basis of the finite element method (FEM). The elaboration of a suitable computational model for this purpose requires a great deal of work and should be supported by interactive preprocessors based on the geometrical model. The major problem here is the idealization of a structure adequate to the problem. Therefore, it may be useful to carry out a verification by means of experiments. For this purpose modal analysis may be employed in which the structure to be examined is triggered by pulses. Transfer functions, eigenvalues and -forms can be computed from the measured values. Both processes, FEM-analysis and modal analysis, can be combined, if only a part of the structure is available for the experiment.

1.1.2.3 Manufacturing Engineering

The more precise are the engineering documents of the preceeding stages of development, the easier it is to continue with the assistance of a computer. An

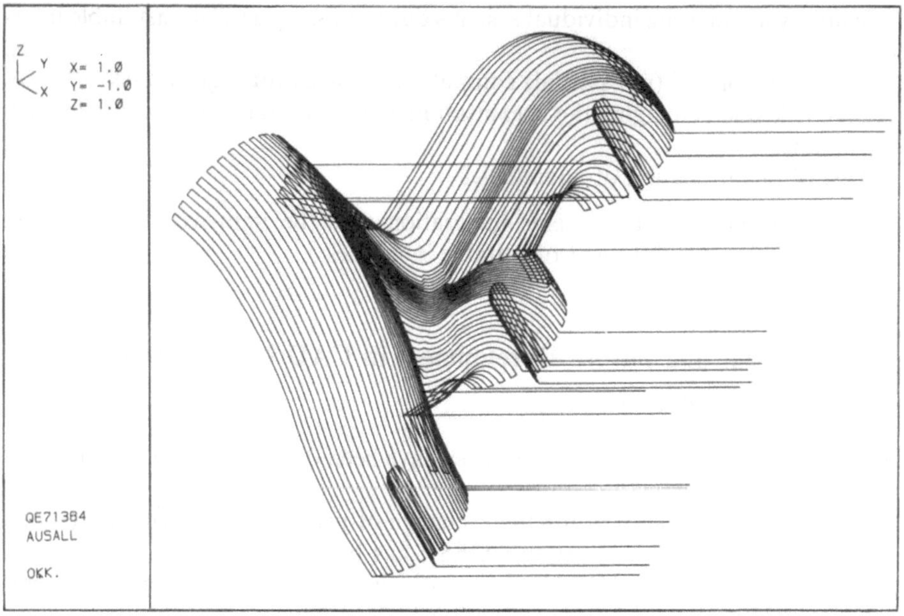

Fig. 1.1.9. NC-machining pathes of an exhaust manifold

example with sculptured surfaces is shown in Fig. 1.1.9. It depicts the milling lines of the above-mentioned exhaust manifold needed for the NC manufacturing of a model, derived from the surface model.

A large application field for computer assisted processing of sculptured surfaces is car body parts (cf. [5]). Here, an uninterrupted automatic data exchange between individual enterprises is necessary since tool production for body parts is generally done in co-operation with other enterprises [6].

1.1.2.4 Assessment in Relation to Objectives

If the present level of application and concatenation of computer assisted processes is assessed using the standards and objectives described in Chap. 1, three different forms of application can be differentiated:

- projects without direct economical use (e.g., examples from Chap. 2.1) (1)
- projects whose results are useful for the development of products, but whose contribution to the above-mentioned objectives are marginal (2)
- projects with considerable contribution to the objectives (e.g., processing of sculptured surfaces in car body parts, Chap 2.3 [5]; systematic application of the FEM method for body structures). (3)

The majority of present-day projects belong to category 2, where, for example, CAD systems are used in an isolated manner (the elaboration of drawings).

The main reasons why integrated projects have been successfully carried out in only a very few cases are the:

- inability to integrate individual systems due to missing and/or unsuitable interfaces
- high costs for full (not partial) computer assistance for a given task
- high risk when changing the organisation while simultaneously respecting target dates
- lack of quantification of advantages

It becomes evident that systems integration must be improved in the future through further development of suitable interfaces.

1.1.3 Current and Future Development in CAD Interfaces from the Application Standpoint

Recently neutral CAD system interfaces have been developed on a national and international basis.

In the USA, a standard for the exchange of product definition data (Initial Graphics Exchange Specification (IGES)) has been developed (cf. Fig. 1.1.10). The basic concept of the IGES interface, which originated at Boeing, was accepted in 1981 as American standard ANSI Y14.26M. Since then, it has been continously developed in the IGES Committee of the National Bureau of Standards.

Initially IGES was designed to exchange CAD drawings for mechanical engineering and for simple 3D wireframe and surface models. Version 2.0 of the IGES standard issued in 1983, included the first steps for the transfer of FEM models and electrical diagrams [7].

Despite the development tendencies IGES, with its structure and elements, is tailor-made for the CAD systems of the 70s [8]. A revision of the standard to accommodate the:

- adaptation to requirements of todays applications,
- adaptation to modern CAD systems,
- improvement of data compactness,
- minimization of processing requirements, and
- increase in quality and quantity of the product definition data,

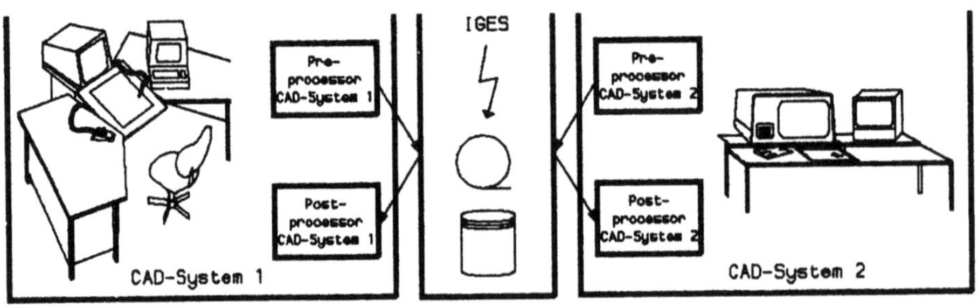

Fig. 1.1.10. Principle of data exchange via IGES

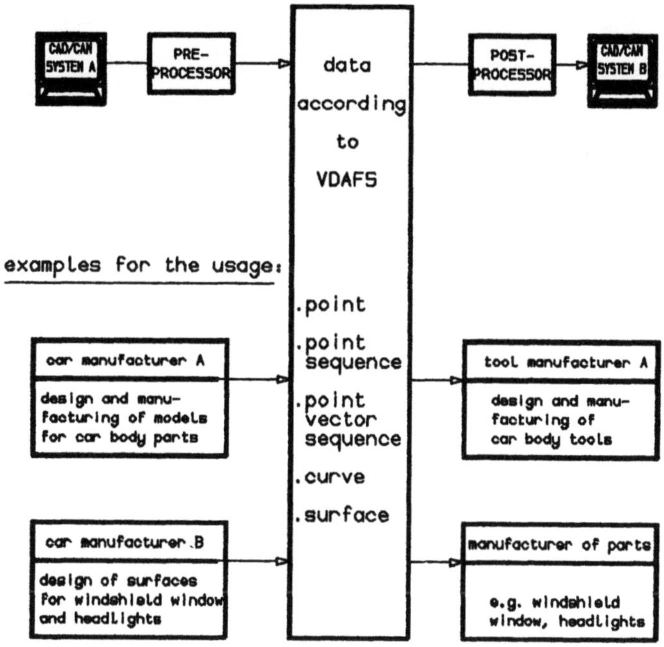

Fig. 1.1.11. Application of the VDAFS-interface

is being worked on in ISO TC 184 SC4 under the project designation STEP (*S*tandard for *T*ransfer and *E*xchange of *P*roduct Model Data) in conjunction with various national standardisation commissions.

The VDA surface interface (so-called VDAFS) was developed in the Federal Republic of Germany by the Association of the Car Industry (VDA) [6], for the exchange of sculptured surface data of car body parts. This specification was adopted at the end of 1984 (cf. Fig. 1.1.11) by the German Standards Institute under DIN 66 301.

Due to its reduced range of elements and its clear and simple specification of the standard the VDAFS is also being employed successfully outside of the automotive industry.

Figure 1.1.12 shows many CAE systems today that have implemented IGES and/or VDAFS processors. The internal and external data exchange via these interfaces is, however, still in the test stage and only special applications transfer data economically at present.

IGES problems stem not only from insufficiencies in concept but also from bad processor implementations. A short-term improvement in data transfer would be conceivable as a result of alterations and extensions of existing processors.

In view of the fact that it will take years until a satisfactory and comprehensive solution can be accepted as a world wide standard, the author's opinion is that a level concept, developed successively and modular in form, must be established for the most important problems (e.g. surface data VDAFS, three-dimensional

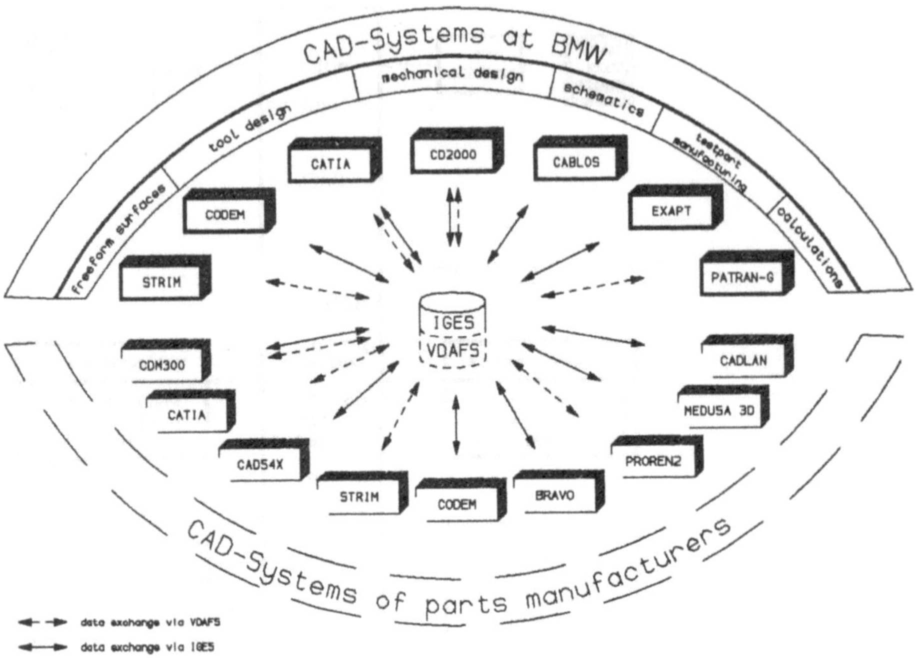

Fig. 1.1.12. CAD-data-exchange at BMW via standard-interfaces

vertex models, drawing exchange, etc.). A stategy for the definition and implementation of the individual levels must not only consider aspects of technical feasibility and scientific precision at each level, but must also aim to maximise the potential advantages.

1.1.4 References

1. Lemon, J, Tolani, SK, Klosterman, A: Integration and Implementation of CAE and related Manufacturing Capabilities into Mechanical Product Development Process. GI-Jahrestagung (1980)
2. Braess, HH: Berechnung, ein wichtiger Teilbereich der Fahrzeugentwicklung. VDI-Bericht Nr. 444 (1982)
3. NN: SAMMIE – Users Manual, First Edition. Compeda, Hertfordshire, England
4. Warn, DR: Lighting Controls for Synthetic Images. Computer Graphics, vol 17, no 3 (1983)
5. Vöge, E: Zur Integration von CAE-Systemen. VDI-Bericht Nr. 501 (1983)
6. Verband der Automobilindustrie (VDA): VDA-Flächenschnittstelle, Version 10. Frankfurt VDA (1983)
7. American National Standard: Digital Representation for Communication Product Definition Data. ANSI Y14.26M (1981)
8. Schuster, R, Trippner, D: Anforderungen an eine Schnittstelle zur Übertragung produktdefinierender Daten zwischen verschiedenen CAD/CAM-Systemen. GI-Jahrestagung, Braunschweig (1984)

1.2 Interfaces and Data Transfer Formats in Computer Graphics Systems

J. Encarnação

1.2.1 Introduction

Based on R. McNall [1] a Graphics System may be seen as a computer-aided environment supporting the application program. The basic elements associated with it are (see Fig. 1.2.1):

- Operator (User)
- Graphics Support System (Services)
- Other User Interface Support System (Services)
- Application Functions
- Generic Action Routines
- Data Base

The kernel for the communication between the different parts of such a system is composed of the different data items associated with the communicating elements.

From the point of view of the user operating such a graphics support system, a simple functional model, again taken from R. McNall [1], may be given (see Fig. 1.2.2) which shows the functional decomposition of the model presented in Fig. 1.2.1. The Graphics System is then based on the following basic functional components:

- User (Operator of the Computer-Aided Environment based on a Graphics Support System)
- Graphics
  - Graphics Viewing
  - Request Processing
  - Graphics Metafiles

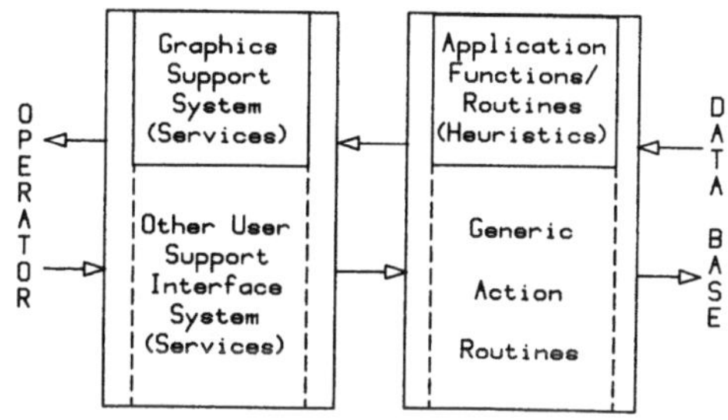

Fig. 1.2.1. Graphics reference Model. (Source: R. McNall [1])

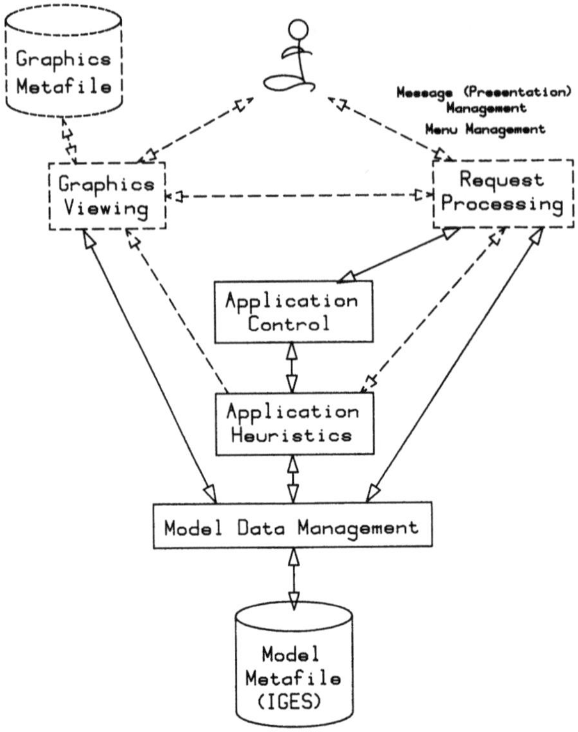

Fig. 1.2.2. Functionality of a graphics system. (Source: R. McNall [1])

- Model
  - Model Metafiles (Design Data)
  - Model Data Management
- Application
  - Control
  - Heuristics

This model implies a clean separation between application system, application control, graphics support system and modèl data management functions. This functionality again is based on the transfer of the associated items stored in the corresponding metafiles (graphics, model).

1.2.2 Data Interfaces

The models shown in Fig. 1.2.1 and Fig. 1.2.2 show the basic functionality of a Graphics System as a computer-aided environment supporting the application program. P. Bono introduced in [2], a model showing the different data interfaces

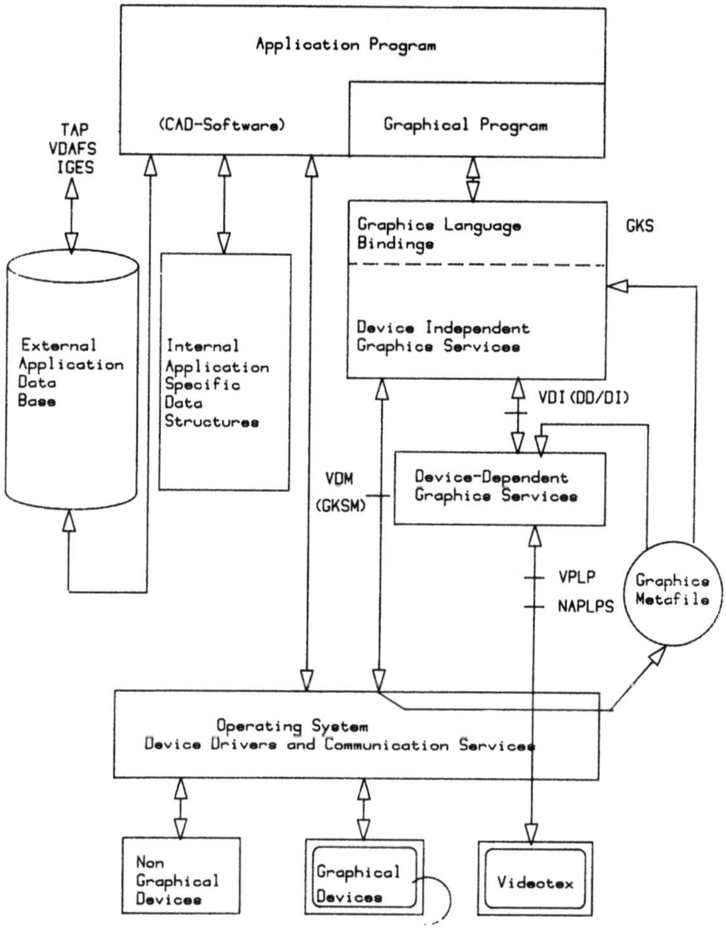

Fig. 1.2.3. Standards and interfaces in a graphics system. (Source: P. Bono [2])

in such a system for which standards have been developed or are in the process of being developed (Fig. 1.2.3); these are:

1) GKS and GKS language bindings; this is also the interface for other graphics standards under discussion (e.g. PHIGS);
2) Virtual Device Interface (VDI);
3) Virtual Device Metafile (VDM);
4) North American Presentation Level Protocol Syntax (NAPLS); this is simply the videotex interface (the European alternative to NAPLPS is VPLP);
5) The Initial Graphic Exchange Specification (IGES) for the interchange of product data in connection with the graphics model; in the Federal Republic of Germany experts have been working with the same goal and have developed VDAFS and TAP;

6) At the application layer special efforts have been made to introduce graphics in the languages for the processing of text (CLPT) and also to develop layers for presentation graphics on the top of graphics standards like GKS.

The coherent and efficient integration of all these standards and developments into a highly functional Graphics Support System is one of the technical goals for the future in the area of Computer Graphics System Design.

Specifically for GKS, three other main activities should be reported

a) the VLSI support of GKS implementations
b) the validation of GKS implementations
c) the design of GKS-based applications for open communication systems (e.g. LANs)

1.2.3 The Standards for Graphics Programming (GKS, 3D-GKS, GKS Output Level 3, GSPC Core and PHIGS)

Several milestones may be considered in the development of graphics standards:

- Formation of the Graphics Standards Planning Committee (GSPC) in 1974 by ACM-SIGGRAPH [8];
- Formation of the Committee for the development of Computer Graphics Standards by the German Standardisation Body (DIN – Deutsches Institut für Normung) in 1975 [3, 6, 7];
- The IFIP WG5.2 Workshop SEILLAC I (Methodology in Computer Graphics) organised by R. Guedj in France in 1976 [9].

The current scenario of these standards is shown in Fig. 1.2.4. This figure shows a distribution of graphics standards based on their dimensionality (2D and 3D) and level of picture structuring (segments or hierarchies):

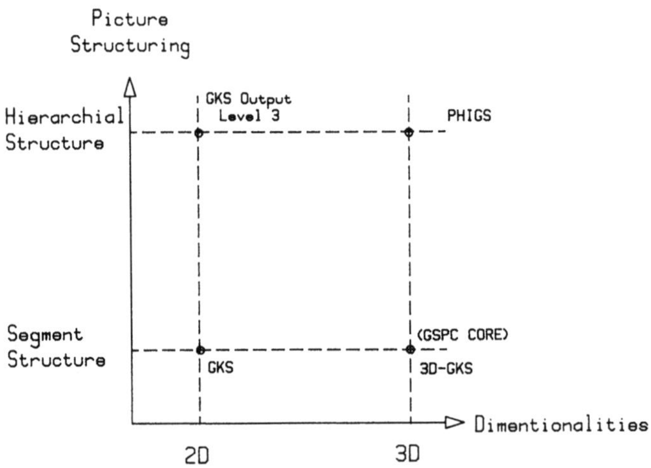

Fig. 1.2.4. Classification of graphics standards and graphics standards proposal

* 2D graphics kernel system
* output primitives
  vector and raster
* output primitive attributes
  individual and bundled
* input primitives
  input types (LOCATOR, STROKE, VALUATOR
  PICK, CHOICE, TEXT)
  request, sample and event input
* picture structuring
  segment and pick ids
* picture manipulation
  segment functions
* output and input transformations
  multiple normalisation transformations
  workstation transformations
* device management
  workstations, parallel output
  input from ws
  workstation dependent attributes
* storage of graphical information
  segment storage - short term
  GKS metafile - long term

Fig. 1.2.5. GKS overview

a) GKS is an already well-established and publicised standard (ISO DIS 7942) [3, 4, 5]. Fig. 1.2.5 gives a short overview of its functionality. GKS will not be further discussed here, since it is well-documented and discussed elsewhere [10] in substantial detail. GKS is the 2D standard; the picture structuring is based on segments.

b) GKS Output Level 3 [11] describes a set of extensions to GKS for segment hierarchy and editing. This GKS level 3 allows a segment to involve other segments; an existing segment may be reopened for editing; elements may be inserted and deleted. The content of segment elements may be inquired. Segment networks may be stored in metafiles. This GKS level 3 demands 15 new GKS functions (see Fig. 1.2.6). GKS level 3 is present only an ANSI working document and has no standard status; nevertheless, it shows a very interesting way of extending GKS to handle segment hierarchies.

c) GKS-3D [12] provides the application program with the following capabilities:

   - The definition and the display of 3D graphical primitives
   - Mechanisms to control viewing transformations and associated parameters
   - Mechanisms to control the appearance of primitives including optional support for hidden line and/or hidden surface elimination, but excluding light source, shading and shadow computation
   - Mechanisms to obtain 3D input

   Figure 1.2.7 shows the GKS-3D viewing pipeline. Existing 2D-GKS applications should run without modification on systems incorporating GKS-3D, since no changes are made to the existing 2D functions. GKS-3D is under very intensive consideration by the DIN group (NI-UA 5.9) and by ISO/TC97/

	New GKS Functions
1	call segment
2	delete elements
3	get element type
4	inquire element number
5	inquire element number from label
6	inquire external name
7	inquire pick path
8	inquire segment paths
9	interpret element
10	reopen segment
11	set element number
12	set external segment name
13	set label
14	set visibility mode
15	write user item

Fig. 1.2.6. GKS output level 3. (Source: ANSI X3H31/84-09R1)

SC5/WG2, the working group of the International Standards Organisation (ISO) responsible for graphics standards. GKS-3D is at present only a first draft and has been submitted to ISO by NNI, the Dutch standardisation body, for further reviewing and processing as a standard.

d) The top-level graphics standards in Fig. 1.2.4 are *GSPC Core* and *PHIGS*: the effort to develop the GSPC Core [13] "was monumental and inspired" [8]; it also very strongly influenced the GKS development in the Federal Republic of Germany and later on in the ISO GKS-reviewing [14]. The technical differences between GKS and the GSPC Core System are shown in Fig. 1.2.8. The GSPC Core never managed to develop to an ANSI standard draft proposal and is not under international consideration within the ISO/TC97/SC5/WG2. The GSPC concepts were the basis for all graphics standards development and a milestone in the development of computer graphics as a technology. The GSPC document itself is now more than five years old (the last report was GSPC79 and no public review on GSPC Core has been done since then) and therefore the standarisation of the GSPC Core seems to have ceased to be viable. The GSPC77 and GSPC79 documents now only serve as historical documentation with very high academic value. The packages most used as examples of "so-called" GSPC Core implementations are DI3000, PLOT 10 and TEMPLATE [15]. Since not FORTRAN binding of GSPC Core has ever been published, all three packages use their own subroutine names and calling sequences; applications using one of these packages can only with very great difficulty be converted to use one of the other packages. Therefore, GSPC Core implementations are mostly only "core-like" and therefore, have their problems, especially at the level of application program portability. From a

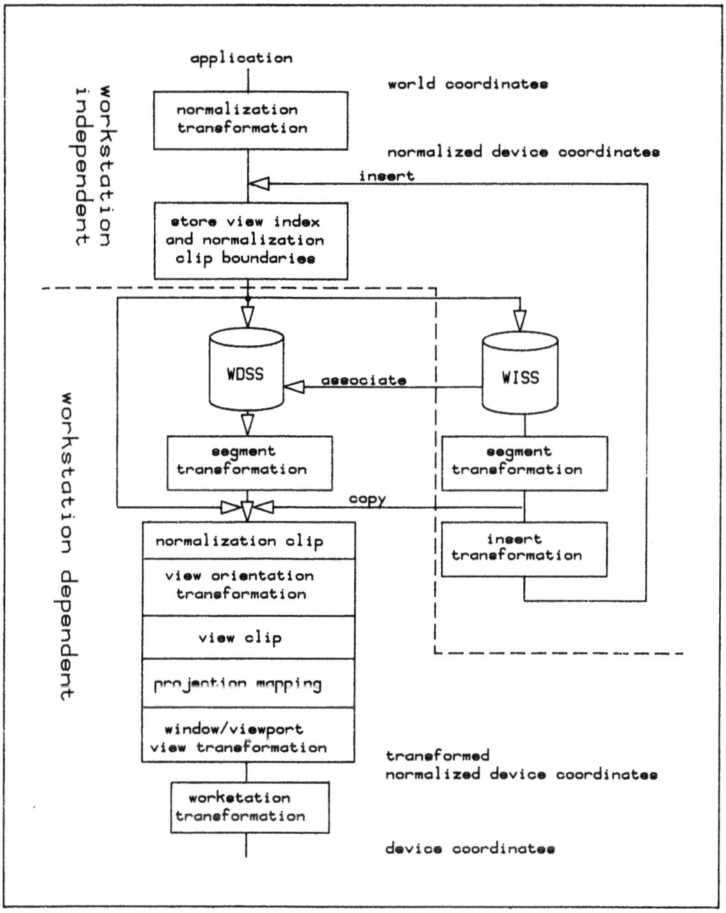

Fig. 1.2.7. Viewing pipeline of GKS-3D

technological point of view, GSPC Core has been eclipsed by the development and reviewing of GKS, GKS-3D and PHIGS.

PHIGS (Programmer's Hierarchical Interactive Graphics Standard) [16] includes in its functionality, three dimensional output primitives and transformations. It has dynamic control over the visual appearance of attributes of primitives within a segment. The goal of PHIGS is to support the most powerful graphics workstations becoming available. The basic functionality of PHIGS is shown in Fig. 1.2.9.

An important issue to be considered in this context is the migration of applications written in the different standards shown in Fig. 1.2.4. The migrations from GKS to GKS-3D and from GKS to GKS output level 3 are no problem since they are guaranteed by the functionality of both GKS-3D and GKS output level 3. The migrations from GKS to PHIGS, from GKS-3D to PHIGS and from GKS

	CORE SYSTEM	GKS
Workstations	Not supported.	Six types defined, three of which are really data storage devices.
Current Position	Uses paradigm of a "robotic pen"; output affects the position of this pen and most output primitive results may depend on current pen position.	Every output primitive is completely specific and is independent of other output primitives.
Viewing Operation	Single window/viewport transformation allowed with entire NDC space mapped screen. Clipping done prior to transformation to NDC space.	Allows multiple window/viewport transformations; to second level window/viewport clips and transforms output primitives from NDC space to screen.
3-D	Supported and integrated into 3-D viewing operation.	Not currently supported.
Attributes	Individual attributes supported.	Individual and bundled attributes supported; workstation dependent and workstation independent attributes defined.
Logical Input Devices	Six types, three modes.	Six types, three modes, but better explained.
Language Bindings	None.	FORTRAN binding specified; others under development.

Fig. 1.2.8. The technical differences (Source: J. Meads [7])

output level 3 to PHIGS still cause some problems because of existing incompatibilities with the functionality of PHIGS. It may be that the current public reviewing of PHIGS will help to solve some of the existing technical problems with the migration of application programs between the GKS-standard and a possible PHIGS-standard.

The "down-migration" of applications from GKS-3D and GKS output level 3 to 2D-GKS may be solved by using the metafile functionality to avoid loss of information (e.g. to store the information which would be lost) on the way down to 2D-GKS.

1.2.4 Graphics Metafiles (GKSM and VDM)

Graphics Metafiles are the standards for file formats for storing/transmitting pictures in a way which is both device and application independent (e.g., for disks)

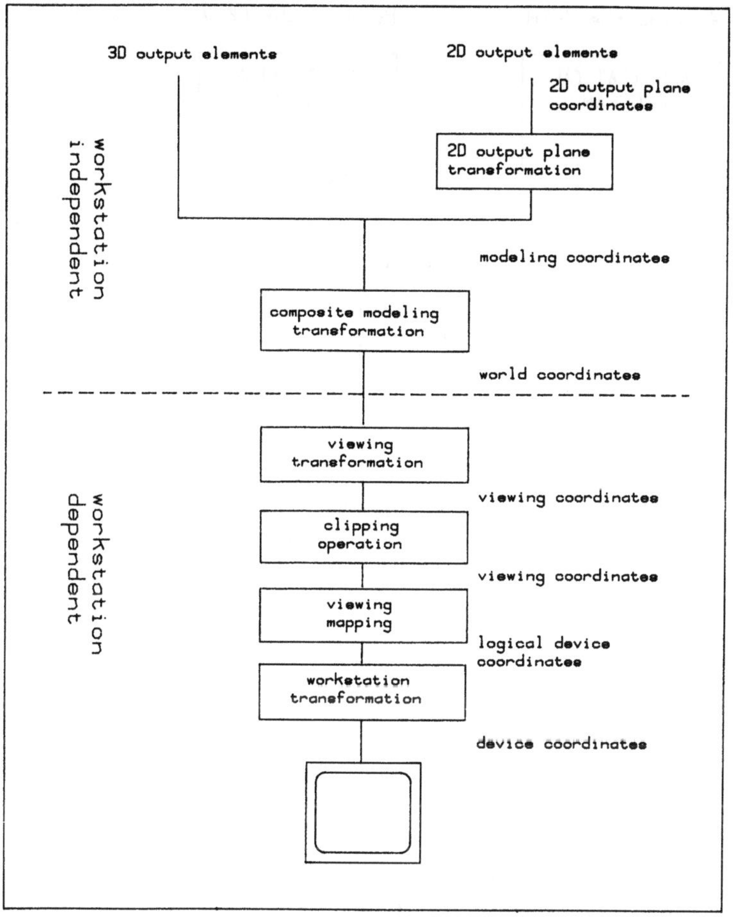

Fig. 1.2.9. PHIGS viewing pipeline

[17]. They are able to interconnect various graphical devices and graphic systems in a standardised way.

GKSM is the GKS Metafile used by GKS; it is a sequential file that can be written or read by GKS and is used for long-term storage and for transmission of the graphical information produced or to be read by GKS [4]. The writing and reading of GKSM by GKS is shown in Fig. 1.2.10. The GKS Metafile contains two-dimensional pictures represented by data records ("items") generated as a result of the GKS functions involved. GKSM contains:

- file header
- picture header
- end of record
- output primitives
- attributes
- non-graphical, application-dependent data

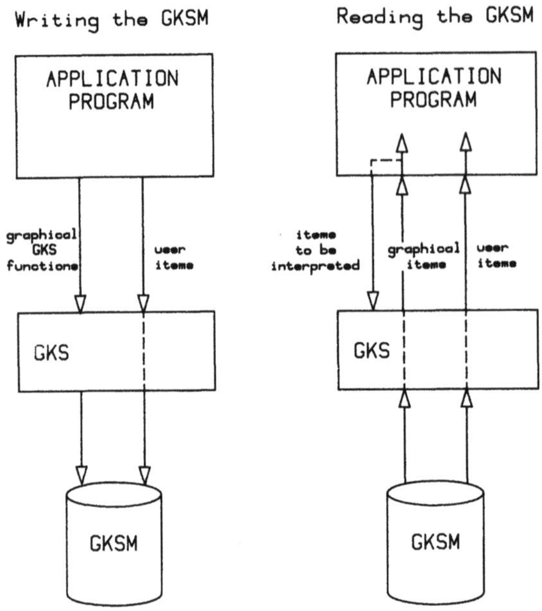

Fig. 1.2.10. Writing and reading the GKSM

GKSM is built up of a sequence of logical variable length data records. GKS addresses GKSM like a workstation. Two workstation types for metafiles are defined in an implementation.

- the GKSM output workstation
- the GKSM input workstation

The GKSM functionality is described in the GKS document [18].

The Virtual Device Metafile (VDM) defines the form (syntax) and functional behaviour (semantics) of a set of elements:

- descriptor elements
- control elements
- picture descriptor elements
- graphical elements
- attribute elements
- escape elements
- external elements

A VDM is a collection of elements from this set of elements. The descriptor elements give the VDM interpreter sufficient data to interpret metafile elements and to make informed decisions concerning the resources needed for display [19].

The relationship between VDM and GKS is shown in Fig. 1.2.11. VDM is expected to be used as a GKS Metafile at level 0a of GKS if protability of VDM for GKS applications has to be ensured [20].

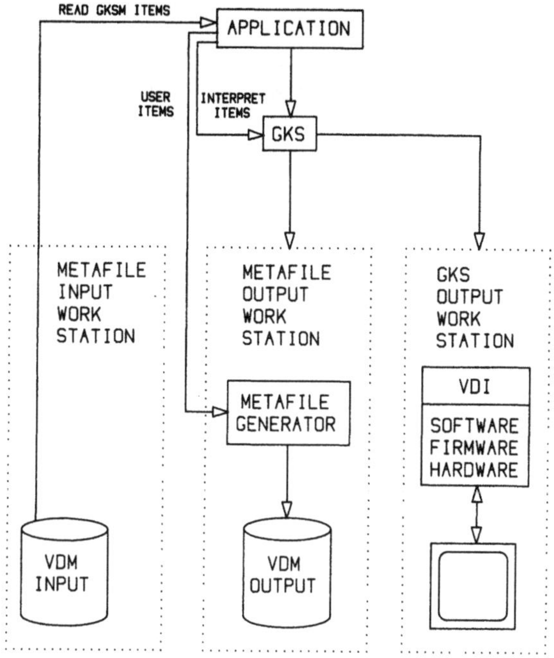

Fig. 1.2.11. Relationship of VDM to GKS

1.2.5 Device and Workstation Interfaces (VDI and WSI)

Between GKS and a Graphical Workstation, there exists an interface separating the device-independent and the device-dependent parts of the graphics system. For highly intelligent devices, this interface will contain most of the GKS functions and thus will be a highlevel interface. For devices without local intelligence, the function set at the device level will be very restricted. Non-existent capabilities will have to be simulated. The highest possible interface is called Workstation Interface (WSI) and the interface to the virtual graphical devices (device drivers) is the Virtual (Graphical) Device Interface (VDI). Whereas the WSI has a standardised fixed set of functions, the function set at the VDI is dependent on the device (see Fig. 1.2.12).

The WSI specifies the functional separation of the GKS Kernel and the GKS Workstations. It allows the operation of GKS in distributed systems and the exchange of information between kernel and workstations of different implementations. The distribution among different hosts does not put any restrictions on the functionality defined by GKS. The WSI is only implicitly defined in the GKS document; a more specific definition is given in [22, 23]. The interface architecture on which the WSI definition is based is shown in Fig. 1.2.13. For some devices, as well as for GKSM and VDM at level 0, the function set at the VDI will coincide with the WSI functions. For most devices, capabilities not present at the VDI have to be simulated. This is done by a Generic Virtual Device

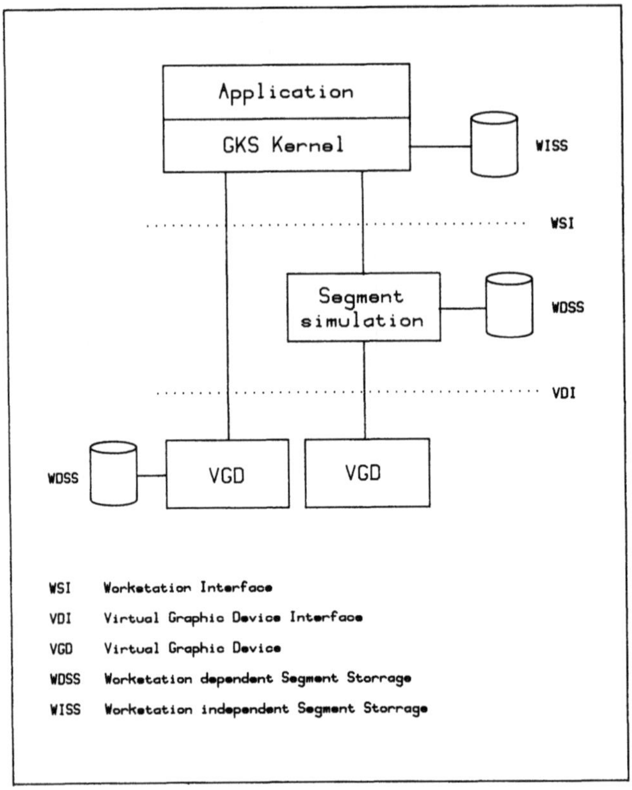

Fig. 1.2.12. GKS workstation interface

Function Set (GVDFS). It contains a standardised set of services (utilities) needed to translate functions at the WSI into a sequence of functions at the VDI.

In [2] the Virtual Device Interface (VDI) is defined as a standardised functional and syntactical specification of the control and data exchange between device-independent graphics software and device-dependent graphics device drivers. A graphics device driver is that portion of the graphics system software that translates commands and data from the VDI into the form required by a particular input/output mechanism. VDI is an interface, which is internally closest to the physical devices and the last point where device-independence can still be achieved.

1.2.6 Videotex Files (NAPLPS and CEPT/VPLP)

The North American Presentation-level-Protocol Syntax (NAPLPS) is a method for encoding visual information, a set of rules and conventions describing how data bytes of information should be formatted, as well as a set of guidelines

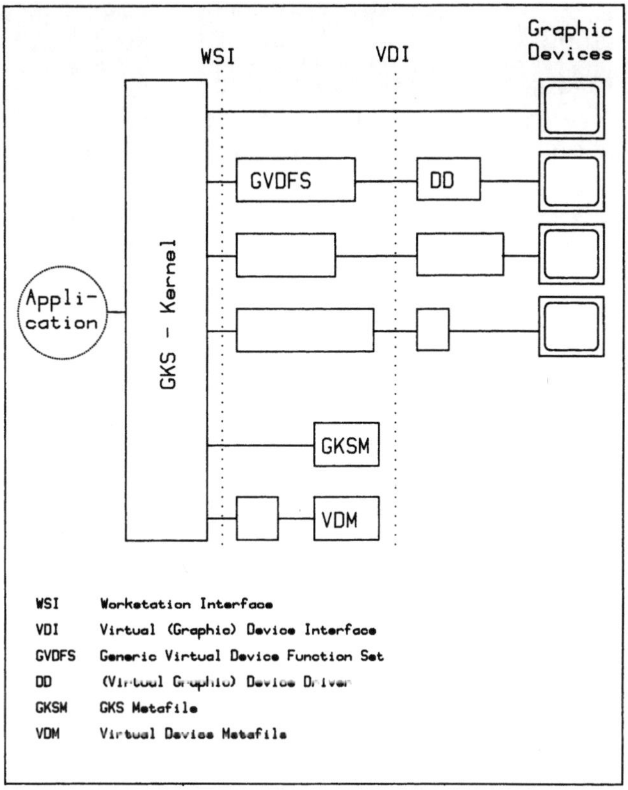

Fig. 1.2.13. Interface architecture

describing what should be displayed when properly formatted data bytes are received by a terminal [23].

NAPLPS includes a method for minimising the amount of information that must be sent over communication lines [24].

NAPLPS code typically needs only 10% of the space used by other graphics codes to define the same graphics and is resolution-independent. NAPLPS is designed to be integrated into the larger communications network through videotape, telephone, television signal and computerised data base. NAPLPS integrates graphics and text and includes a colour look-up table that allows the colour of any part of a picture to be altered instantaneously.

In the character-coded method of describing alphanumeric characters and pictorial information, particular codes are identified by an 8-bit code sequence in which seven of the bits are used as an index into a 128 character code table and the eighth bit is used for parity error checking or extension to another code table of 128 characters. The coding of alphanumeric characters is mainly based on ISO DIS 646 (ISO 7-bit and 8-bit coded character sets for information interchange).

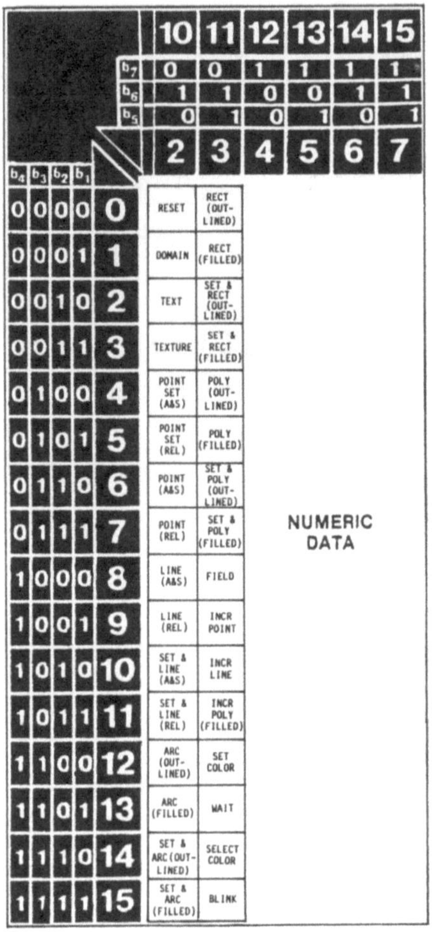

Fig. 1.2.14. PDI code sets

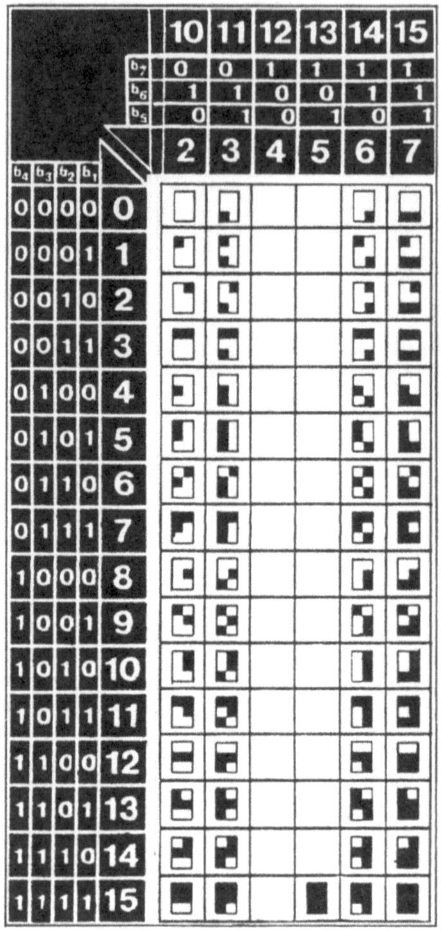

Fig. 1.2.15. Mosaic set

The coding of the pictorial information is based on:

a) Picture Description Instructions (PDI)
b) Mosaic Set
c) Macro Set
d) Dynamically Redefinable character Set (DRCS)

Independence of display hardware is achieved by using simple geometric picture description instructions as the basis of the coding scheme. The geometric drawing commands are defined in terms of an abstract unitary coordinate space (unit screen concept) and the text oriented commands are defined in terms of a variable character size, which permits different size characters to be displayed on the screen [25].

Picture description instruction (PDI) is composed of an Op-code, followed by one or more operands and constitutes an executable picture drawing or control command (see Fig. 1.2.14). Mosaic is a rectangular matrix of pre-defined elements, that can be used to construct block-style graphic images (see Fig. 1.2.15). Macro is a locally-stored string of presentation code, represented with a single character name. When the macro name is used, the locally stored string is processed in its place. The dynamically redefinable character set (DRCS) is a code set containing definable characters whose patterns can be downloaded from the host.

The CEPT/VPLP videotex file format is the European videotex proposal with a similar-function to NAPLPS. Both differ from each other in some details. Efforts are being made to achieve compatibility between the two proposals [26].

1.2.7 Product Data Transfer Formats (IGES, VDAFS, TAP, EDIF)

The Initial Graphics Exchange Specification (IGES) is a neutral data format which serves as a communication file to transfer data between CAD/CAM systems (see Fig. 1.2.16). IGES is structured as a five section file [27], containing a

- Prolog section: user defined text header for the file
- Global section: contains information about the system on which the part was developed, including numeric accuracies, scale factors, units of measurement and other environmental parameters. The object data in the file is composed of individual entities.
- Directory entry section: contains an index to all the entities as well as descriptive attributes for each.
- Parameter data section: contains the actual data defining each entity.
- Terminator section: acts as a bookkeeping record to check the number of records received and processed.

IGES files are coded in ASCII, with 80 characters per record and appear logically as a card deck. The new versions of IGES allow a binary file structure to reduce data volume. The binary file structure utilises data definitions and relationships identical to the ASCII version, but trades substantial data compression for increased processing complexity. The IGES file concept is strongly directed to the "transfer of drawings" and related information between CAD/CAM systems.

IGES includes three entity types:

- geometry (includes point, line, circle, conic, parameter spline, surface of revolution, etc.)

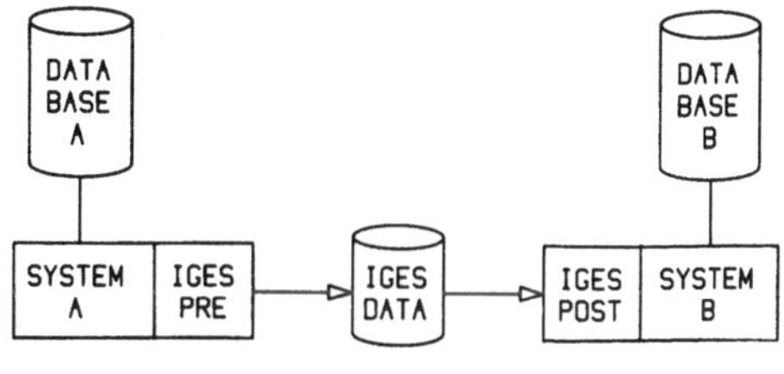

Fig. 1.2.16. IGES interface methodology

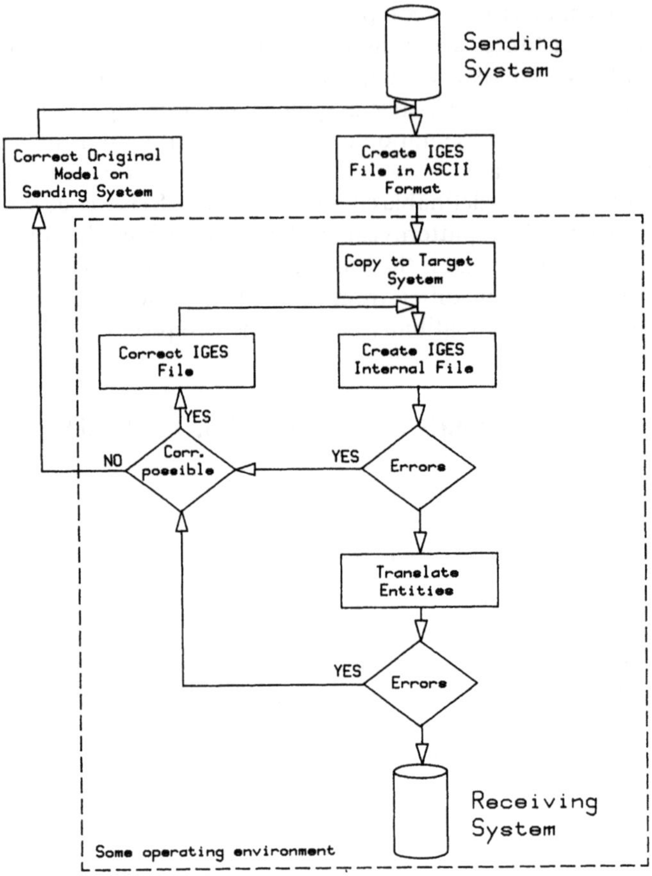

Fig. 1.2.17. IGES error correction cycle

- dimensioning/annotaton (includes angular dimension, centreline, label, etc.)
- structure (includes standard and user defined associations, drawing relationships, font relationships, view relationships, etc.)

The IGES translator is basically composed of two programs: The Edit program deals with the problems which are related to the format of IGES and the Exchange Program deals with exchange and translation of the entities themselves. Both the Edit and the Exchange programs check their data for correctness and produce appropriate reports. This information is used either to correct the original IGES file with the help of a text editor, or to send the IGES file and the error reports to the originating system [28] (see Fig. 1.2.17).

Other standard proposals with similar functionality to IGES are SET (Aerospatiale, France) and XBF-2 (CAM-I).

The German standards organisation DIN has taken an interest in standards for graphics and CAD systems interfaces for a number of years. At the beginning of 1983, when the demand for standards in product definition data exchange began to be expressed more acutely, a new DIN Working Group was formed. It was named "Transfer and Archiving of Produce Definition Data" (or briefly TAP). This Working Group is concerned with issues very similar to those of IGES in the data exchange between CAD systems, as well as the medium or long-term storage of such data [29].

In the area of automotive engineering in Germany, the Association of Automobile Manufacturers (VDA) has recently developed a standard format for exchanging curve and surface data, called the VDA Sculptured Surface Interface (VDAFS) [30].

The approach taken here may serve as an example of a low redundancy lean entity set solution. The interface is limited to geometry entities (and comments) and contains only the following set:

POINT
POINT SET
POINT-VECTOR SET
COMPOSITE CURVE (INCL. PARAMETRIC SPLINES)
PARAMETRIC SPLINE SURFACE

Any geometric representations not contained in this basic set are converted to the standard by the sending system and later reconverted into the local representation of the receiving system. The VDA proposal is currently under review by DIN as a basis for a German national standard. Pilot implementations exist and have been tested with success. The VDAFS will also be submitted for international reviewing.

By the end of 1983, a new Electronic Design Interchange Format (EDIF), with similar goals of IGES, has been developed by the main semiconductor and computer companies [31]. EDIF enables the communication of various types of electronic data among CAD/CAE tools and systems. The EDIF file consists of four kinds of information blocks:

- Status blocks – contain accounting information, such as data, author's name and software level.
- Design blocks – provide entry points to the EDIF file contents by indicating which cell in which library contains the top-level description of the design conveyed by the file.
- Cell-definition libraries – contain all relevant design information
- User data blocks – catch-alls to handle information not otherwise expressible in EDIF.

The EDIF file does not concentrate as much as IGES on the drawings and related data, but more on electronic design information and corresponding data. This file is still in a very early stage of reviewing; the companies involved in this reviewing process are, among others, Daisy Systems, Mentor Graphics, Motorola, Semiconductor, Tektronix, Texas Instruments and University of California at Berkeley. There are also efforts to use IGES for PCB design [32].

1.2.8 Graphics in the Processing of Text Documents Which Include Graphics (CLPT)

The document Computer Languages for the Processing of Text (CLPT) [33], includes a Part 8 "Binding to the Graphical Kernel System (GKS)." This part specifies the binding of GKS to the text processing programming language, to allow the integrated processing of illustration (raster and vector graphics) and text. The work in progress here is very close to the GKS-Ada-binding developed by ISO/TC97/SC5/WG2. Part 6 of the document discusses the functionality of the "Standard Generalised Markup Language" (SGML); the interface between Graphics and SGML is being developed based on the Graphics Metafiles (GKSM, VDM).

All these activities are still in a very early stage of standardisation; first concrete results are expected 1985.

1.2.9 Presentation Graphics Layer on Top of GKS

This layer is based on the model shown in Fig. 1.2.18. There are three interfaces to be specified:

a) Interface "GKS – Presentation graphics package"
   – primitives

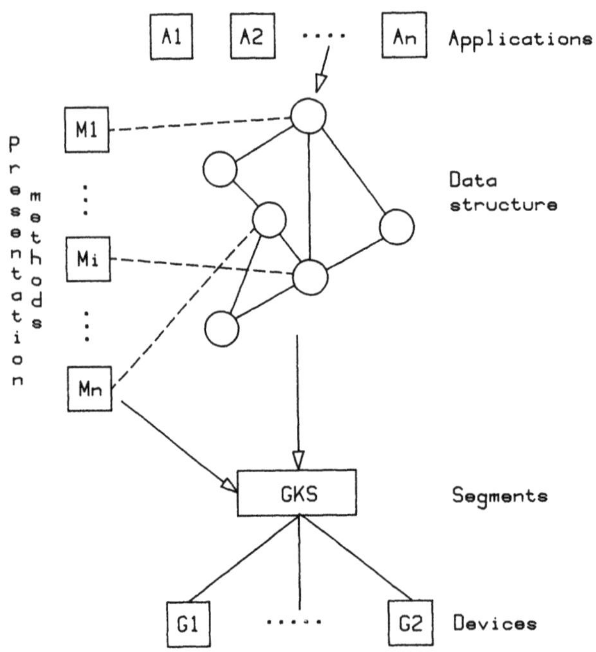

Fig. 1.2.18. Model for presentation graphics on top of GKS

- data structure
- clusters/levels (functionality)

b) Interface to the environment
- operating system
- language binding
- interface to the data handling utilities
- interface to the methods handling utilities

c) Operator interface
- passive/interactive
- dialog
- interaction techniques

Based on such a specification, special implementations of a presentation graphics package can be realised which at the application layer differ from each other.

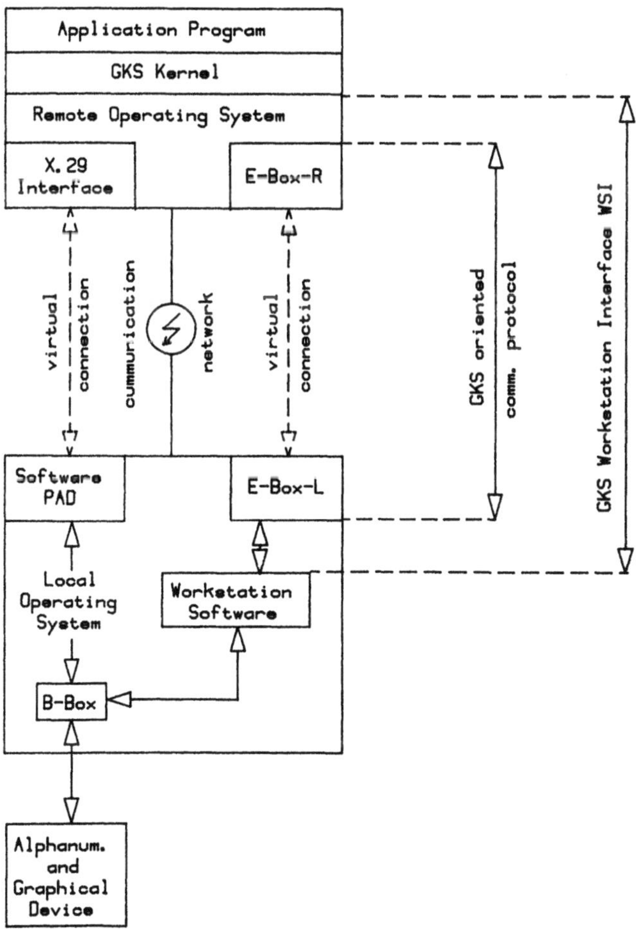

Fig. 1.2.19. The GKS communication system (Source: DFN 36])

Their efficiency is then dependent on the methods library and on the data structure handling utilities used. The Working Group of the German GKS Verein (GKS Association) is working on the development of common interfaces a), b) and c) on top of GKS, to achieve more flexible capabilities for system integration [35, 36].

1.2.10 GKS in a Network Environment

The WSI (Workstation Interface; see "Device and Workstation Interfaces") of GKS opens the possibility of using GKS in a network environment. The communication is based on the concept of a Graphic PAD (G PAD), which is an extension of the CCITT standard proposal for alpha-numeric communication (PAD). Such a G PAD is a software module, with the functionality of channeling the information received either to an A/N Terminal, or to a given process running under the local operating system; this process implements the GKS Workstation. The GKS oriented communication protocol is a special implementation of the G PAD concept, based on a Software PAD and on two special processes called E-Box-L(ocal) and E-Box-R(emote); they implement the transmission of graphic data based on the WSI of GKS. If both types of communication (alphanumeric and graphic) are supposed to run on one device, another software module B-Box is needed to coordinate the alpha numeric and graphic data flow. Such a GKS-oriented communication system is shown in Fig. 1.2.19 [37]. In Germany, several institutions are involved in designing and implementing these concepts; these activities run under the sponsorship of the German Research Network DFN (Deutsches Forschungsnetz).

1.2.11 References

1. McNall, R: Graphics Reference Models – Very Preliminary X3H3/84-005R0 (January 1984)
2. Bono, P: Graphics Standards. In: Tutorial T3.1 CAMP '83, Berlin (March 1983)
3. Encarnação, J, Schlechtendahl, EG: Computer Aided Design: Fundamentals and System Architectures. Springer, Berlin Heidelberg New York Tokyo (1983)
4. Enderle, G, Kansy, K, Pafff, G: Computer Graphics Programming GKS – The Graphics Staqndard. Springer, Berlin Heidelberg New York Tokyo (1984)
5. Encarnação, J, Straßer, W (eds): Geräteunabhängige graphische Systeme. Oldenbourg, München (1981)
6. Hopgood, FRA, Duce, DA, Gallop, JR, Sutcliffe, DC: Introduction to the Graphical Kernel System (GKS). Academic Press, New York (1983)
7. Meads, JA: The Graphics Standards Battle. In: Datamation, pp 76–84 (1984)
8. Guedj, RA, Tucker, H (eds): Methodology in Computer Graphics, Proc. IFIP WG5.2 Workshop SEILLAC I, May 1976. North-Holland, Amsterdam (1979)
9. Duce, D, Hopgood, FRA: Lecture Notes of GKS Tutorial at EUROGRAPHICS '84, Copenhagen (1984)
10. Steinhart, J: Proposal for GKS Output Level 3, ANSI X3H31-09R1, ANSI X3H35/84-02 (1984)
11. GKS-3D. ISO TC97/SC5/WG2 N237 (June 1984)
12. GSPC '79: Status Report of the Graphics Standards Planning Committee Computer Graphics 13, 3 (1979)

13. Bono, P, Encarnação, J, Hopgood, FRA, ten Hagen, PJW: GKS – The first graphics standard. IEEE Computer Graphics and Applications, vol. 2, no 5, pp 9–24 (July 1982)
14. Straayer, D: Computer Graphics Standards: Where they are. In: Techniques: vol 7, no 3/4, pp 8–14 (1984)
15. American National Standard for the functional specification of the Programmer's Hierarchical Interactive Graphics Standard (PHIGS). ANSI X3H3/84–40 (February 1984)
16. Hindin, H: Graphics Standards finally start to sort themselves out. In: Computer Design, p 167 (May 1984)
17. Information Processing – Computer Graphics Graphical Kernel System (GKS) Functional Description. ISO DIS 7942 (1982)
18. Information Processing Computer Graphics Virtual Device Metafile (VDM) – Functional Description. ISO TC97/SC5/WG2/N229 (December 1983)
19. Comments on and questions about the "Virtual Device Metafile (VDM)" Contribution from DIN-NI-AU 5.9.4. ISO TC97/SC5/WG2/N230 (May 1984)
20. Information Processing Computer Graphics "Virtual Device Interface (VDI)" – Functional Description. ANSI X3H3-84/85 (March 1984)
21. Structure of a Workstation Interface. Position paper, DIN-NI-AU 5.9.4, ISO TC97/SC5/WG2/N238 (May 1984)
22. Davidson, J: Integrating Videotex with the Personal Computer NAPLPS-Based Products Offer the Solution. Computer Graphics World, vol. 7, no 5, pp 11–18 (May 1984)
23. Flemming, J, Frezza, W: NAPLPS: A New Standard for Text and Graphics. Byte vol 8, no 2, pp 203–255 (February 1983)
24. Videotex/Teletext Presentation Level Protocol Syntax (1982) North American PLPS, ANSI X3L2.1: CVCC/CSA/WG Videotex CEPT
25. CEPT CD/SE: Videotex Presentation Layer Protocol (VPLP) Draft 2.1 (September 1982)
26. Liewald, H: The development and testing of IGES interfaces. Tutorial T3.2, CAMP '83, Berlin (1983)
27. Weissflog, U: Experience in design and implementation of IGES translators. Proceedings of CAMP '83, Berlin, pp 1499–1516 (March 1983)
28. DIN Working Group NI-AK 5.9.5: IGES review and proposed extensions. Transfer and Archiving of Product Definition Data (TAP) (February 1984)
29. VDAFS (VDA/VDMA – Sculptured Surface Interface) (1983) German Version. Verband der Automobilindustrie e.V. (VDA)
30. Workstation Alert (June 1984), vol 1, no 4
31. Parks, C: IGES Update. In: Computer Graphics World, pp 43–50 (March 1984)
32. Information Processing Systems: Programming languages Text Interchange and Processing. ISO TC97/SC5/WG12 (X3J6) (1984)
33. Minutes of a meeting of the DIN Working Group NI-5.9.6 "Text and Graphics"
34. Paller, A, Harendza, HB: Management Graphics. CAMP '83 Tutorial, Berlin (March 1983)
35. Minutes of a meeting of the ad-hoc-Group of the GKS-Association on "Presentation Graphics" in Darmstadt on 10. February 1984
36. Deutsches Forschungsnetz – DFN: Graphische Kommunikation in offenen Netzen Version 1.0 (April 1984)
37. Encarnação, J: Aspekte der graphischen Datenverarbeitung in Rechnernetzen. Symposium von DECUS e.V. München, Darmstadt (March 1984)

1.3 CAD/CAM: Integration in the Automobile Industry

H. G. Wilfert and H. Seeland

1.3.1 Introduction

Working out a long-term holistic strategy for introducing CAD and CAM into all areas of the process chain of a firm has decisive influence on the selection of hardware, operating software, CAD/CAM user software and the design of the necessary communication structures between the participating areas of the firm.

To say CAD is to imply CAM, no doubt should exist about this from the beginning. This makes it a requirement that *before* the introduction of CAD all areas participating in the process chain, from the design to the manufacturing of a product, sit down at a table and develop a holistic conception in the sense of a top-down analysis. This holistic strategy should also include apparent fringe areas in its considerations. (It is certainly not immediately obvious what the introduction of a CAD system in the design area has to do with the definition of tasks in the department of technical documentation.)

The "bottom-up" approach practised up to now in many firms, in which CAD/CAM systems have been introduced piecemeal, in design or manufacturing, leads to an uncontrollable interface jumble with all of its most unsatisfactorily solved problems (Fig. 1.3.1).

A holistic strategy must answer the following questions without contradiction:

- Where should CAD/CAM be introduced in the firm and which goals are to be attained?
- Where are isolated solutions permissible and where is universal accessibility of functions and data necessary?
- What kind of requirement profile exists for each of the areas participating in the process chain?
- Are these requirements achievable with *one* uniform CAD/CAM system?
- If not, then which workable common denominator can be found in order to attain the goal of a system solution which is as homogeneous as possible within the process chain?
- How do the data bank and communication structures aim to attain an optimal data accessability in the process chain? How can once-produced information subsequently be used as often and as variously as possible?

The goal of an integrated CAD/CAM concept must be to transmit the required quantity of alphanumeric and graphical information via the most efficient com-

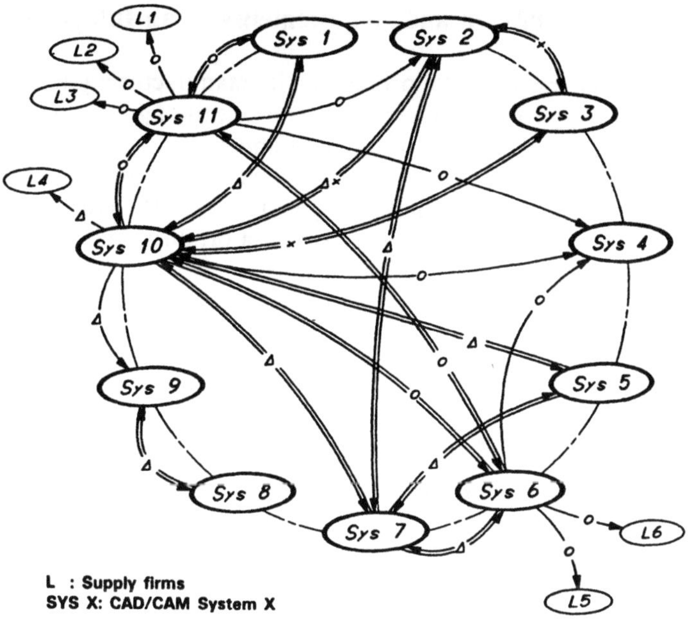

Figure 1.3.1. Interface jumble

munication paths in order to connect the phases of product preparation listed below.

The relevant members of the process chain are:

- Planning
- Design/Computation
- Testing
- Production engineering
- Calculation
- Production preparation/Production tools construction
- NC-manufacturing
- Quality checking
- Technical graphics/Scales
- Documentation/Parts lists

The more homogeneously the whole system (consisting of hardware, operating software, user software, communication software) can be made, the lower will be the overheads resulting from incompatible system components.

The following contribution is a plea for the most possible uniform system without developmentally complex and operationally expensive interfaces; and for custom-tailored interfaces in those places where firm-specific software programs are tied together, insofar as they cannot be tied in through an interface which is comfortably accessible to the user in the CAD/CAM system.

1.3.2 Demands on and Requirements of an Integrated Concept

While the use of data processing in manufacturing technology has already reached a high level, for a long time no-one thought much about what help could be given to the designer in order to improve the quality and produtivity of his work. Therefore a very high percentage of the responsibility for the costs of a product lay precisely with the designer (Fig. 1.3.2). Design changes are something self-evident in the formative history of a product, and are most easily done and most cheaply made at the design stage.

The fundamental questions asked by a design department

- does it work
- does it fit
- is it durable
- is it produceable,

are made difficult to answer because of an abundance of restrictive limiting conditions (Fig. 1.3.3).

The room for manoeuver in the solution of an assigned task becomes progressively smaller while the demand for effective assistance becomes progressively louder.

So, from the beginning, the emphasis of computer support has lain in the design area as the source of product information. But the real success of CAD in a firm essentially depends on how comprehensively all the areas of a firm affected by CAD are tied together, both horizontally and vertically, in a holistic strategy.

CAD which is restricted to the design department is *locally* highly effective but seen globally it is expensive. The future success of a CAD/CAM system depends on its capacity for integration into the entire operational picture. The ideal state is *one* CAD/CAM system which fulfills all requirements of the individual areas inside the process chain. This results in the fewest integration problems (Fig. 1.3.4).

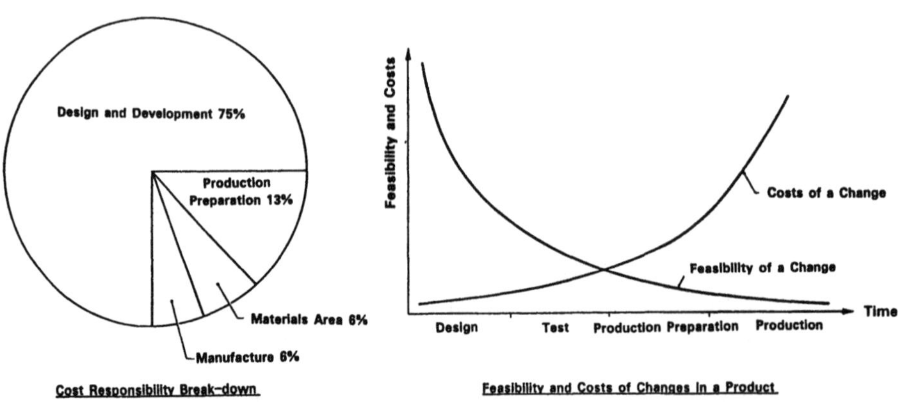

Figure 1.3.2. Cost responsibility of the designer

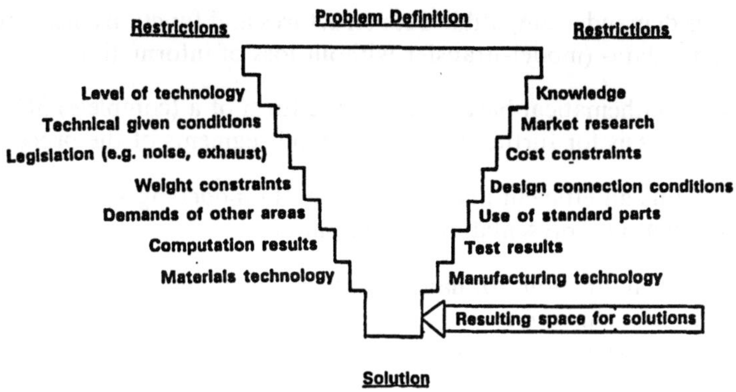

Figure 1.3.3. Limiting conditions in the design process

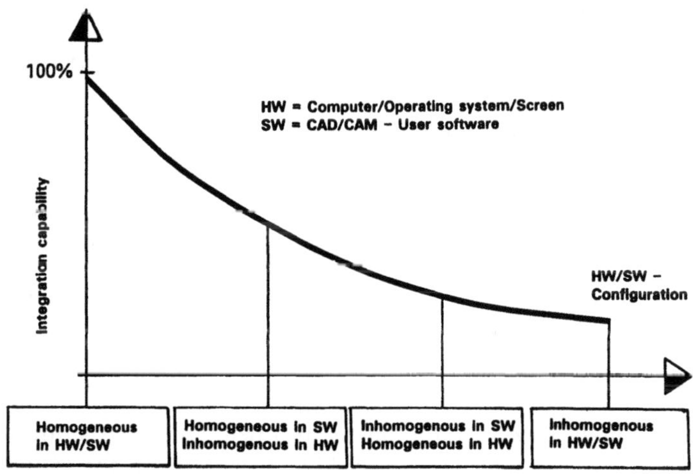

Figure 1.3.4. Integration of the sub-areas along the process chain

Different software systems and different hardware in the various departments create interface problems among the various CAD systems, which are at present solved in a most unsatisfactory way.

With the introduction of CAD/CAM technology in a firm, the mistake is often made that in the short-term (or short-sightedly!) functional aspects of a CAD system are overvalued in favor of a certain area, rather than the strategic aspects for the entire firm being considered.

Obviously even the best strategy is not useful if it is not supported by an efficient software system having, above all, development capability.

What are the most important requirements of a successful CAD/CAM concept, of which maximum integration is expected; and which requirements have to be established?

- Single preparation of basis data and multiple use of the data and functions.

This demands compatible data structures and functions inside the process chain, and a data- (model-)transfer without loss of information.

- A mathematical base model in the form of a (complete) 3D surface model as the basis for further processing in all segments of the process chain.

For this an efficient and expandable 3D modelling system for surface-oriented product data presentation is necessary.

- Special functions for handling special distinctions in the individual parts of the process chain, e.g.,
  - Drawing generation/Word processing
  - 2D/3D kinematics/Basic calculating functions
  - NC model generation/NC processing
  - Cast part, form, and core generation

Necessary in addition are

- comprehensive, efficient and expandable CAD/CAM functions, and
- the direct exercise of influence on (up to cooperation with) the system creator for the developmenmt of special functions.

- Uniform product identification and product data management within the process chain. Common data base, data integrity, data protection, fast access.

This is possible on the basis of a modern data bank with central data storage and data management.

- Integration of firm-specific processes and functions.

Absolutely necessary for this is an open system structure with a comfortable accessible user interface serviced by the system creator. (Source code availability – departure from the "turn-key mentality").

- Fast communication between all parts of the process chain without loss of information. Access from every node in the network to functions and product data. Communication throughout the firm in a uniform communication system.

The requirement for this is a uniform hardware and operating software base under uniform control mechanisms without complex logging and procedure conversion. (Homogeneous information and communication technology).

- Uniform workstations with a uniform service strategy and more flexible equipment matched to the task to be performed.

This requires an expandable "workstation" with standard user interfaces (virtual terminal concept) and a comprehensive selection of peripheral components.

- Horizontal and vertical software portability under a uniform operating system strategy.

This is made possible by means of a computer family with different performance characteristics but with uniform operating control.

- Good computational performance, accuracy, and availability, and adequate response time behavior. Flexible adaptability to the state of the art in DP technology and to future user demands.

This is attained by means of an expandable and adaptable computer system within the framework of a computer family with 32/64 bit processors on the bases of standard hardware and operating software (processor – main storage – channel expansion).

- Consideration of the engineering aspects of calculation, manufacture, and testing in the design process.

The prerequisite for this is that all those involved in developing the system-strategy, but especially those responsible for design, base their approach on a broad overview of the complete process chain.

1.3.3 The CAD/CAM Process Chain in Automobile Manufacturing

Figure 1.3.5 schematically depicts the stages of product development in automobile manufacturing – beginning with the idea and ending with production. Between these stages are regulators, such as the diverse clearing processes or technical planning considerations, which regulate communication between the stations.

When one observes the traditional communication along the process chain, it can be determined that the kinds and means of communication were developed, integrated, and thereby standardized and accepted over decades (drawings, piece lists, documentation, records). The use of CAD/CAM in many cases initially conceived of as a local replacement of the drawing board, increasingly succumbs to the same conformity.

CAD/CAM applications which are essentially limited to specific stages in the process chain, and which largely differ from stage to stage both in the CAD/CAM system used, and in the definition of the product model require integration into the existing process chain environment, and specifically in accordance with *functional, data-technical, technological, and organization integrity conditions.*

This integrity can be attained only when a conversion between different product models along the process chain is avoided. Modifications with differing mathematical procedures along the process chain can also critically affect the product model and reduce its quality. So, for example, the diverse mathematical surface definitions in the respective product models demand different generation and manipulation procedures which are not always identically transferable.

1.3.3.1 Product Model and Data Management

The central element and integrating factor within the process chain is the computer-internal product model, which is needed with various distinctions in all phases of product creation (Fig. 1.3.5).

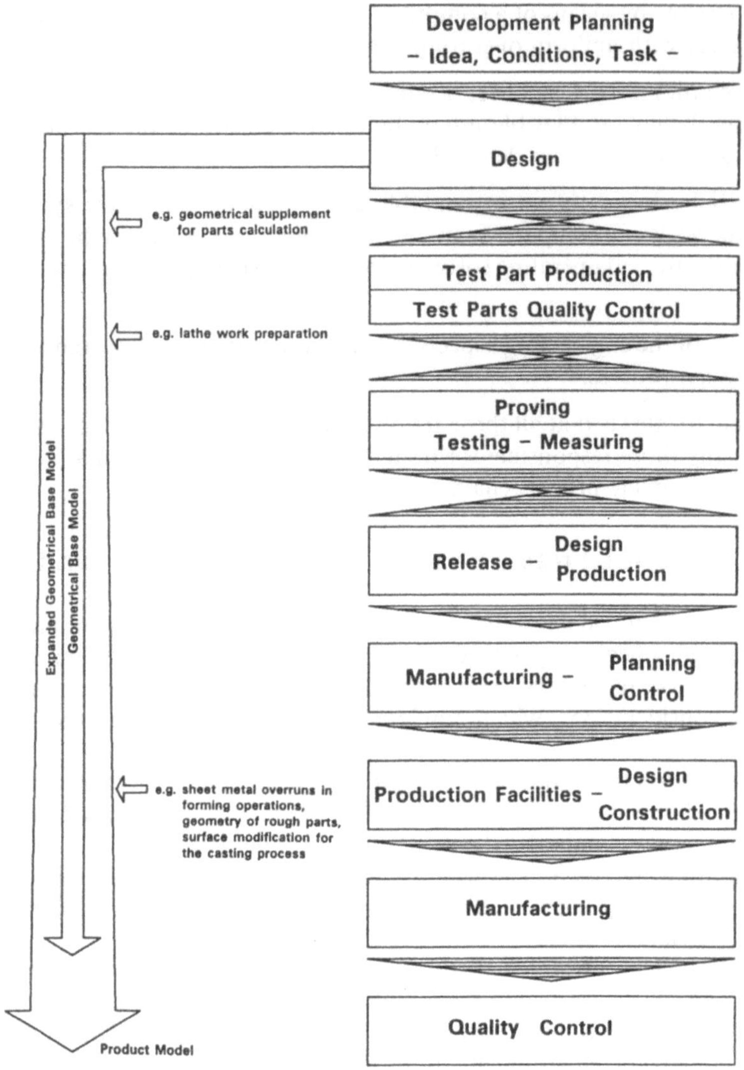

Figure 1.3.5. CAD/CAM process chain: The stages of product development

The mathematical model of a production component, the *geometrical base model* as it is created in the design department, requires for its further use in the framework of an integrated CAD/CAM processing, an adaptation to its new intended use in the process chain. The higher the information content of the base model is, the lower the resulting adaptation expense. Inside the computer the geometrical base model is a mathematical surface model with fully described external and internal surfaces, which, for example, can be created by solid modelling, with additional technological and organizational information.

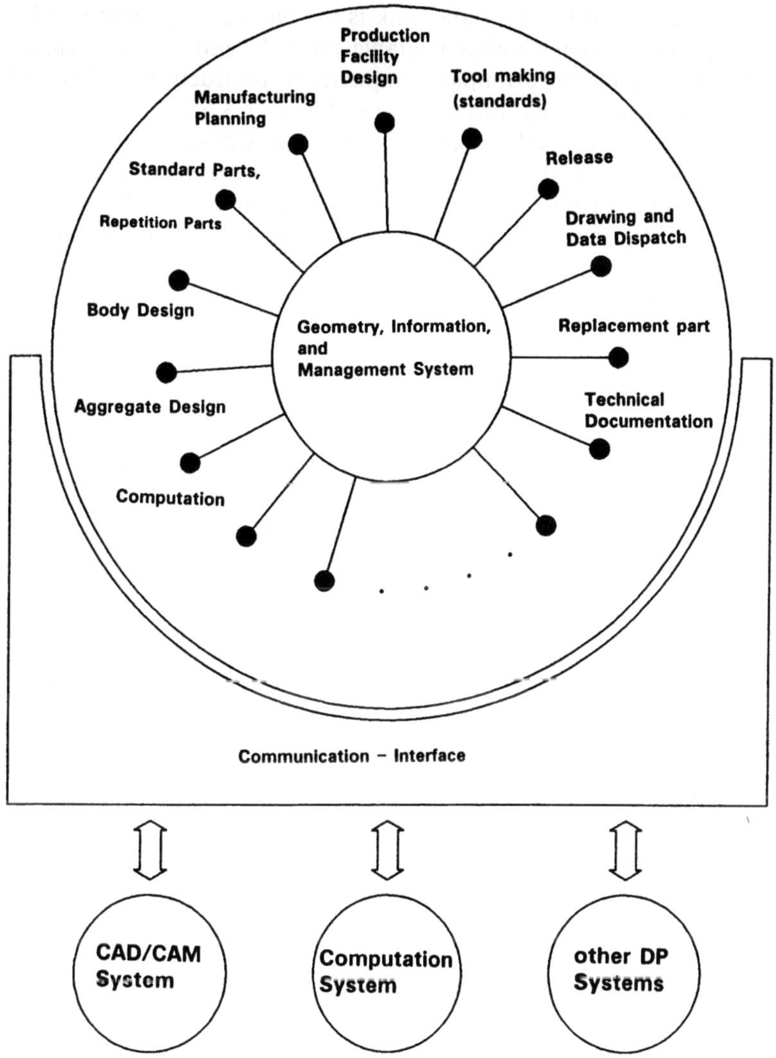

Figure 1.3.6. Product data bank

The representation of the base model within the computer is delineated by the underlying mathematical modelling procedure as it exists in CAD system application.

Essential for the further processing of the geometrical base model is that identical algorithms for manipulating the representation inside the computer, e.g., for the handling of surfaces, be made available in the downstream parts of the process chain.

The geometrical base model, as it is processed in the design department, should be available to areas working farther along the process chain through a product data bank. This data bank is the basis of a *geometry, information, and management system* which is available along the entire process chain and records all derived data, for example, computation, production facility and equipment design, manufacturing, product data. (Figure 1.3.6 shows a basic structure).

Already existing DP systems – mostly purely alphanumerical – have to be tied into the CAD/CAM system and into the geometry, information, and management system, for the future use of the product model and for integration into the CAD/CAM process chain. In order to safeguard integrity and avoid data redundancy, only a functional coupling can be selected here (see for this the section "Internal and External Interfaces").

1.3.3.2 Information and Communication in the Process Chain

Integrated information processing exists when the conception as well as the hardware and software components of the organization's system (in our case the CAD/CAM process chain in automobile manufacturing) are matched to each other and function as a whole. In this way information can be provided which is based on the data of several departments or fields.

The goal of integrated information processing within the CAD/CAM process chain is to make available to the user the most *uniform tools* possible in the form of workstation, user guidance, and user software in a uniform system environment, for the processing of a *binding base-data set in the entire process chain* (geometrical base model).

In the following the most important parts of the process chain and their role in the CAD/CAM environment are described.

1.3.3.2.1 Design and Computation

The design activity in automobile manufacturing, under the coordination of the overall design management, is divided essentially into the following areas:

- Designing and stylistics with model building
- Body design and engineering
- Chassis design
- Aggregate design with
  - Engine design
  - Transmission design
- Design of electrical equipment

Today CAD support is used in all areas, with highly different demands on the functionality of the CAD support; which is not to say that these functions cannot be made available in one and the same CAD system.

So in car body design the surface description of the external surfaces of the car body, building on the raw data supplied by the designer model, stands in the foreground, whereby the quality of the mathematical surface approximation plays a decisive rôle (Fig. 1.3.7).

In aggregate design the method of 3D-shape-orienting (solid) modelling will be adopted for the design of parts (Fig. 1.3.8).

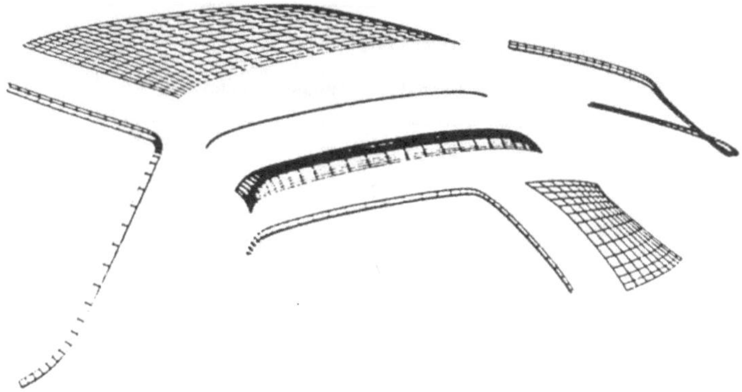

Figure 1.3.7. Surface model in car body design

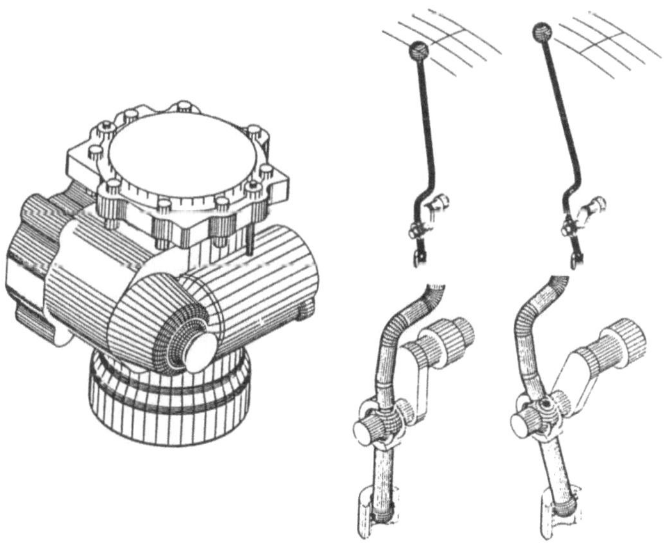

Figure 1.3.8. Solid model in aggregate construction

The *solid model* yields a complete and exact description of the part's geometry. All *surfaces,* interior and exterior, of a volumetric model are completely defined. However, the requirement is that the available basic elements allow the component to be completely recorded geometrically.

The integration of surfaces of higher orders into the basic solid model, which is defined by surfaces of the second order, particularly needs a satisfactory solution.

The model data processed in *one* area serves as a base or as reference data for the other areas. On the way from the first design up to the product model for testing or series release, numerous iterative adjustments and matchings are neces-

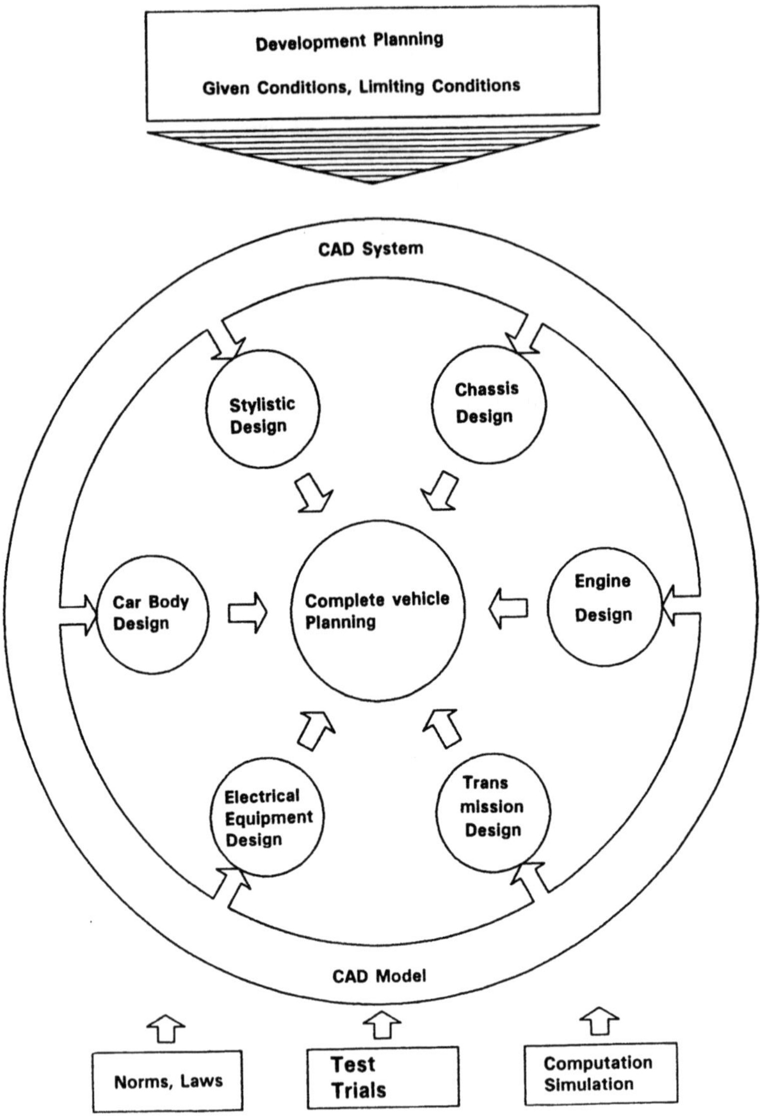

Figure 1.3.9. CAD communication in the design area

sary within and between design areas. This means that the different design departments must then enter into close communication via terminal on the basis of the geometrical base model (Fig. 1.3.9).

For example, the testing of the engine lay-out and mounting, along with the engine's additional aggregates in the vehicle engine compartment, requires information from the areas of car body design, aggregate design, and chassis design (Fig. 1.3.10).

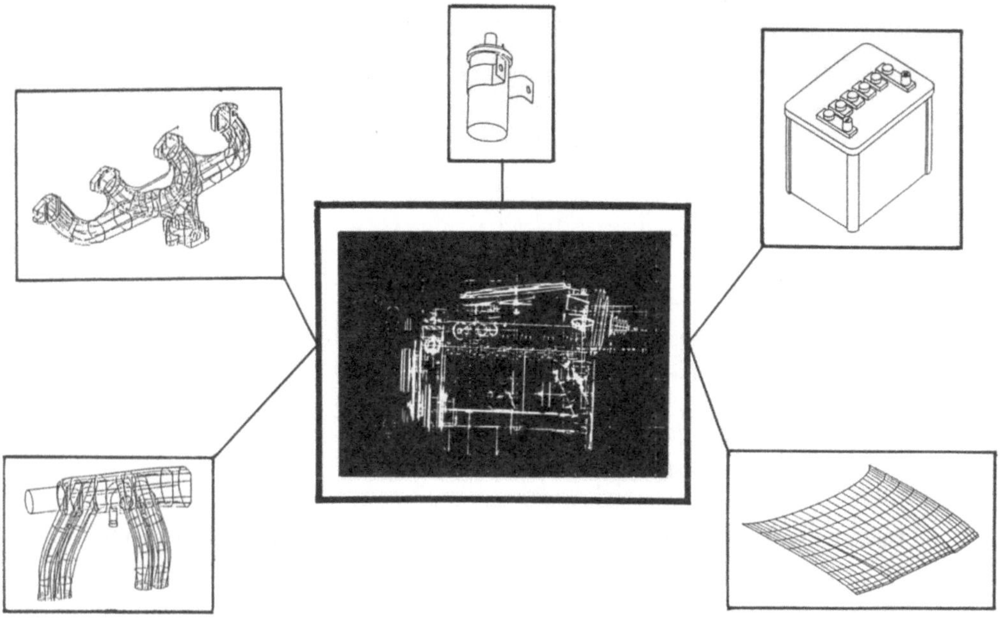

Figure 1.3.10. Integration in vehicle design

Speedy communication between the areas supports, among other things,

- the demand for reducing development time;
- a quicker adaptation to engineering knowledge;
- the demand for higher product quality with simultaneously lower costs through an intensification of the design work, in part through the processing of more design variations;
- the avoidance of existing data redundancy between areas.

It may be necessary along the process chain that a preceding area has to put an excess of information into the geometrical model description in order to make this data available to the following areas.

The possibilities of mathematical part modelling currently available in CAD systems form the foundation for a close integration of computation into the design process.

Certain computation functions are made available in the CAD system itself and use the component model *directly* for the computation of physical parameters such as weight, volume, and moment of inertia.

Kinematic functions are member functions of the CAD system which are used in connection with the part description (Fig. 1.3.11).

The 3D part model is *indirectly* the basis for computation tasks which are solved with the help of the finite element method or of similar computation procedures.

Based on the CAD geometry description (for example of a surface model), the finite element structure consisting of nodes and elements is built up over the topology description (see Fig. 1.3.12).

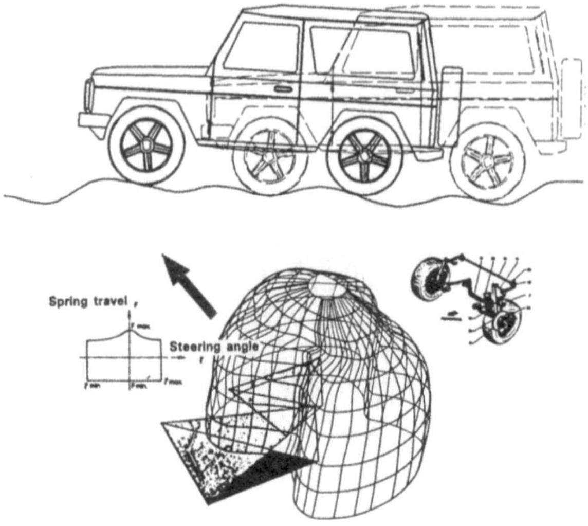

Figure 1.3.11. CAD design support: 3D-Kinematic – Example: tire enveloping surface

Computational engineers and designers come to their user programs at the same work place and in a uniform system environment. The exchange of information between designer and computational engineers can take place in the shortest, most interactive way.

Figure 1.3.13 shows in summary the demands of DP supported computation on an integrated CAD/CAM concept.

1.3.3.2.2 Standard and Repeat Parts

With standard parts one has to make a thorough distinction between DIN norms and internal factory norms. Making DIN standard parts available is a task which overlaps firms. Standard parts could be made available through an expanded IGES-interface. The availability of factory (or in-house) standard parts can be achieved directly through the CAD-system in use.

The use of standard and repeat parts becomes interesting and completely effective for the CAD designer when he selects the parts directly in his CAD system via the central geometry, information, and management system or by searching (norm number, designation, catchword, etc.) with graphically backed fulltext. Depending on the definition of the norm, the part is made available to the designer by means of selection of the variant or of determination of the specification parameters in 3D or true to view (with or without measurements) for inclusion in his design. This requires parametric procedures within the CAD-system to compute the desired dimension of the actually selected standard part.

Figure 1.3.14 shows the external tie-in of DIN parts. Figure 1.3.15 shows an example of standard-part search with final transfer to and use in the CAD system.

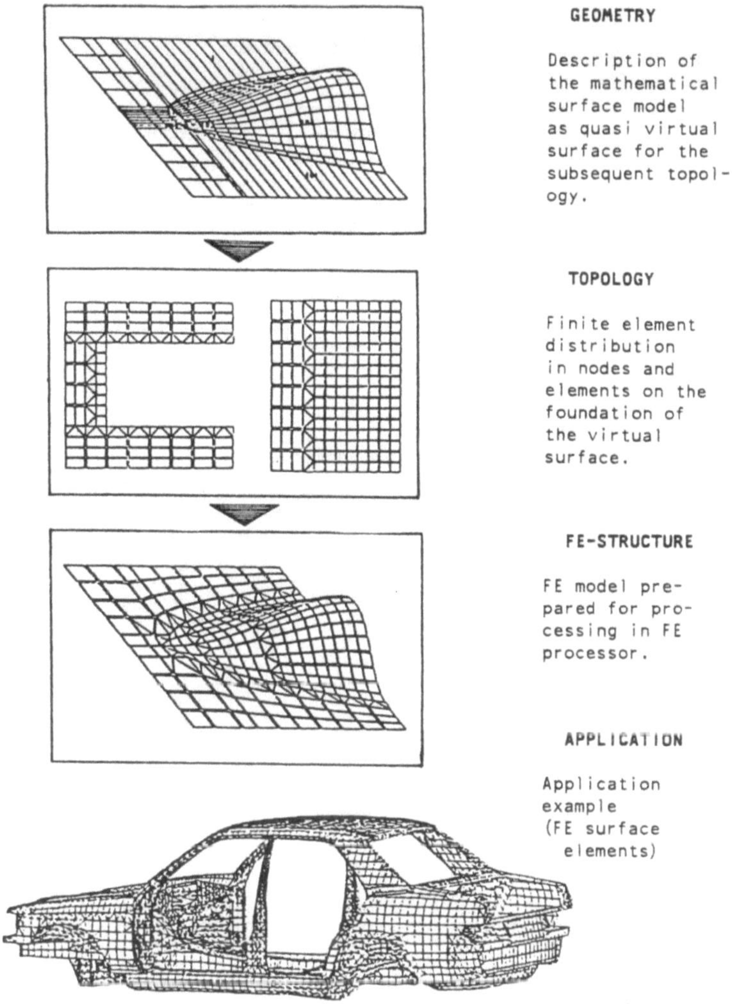

Figure 1.3.12. Computation: CAD support of computation with FEM model generation

Demands from the viewpoint of DP-supported computation	CAD/CAM requirements
- Direct exchange of 3D geo-metry over program interfaces (complete piece description)	- Geometrical base model; Geometry, Information and Management - System
- CAD functions for modelling tasks in the computation	- CAD/CAM system, geometry processing modul
- Free movement of data and applications	- Homogeneous DP environ-ment

Figure 1.3.13. Computation: Demands of DP supported computation

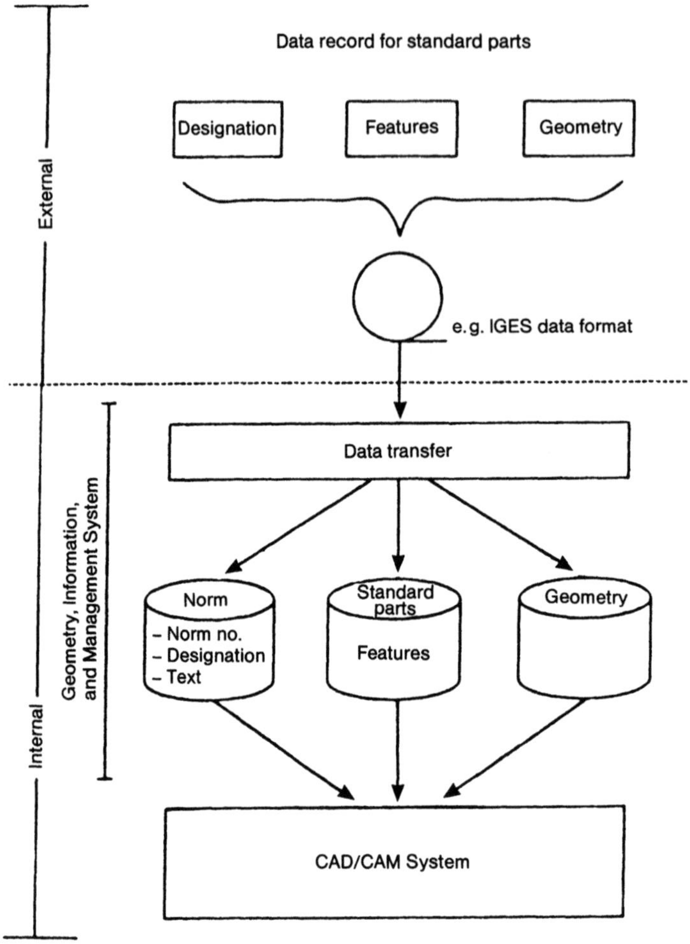

Figure 1.3.14. Transferance of CAD standard parts

```
SEARCH  -  Searching in fulltext procedure:
           + Standards number
           + Designation
           + Features
           + Measurements
           + Keywords, ...

SELECT  -  Determine delineations:
           + Selection of table column/line
           + Selection of variable parameters
        -  3D solid model and/or
        -  Selection of desired view
        -  with/without dimensioning, ...

Present -  Positioning and aligment on the
           CAD/CAM screen
```

Figure 1.3.15. Standard and repetition part retrieval in design

1.3.3.2.3 Production Planning and Engineering

In the area of production tool design, essentially the same CAD functions are needed as in the area of product development. Production tools are necessary for the production, testing, transport, etc., of a manufactured part. Direct communication between the product designer and the production tool designer, in the same system environment, allows the production designer to get the earliest possible information for the fulfillment of his task, independent of location.

Figure 1.3.16 shows the machining equipment for an exhaust manifold. Here, as in the next example, the correct part description (here: surface description) for the design of the equipment has to be submitted.

Figure 1.3.17 shows the design of a trunk lid drawing die. The trunk lid surface itself was determined in the car body design and transferred directly and without loss of accuracy. This means that a mathematical conversion of the surface data of the trunk lid was avoided.

The most lasting changes will come through the introduction of CAD systems in the design area, in the relation between design and manufacture, and in the *manufacturing area* itself.

The traditional interface between design and manufacture was hitherto the drawing. The quality of the information for the production engineer was largely determined by it. The quality and quantity of information are being decisively improved through the introduction of CAD systems in the design area. The design department's geometrical base model is the *foundation* for the subsequent work of *production engineering*, which supplements the geometrical component description with additional information corresponding to the chosen method of production.

In the past, design, production engineering, and production acted clearly and finely divided. The NC programming group in production recorded the geometry

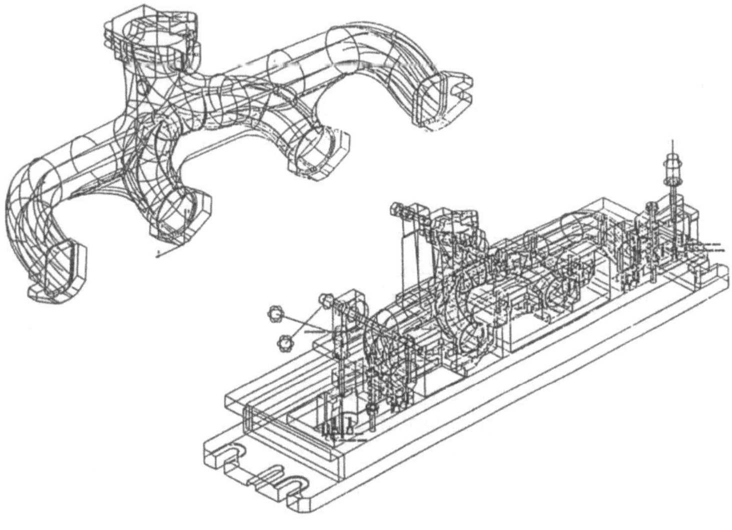

Figure 1.3.16. Equipment construction: Designing with solid and surface elements

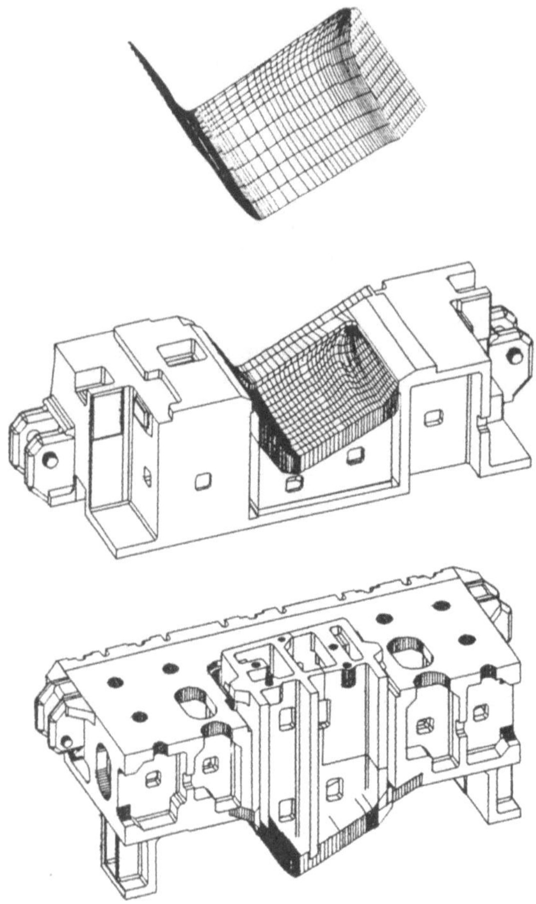

Figure 1.3.17. Production tool design: Transferance of surface data

of the component again and described it in the geometry part of the NC program. The basis for this was the design drawing, even when it was done with the help of a CAD system. The geometrical model of the component stored in the CAD data bank was only *indirectly* used.

In cutting or non-cutting manufacturing processes, the part description has to be specifically supplemented and/or adapted. Additional information, e.g., conditions out of the computation programs such as fluidic limiting conditions for pipe cross-sections, are given on as additional information to the production engineers.

In the future designer and production engineer will work side by side, with a positive effect on design suitable for manufacture and the efficient and cost-cutting creation of NC programs.

The dialogue between designer and production engineer will be a dialogue via terminal, with the gaol of optimizing the functionality and manufacturing suitability of a part. This dialogue becomes more efficient, the integration of design

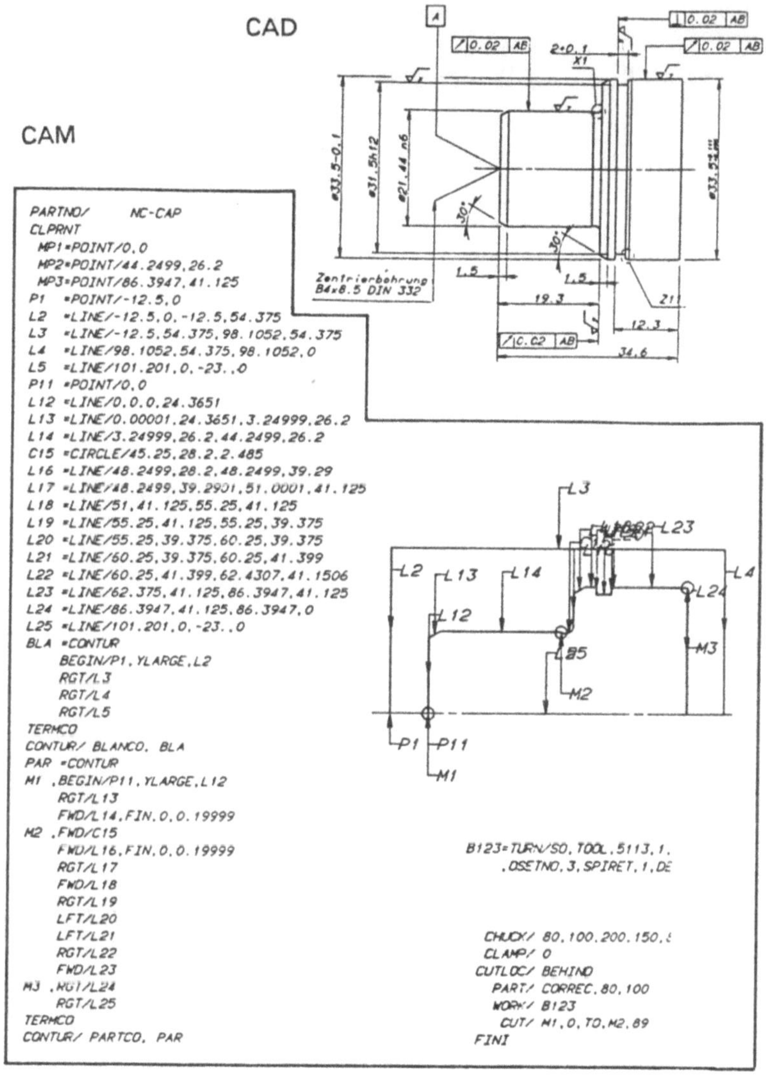

Figure 1.3.18. Graphically interactive NC part programming: Example – lathe work

and production more successful, *the more homogeneous the system environment is in which both move.*

The future workstation of the *production engineer* will consist of an alphanumerical and a graphics screen. On the graphics screen all CAD functions which are also used in the design area will be supplemented by the CAM functions which he needs for the requisite production preparation of the part (Fig. 1.3.18) On the alphanumerical screen complete control of the *work flow planning* will take place.

Figure 1.3.19 shows the basic flow of computer supported production planning and engineering.

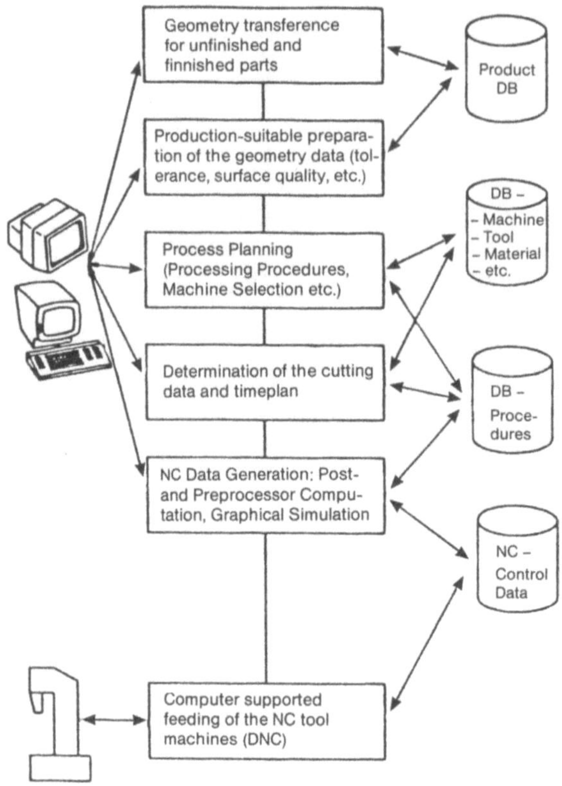

Figure 1.3.19. Production planning and engineering

The task of production planning becomes more *complicated* when procedure-conditioned peculiarities are introduced, such as form distribution, extraction angles, and consideration of the amount of shrinkage in the production of a casting.

It is precisely in the sense of making production facility preparation efficient that a close collaboration between product design on the one hand, and production planning and production tool design on the other hand, is absolutely necessary, in the framework of a CAD/CAM system environment that is as homogeneous as possible.

Existing systems (e.g., NC systems, alphanumeric planning systems) have to be integrated into the CAD/CAM process chain (see also the section "Internal and External Interfaces").

1.3.3.2.4 Quality Control/Quality Assurance

The task of *quality testing* consists, in part, of the comparison of the *desired values* specified by product development with the *actual values* achieved in manufacturing.

These desired values will be made available by CAD systems to an increasing degree in the future.

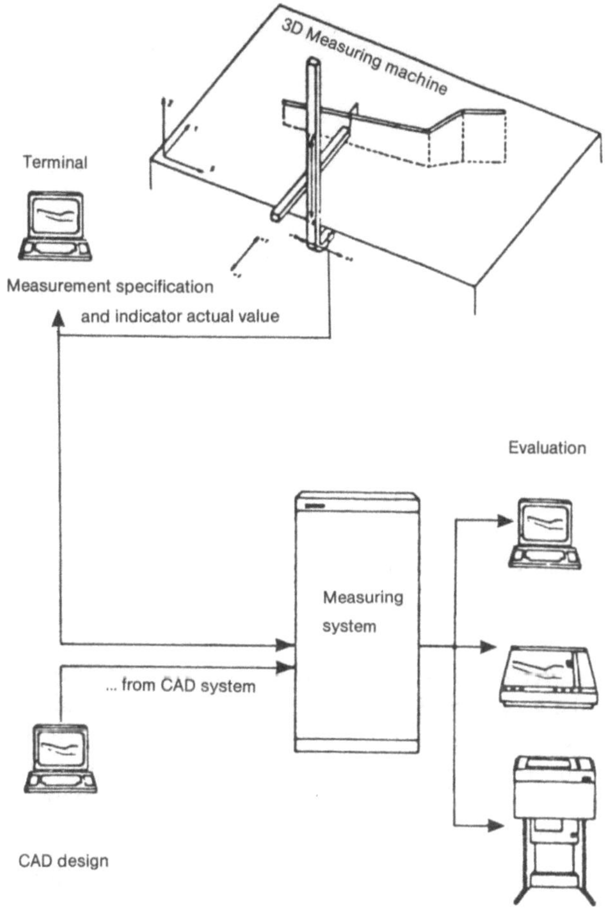

Figure 1.3.20. Quality control: Pipe measuring

Without going into the job area in detail, it is conceivable that the mathematical model of a part will be "loaded down" into a dedicated quality measurement system, where it will be provided with a measurement specification by the measurement engineer, and then the desired-value/actual-value comparison will be performed with log output and possibly feedback information to product design.

Figure 1.3.20 shows the desired-value/actual-value comparison: design of the pipe by means of geometry functions, production of pipe-bending data, generation of measurement specifications, measurement of the bent pipe, comparison of the pre-specified and measured data.

1.3.3.2.5 Fringe Areas

A number of areas not immediately participating in the production of the product will be able to use the geometrical base model in order to make their own work flow more efficient. As examples two areas will be mentioned:

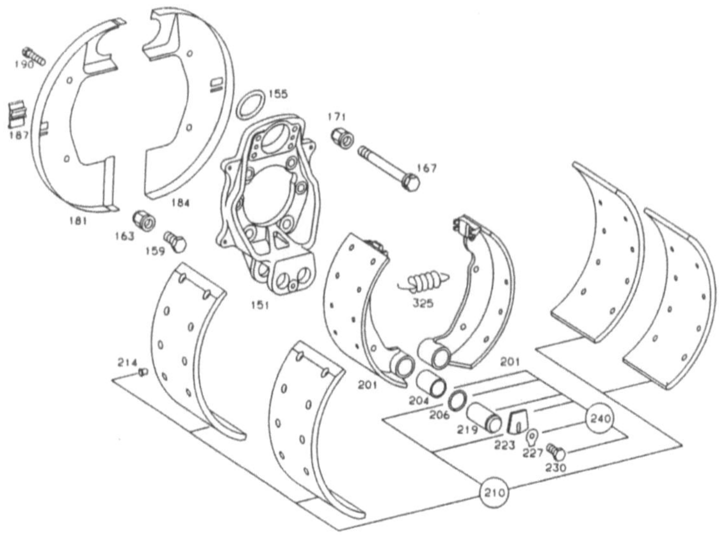

Figure 1.3.21. Information transfer in the process chain: Example – Technical Documentation

1. *Technical Documentation.* The technical documentation department will use the geometrical base model for the computer aided preparation of replacement part catalogues, operating and service center forms, et al. (Fig. 1.3.21), either directly or as layout help for a commercial artist. Although not yet satisfactorily solved, it is here absolutely essential that there be a comfortable mixture of graphics and text.

2. *Sales/Acquisition et al.* The primary possibility here is the processing of the base model for sales, advertisement, and education materials in animated or non-animated form (films, simulations, paperware). In addition to the requirements from (1) for graphics and text layout, technicians will be needed for artistic shaping and for motion simulation (vision simulation).

Secondary, the evaluation of the technical and organizational data from the geometry, information, and management system will vouch for product information and product controls.

1.3.3.2.6 Internal and External Interfaces

When one looks at the present situation in the automobile industry along the stages of the process chain, one frequently finds the system environment as it is shown in Fig. 1.3.7.

When one looks at the communication between these systems one sees that, because these systems usually possess their own DP field, no *functionally interactive coupling* is realizable; only a data coupling at a systems technologically low level is possible (Fig. 1.3.22). This data coupling, however, does not fulfill the integrity conditions as they were demanded at the beginning in the section "The CAD/CAM Process Chain in Automobile Manufacturing."

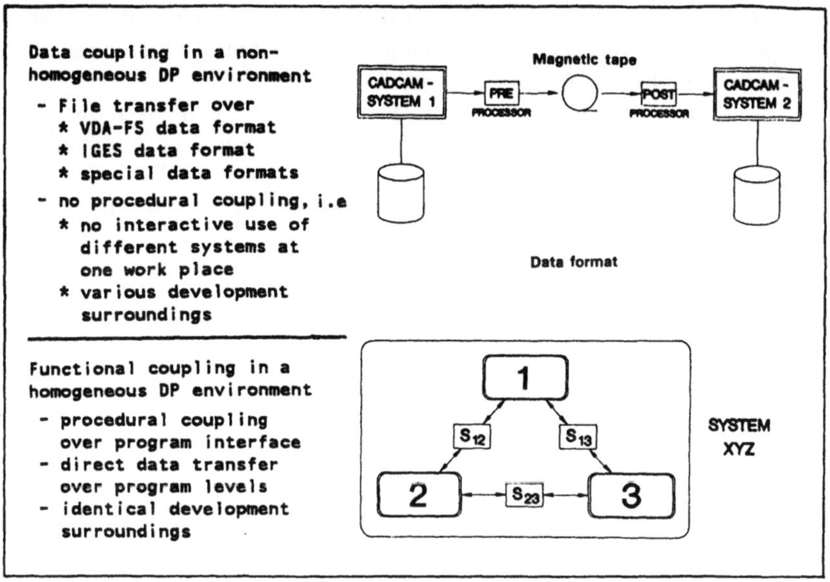

Figure 1.3.22. CAD/CAM interface types: Functional and data-technical coupling

For an optimal transferrance of a product model from one CAD/CAM system to another on the *level of pure data coupling* only the data format IGES (Initial Graphic Exchange Specification) is currently available. Here, although the product model is transformed as well as possible, the transformation is not complete in the sense of a 1:1 image.

The advantages of IGES are:

- in discussion as an international standard
- general DP-engineering format
- pre-processors and post-processors are prepared in part by the CAD/CAM distributors

On the other hand, the disadvantages at present are:

- bulky data storage
- complex programming and conversion
- definition in syntax and semantics equivocal
- no clear programmer instructions derivable
- missing or defective structure definitions
- no implementation steps given; therefore the performance ranges of the pre-processors and post-processors from producer to producer are different and hardly comparable
- the previous test library had to be discarded because of defects; i.e., there is at this time no test spectrum for the processors
- important geometry elements are not supported
- no support of the clear, unequivocal transfer of standard elements

Even with the removal of all the weaknesses of IGES it will remain a data transport format; this is indeed its defined task; it cannot provide the interactive functional coupling of graphic systems.

Another situation arises in the interaction with supply firms of the automobile industry. Here, at present no need for functional coupling is in sight. In data exchange the development of a "minimal" interface, the VDA-FS data format, has become a speciality of the automobile industry and is currently the preferred means of transferring surface data.

1.3.4 System Engineering Aspects of an Integrated CAD/CAM Concept

1.3.4.1 A Possible Hardware Architecture

The conceptual guidelines for achieving an integrated CAD/CAM concept in the automobile industry can be outlined briefly as follows:

- As far as possible, a *homogeneous system environment* should be aimed at, without complex logging, procedure, and data format conversions.
- The number of computer levels should be reduced to the necessary minimum in order to guarantee control of the network (Fig. 1.3.23).
- Beneath the general-purpose computer level, real time process systems can be installed a long side the CAD/CAM workstations; for instance, allied to the CAD/CAM process chain in the areas of tool machine control (DNC), test-data recording and processing in quality and precision engineering, and manufacturing control.

1.3.4.1.1 CAD/CAM Work Places (Workstation Concept)

As hardware architecture, a two-level computer hierarchy seems sensible for the integration of CAD/CAM into the automobile industry (Fig. 1.3.23 and Fig. 1.3.24):

- A powerful large-scale computer system with centrally available mass storage. The system may have access to accurate, high performance computing power.

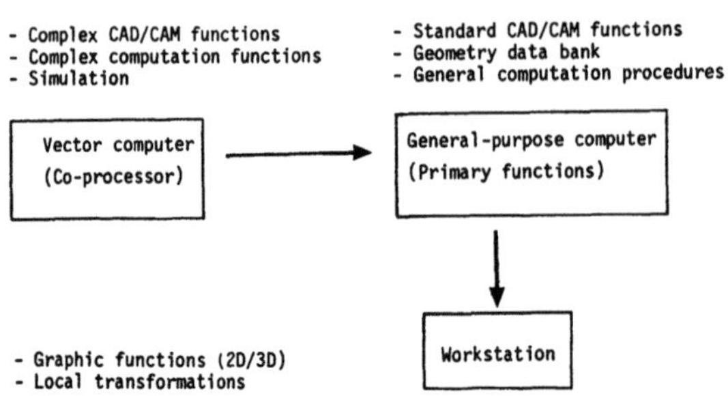

Figure 1.3.23. Future developments in computer hierarchy

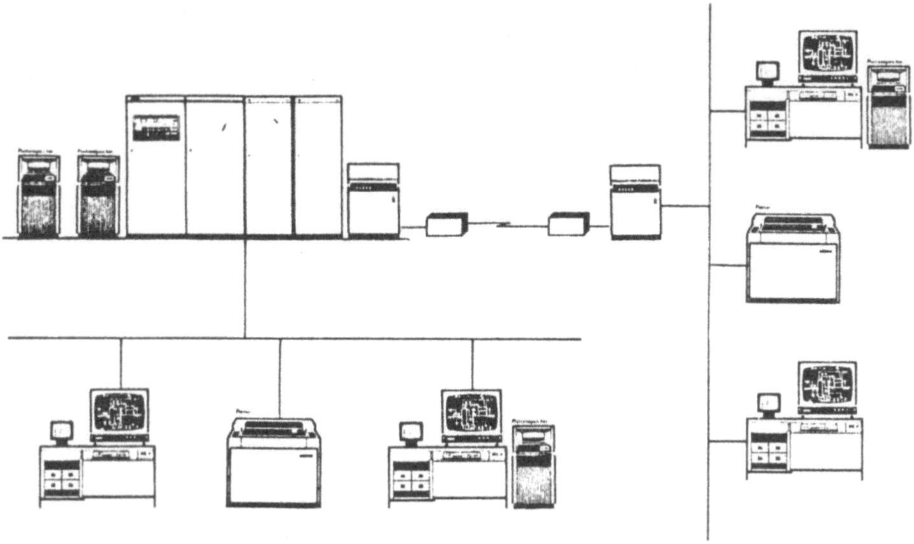

Figure 1.3.24. Central computer with CAD workstation (local and remote)

The CPU work load should not, on average, exceed 70% in order to ensure satisfactory response time.

- An efficient CAD workstation with 32-bit processor(s), color raster screen and flexible peripheral equipment which is adaptable and expandable (Fig. 1.3.25).

Intelligent operating system software and communication software, as well as a revised software structure (as opposed to present CAD systems) will make distributed processing possible, in the framework of an interactive communication between both processors. The possibilities of performance control on the central system thereby guarantee that a demand coming from workstation is processed with priority. 2D/3D graphic functions and simple CAD functions will run locally in the workstation computer.

All model-changing functions which require high computational performance (connective functions in volume modelling, model cross-sections, kinematic function, surface penetration, real-time hidden line, et al.) will run, *automatically* triggered, in the powerful central computer.

The growing performance capacity of microprocessor systems and even lower mass storage costs lead to an increased storage of functions in the workstation computer, with *local* data storage. In future, standardized CAD/CAM functions will be integrated as firm-ware into the CAD workstations.

The advantages and arguments for these ideas are summarized in Fig. 1.3.26.

1.3.4.2.1 Computer and Operating System

The performance demands of complex 3D-CAD/CAM systems (Fig. 1.3.27) require corresponding computer and operating systems. The call for expansion in

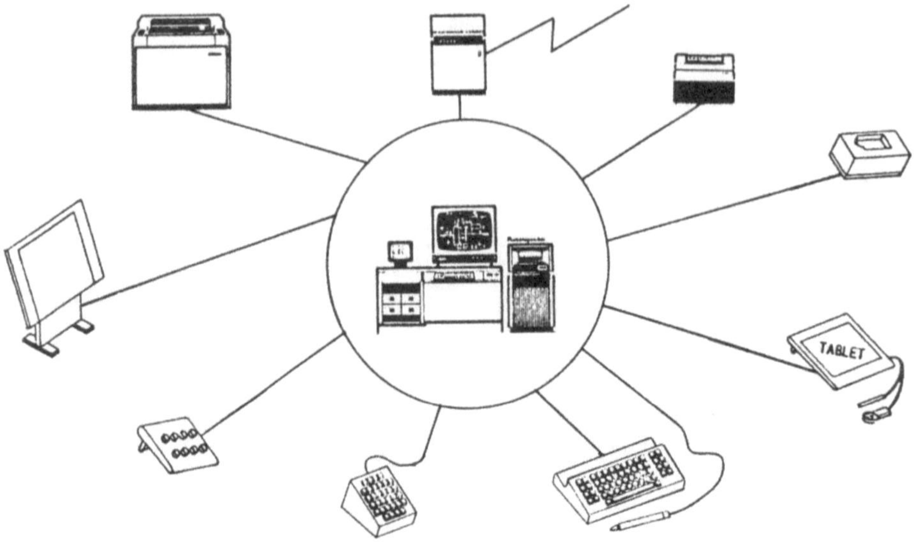

Figure 1.3.25. CAD workstation (configuration)

Workstation concept

- 0 Avoidance of multiple computer levels
- 0 Direct and efficient connection to the host
- 0 Local functions at the workstation
  - Processing
  - Presentation
  - Storage
- 0 Function as standard terminal
  - Softkey switching
- 0 No activities foreign to the application at the workstation (daily backup, operating)
- 0 Configurability of the Workstation according to the area of application
  - Storage expansion
  - Digitalizing tablet
  - Printer
  - Hardcopy equipment
  - Valuator
  - Plotter
- 0 Graphic screen
  - Raster technology (standard)
  - High resolution >=(1024 x 1024)
  - Color
  - Vector-refresh technology (simulation)

Figure 1.3.26. CAD/CAM work places as workstations on the host system

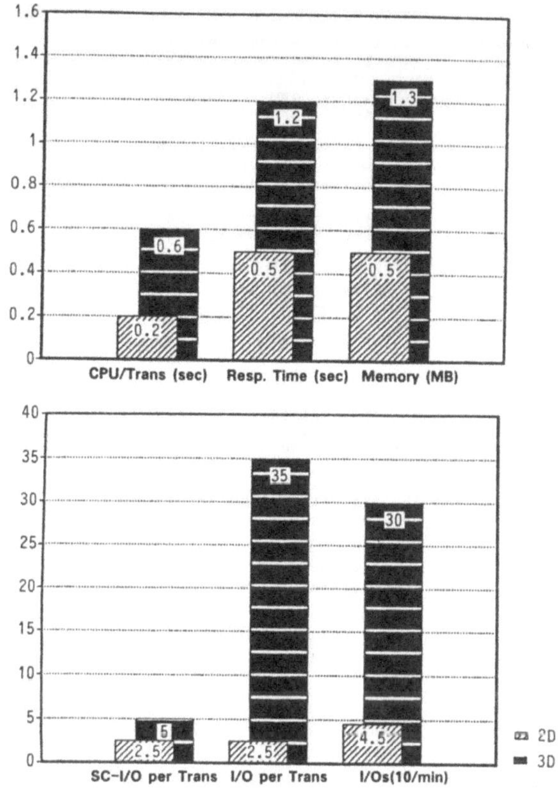

Figure 1.3.27. Performance of CAD/CAM systems

the quality and quantity of CAD/CAM applications requires an expandable computer family under common operating system control.

1.3.4.2 Network Architecture

The communication between the parts of the process chain and the different computer localizations can be safeguarded only by a *uniform network and communication architecture* (Fig. 1.3.28). Through this an application and data tie is guaranteed in the same location and over different locations (Fig. 1.3.29).

1.3.4.3 Software Architecture

In addition to the requirements of modern system architecture of the CAD/CAM system (with the components of monitor control, dialogue management, model management), components for fast interactive *"task-to task" communication* between the host computer and the more powerful graphical workstations are becoming increasingly necessary.

The software has to be loadable from the host computer into the CAD workstation and has to recognize the current configuration of the CAD workstation.

Network - Functions realized for the user through software products

* Network communication programs
* Network control programs

- Construction specification for all communication hardware and software products.

- Structuring of all of the functions necessary for communication into funtion layers.

- Validity of all components in the Network connection.

- All data avaible in a network is reachable from every point in the network.

- All applications, regardless of which computer they run on, are reachable from all terminals in a network.

- The applications in the network can communicate with each other.

- The configuration possibilities for networking are such that hardly any constraints result from the network topology.

- Public networking and satellite links for transcontinental connections are possible.

Figure 1.3.28. Network architecture I: requirements

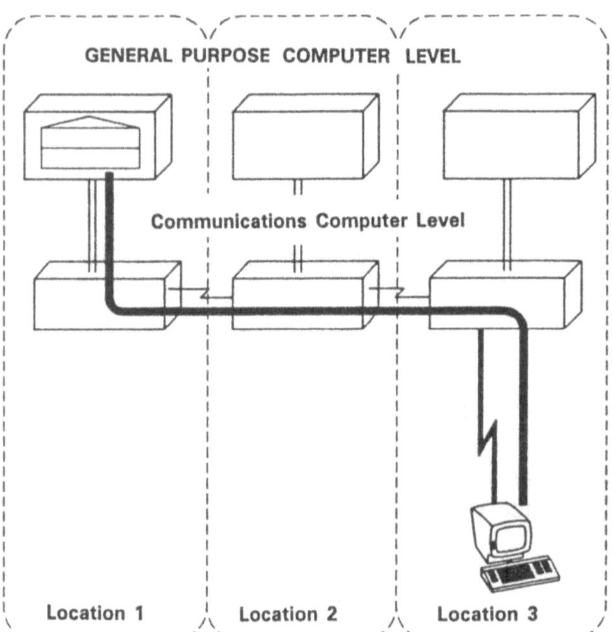

Figure 1.3.29. Network architecture II: applications

The use of the full 3D functioning of these stations requires corresponding universal drive-software.

An integration of a CAD/CAM system into the firm's existing DP environment or the introduction of firm-specific CAD/CAM functions into a CAD/CAM system can take place only on the basis of a *functional and interactive coupling,* if time-wasting and expensive conversion processes are to be avoided. For this coupling the CAD/CAM system requires a program-engineering development level in the form of an open and standardized *graphical operating system,* which is prepared and maintained by the CAM/CAD configurator, and which is matched to the relevant hardware, operating system, and software engineering developments (Fig. 1.3.30).

The graphical operating system of a CAD/CAM system has to make available the following functions in the form of program calls in a standard language for the tying-in of self-developed user modules:

- Program control
- Graphical screen management with
  - Menu control
  - Drive of the local terminal functions
- Model access
- Model management
- Operating system communication
- Program library
  - Graphical basic program
  - Mathematical basic program
  - General service performance program

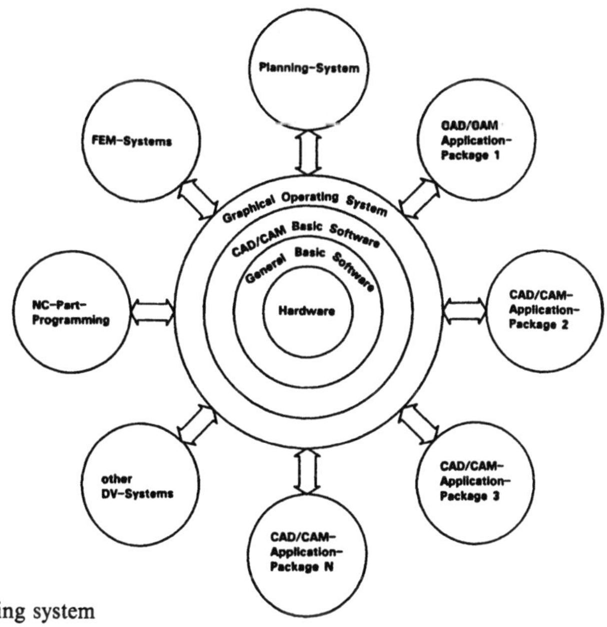

Figure 1.3.30. Graphic operating system

A CAD/CAM system configurable in this way first of all makes the CAD/CAM basic functions available along the entire process chain, and furthermore, makes possible the integration of process-specific function complexes (Fig. 1.3.31).

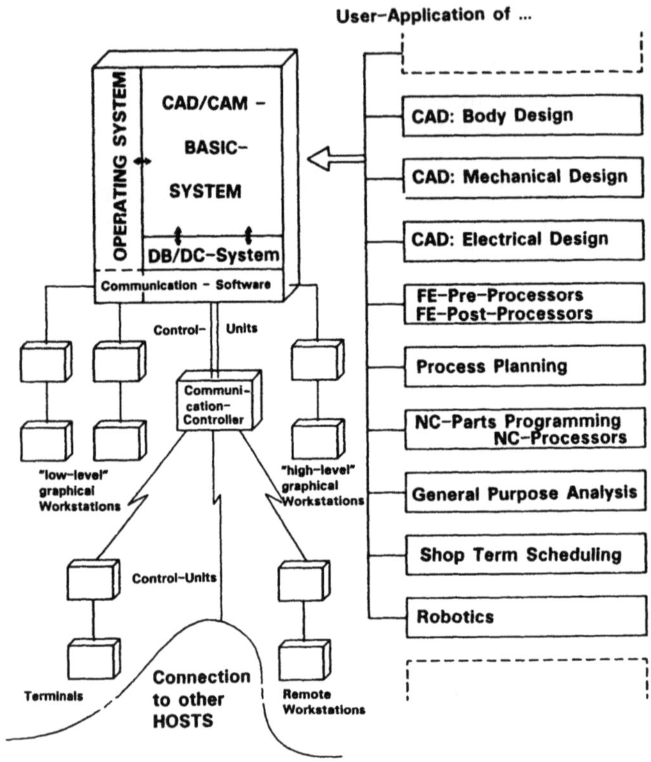

Figure 1.3.31. Applications along the process chain

1.4 Interfaces for CAD Applications

K. Pasemann

1.4.1 Introduction

IGES and lately VDAFS are the key concepts when discussing CAD-interfaces. CAD-interfaces are a major topic in the realm of CAD-integration. Up to the present time it has been the task of the CAD-systems analysts in industry to introduce and support particular design processes i.e. to develop or adapt appropriate CAD-systems. The emphasis was on the human interface in its fullest sense between a designer and his CAD-workstation. Since a vast amount of CAD-data has been generated which is benefical not only to the design process but also for many other branches in a company, CAD-data has to be made available to those other systems i.e. users. Eventually CAD must have an impact on the corporate data structure. This is a natural consequence of having CAD-data since these data contain the most complete geometrical description of the products. Due to response time requirements, the kind of CAD-modeling involved and the operating systems, CAD-data is structured in many extremely complex ways. Each CAD-system has a different structure.

The CAD-interfaces are the bridges between different data structures. Those available are of some help for industrial applications. Much is left to be done. The CAD system vendors will have to provide neutral interfaces. It is the task of the users to make this happen.

All larger industrial companies have different CAD-systems for various applications. This applies also to their suppliers. A keen interest among user companies has been generated to force the system vendors, with the help of standardization bodies, to supply neutral CAD-interfaces.

In this paper the current possibilities and the underlying subjects, CAD-systems, communications, interface formats and data bases, are discussed as they relate to the present possibilities and requirements of CAD interfaces. For all of the areas mentioned, standardization is the most important prerequisite. Up to now standardization has had practical consequences only for communications (ISO-OSI) and for interface formats (IGES).

1.4.2 CAD Systems

Today all large industrial companies have introduced CAD to some degree. A few American, Japanese and French companies have developed their own systems in house starting some 15 years ago. Due to the constraints of that time they were developed on general purpose computers. Some of these systems are now offered on the marketplace. Most of the other companies have acquired CAD turnkey systems over the last few years. Drafting has been the prevailing application area. In recent years surface and wire frame modeling has come into use by designers. Solid modeling is about to enter the design office. However none of the present CAD-systems is capable of processing and storing all details of a geometrical model of an industrial product. It also means that up to now no single CAD-system covers all reasonable requirements for designing complex products. Different types of systems have therefore been introduced within recent years in large companies for various application areas in different locations.

Many facets of mechanical and electrical CAD-system features apply to car design. The emphasis is on mechanical design, and it alone will be considered in this paper. All features of CAD-systems for mechanical design are required in the car industry. This implies that all kinds of geometric modeling, ranging from schematics and drawings to solid modeling, are involved. The modeling of smooth surfaces is the most important.

Up to now different CAD-systems have been necessary to meet the various application requirements, thereby forcing the development of interfaces between these CAD-systems. The applications adjacent to CAD are FEM-computations and NC-processing. They also have to be connected via interfaces which must be capable of transferring the geometrical data generated in the CAD-systems.

The ultimate benefit of CAD application in industry however will result from integration of the various systems. This includes analysis, NC-systems and -processors and more importantly the corporate data structure i.e. the commercial systems side. Integration means first of all well functioning interfaces between these systems providing internal or external communication of product data. This is a natural consequence of having modular systems.

1.4.3 Interface Possibilities

The application areas extend from drafting to modeling of complex surfaces and volumes. Different systems were required to accomplish a reasonable support for the multitude of individual applications. This has been the only way by which CAD could be introduced. Unfortunately the different systems have different user interfaces, run on different mainframes and operating systems, use different CAD workstations and have a multitude of additional different features and philosophies.

The implementation of the GKS-standard for CAD-systems would make these systems independent of the graphical input/output i.e. independent of the CAD workstation and somewhat portable at the same time, see Fig. 1.4.1. The GKS (Graphical Kernel System) has almost passed the final standardization procedures in Germany, in the US and in the ISO.

In recent years the traditional drafting oriented systems have been enhanced so that they also support 3-dimensional (3-d) design work. Other, newer systems, which have initially been developed for 3-d or solid modeling design, have ap-

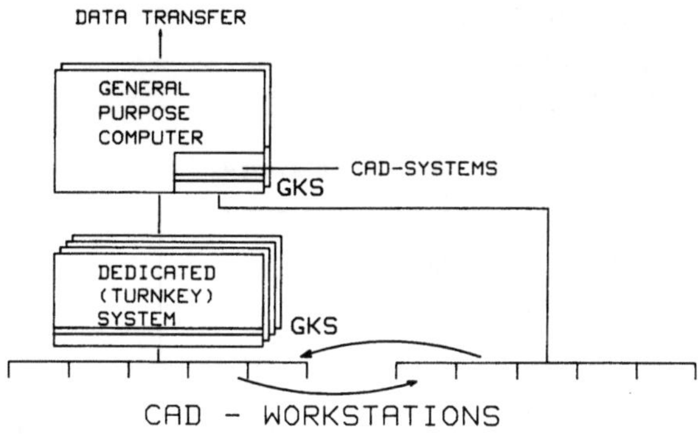

Fig. 1.4.1. Portability of GKS

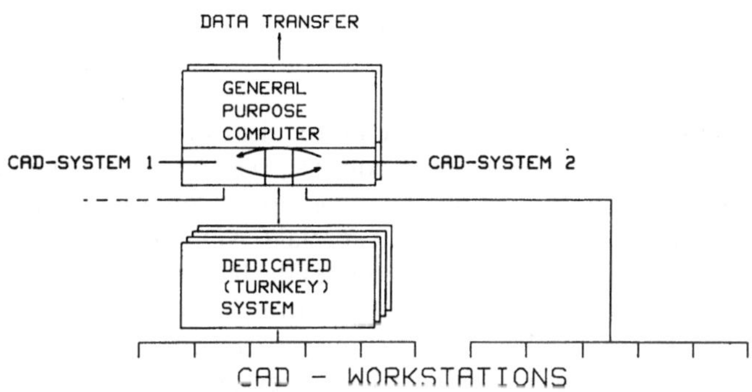

Fig. 1.4.2. Portability of CAD-systems using general purpose computers

peared in the marketplace. They have been extended into 2-d drafting. There is a general tendency whereby the CAD-systems with different roots and philosophies are developed into very general systems supporting all important aspects of mechanical design and drafting. These more general systems will alleviate some of the problems mentioned, representing a limited step towards integration, since many different systems will not be required any more, see Fig. 1.4.2.

Standardization of the user interface would represent a large step towards CAD-integration, in that applications and end users would then be portable, and in this way the different sources of CAD-data streams could be limited, see Fig. 1.4.3. At present the designers have to master the intricacies of different user interfaces and their philosophies, which is much too costly.

The use of general purpose computers for CAD application will ease the interface problem. It is therefore an obvious tendency in all large companies to limit the variety of CAD-systems and their respective systems environments as a practical approach towards integration. The standardization with respect to CAD-systems leaves much to be desired; it has not even started yet, for obvious commercial reasons. As a consequence, de facto standards will evolve in the marketplace. The remainder of this paper will discuss the interfaces which are of immediate practical importance for CAD applications.

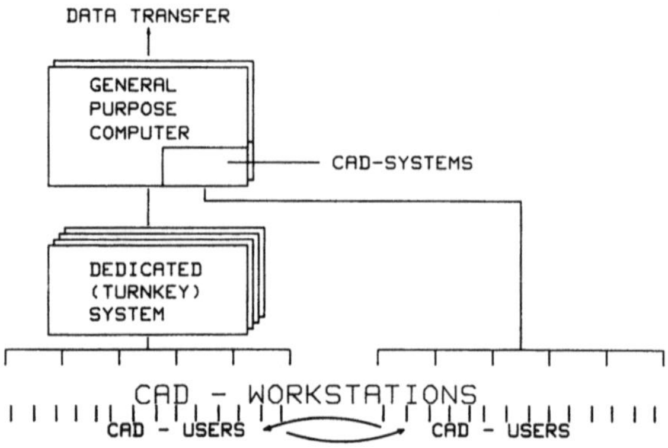

Fig. 1.4.3. Portability by common user interface

1.4.4 Communication

Communication is one of the prerequisites for CAD-integration. The ISO-OSI-layer model is applied as a concept, see Fig. 1.4.4. The layers 1 through 5 are considered in this section under the topic "Communication". It provides the basis from which on can implement special CAD interfaces, in a way similar to that in which an operating system provides the basis for application programs. There are many ways in which the layers 1 through 5 are implemented and used in CAD. Some vendors deliver LANs (Local Area Networks) for communication between computers and/or intelligent CAD-workstations. These LANs will then typically also have a gateway to general purpose computers.

In terms of the layer model the layers 6 and 7 represent the CAD-interfaces, which will be discussed in the next section.

In conjunction with the standardization in this field and the evolving related products, a reasonable base for CAD-integration will be available within the next few years.

Layer		Realisation	
		Technology	Application dependent
7	Application		CAD/CAM Systems, User Dialog
6	Presentation		GKS, IGES, VDAFS
5	Communication control		Supervision of Information exchange and Access
4	Transport		Delivery of Data
3	Network	X 25 Packet switching	Data transport, Selection of Communication Paths
2	Datalink	HDLC Error correcting Codes	Reliability of Transmission
1	Physical	V 24, Koax, Basis band	Physical Connection

Fig. 1.4.4. ISO-OSI 7-layer model

1.4.5. Interface Requirements

Interfaces or CAD interface formats are crucial for CAD integration. They must be developed within the CAD realm due to their application dependency, whereas communication facilities are more general and should preferably be delivered as a general purpose network, like an operating system.

Interfaces provide a format by which all product definition data, including geometrical modeling and drafting data, can be transferred between systems. The CAD-systems have different internal data formats structures and semantics. A particular application will only use a fraction of the full set of possibilities. These various subsets have to be mapped one onto the other without loss of information via the interface. This will most likely not be achieved. There are promising standardization efforts underway, since the importance of interfaces has been universally acknowledged. This has led initially to different formats and more importantly to extensive national and international standardization efforts.

International standardization is an absolute requirement for of the following reasons:

- Different CAD-systems stemming from different countries are in use in the same company.
- International companies have to ship their data between different subsidiaries in different countries.
- The network of national and international trade and the division of labour will require general exchange of product definition data.

The latter point will always be important no matter how unified companies might be within themselves. Different systems will have to handle product definition data within companies such as in the realm of CAD, FEM and NC. The multitude of systems in different corporations will be even larger. Therefore an international standard will be the only promising future solution.

1.4.6. Interface Standards

The most important Interface Standard is the IGES (Initial Graphic Exchange Specification) effort. IGES was developed and standardized in the US. Almost all major US CAD-vendors and industrial users are actively working in their respective NBS committees. Due to the wide support, most vendors currently offer partial implementations of this standard. They are continuously upgraded as the experience and requirements of the users demand more features and more reliability. The present implementations provide for the transfer of limiting modeling data.

The IGES effort was initiated with the classical 3-d wire frame model and with some preliminary solutions in mind. It is not based on a consistent concept, and was developed and standardized in a very short time frame.

Present experience confirms this initial limitation. As an evolving standard the IGES-implementations will provide for exchange of drafting and limited geometrical modeling data. There is currently much work being done in the US and some in Europe to make IGES a more concise and more general standard as the next versions are developed.

The representatives of the German car manufacturers and their suppliers, working together in the VDA (Verband der Deutschen Automobilindustrie), realized in 1982 that product defining data must be transferred to the CAD-systems of the tool suppliers. Since IGES version 1 was too limited to allow the transfer of complex car body surfaces, the VDAFS (VDA-Flächen-Schnittstelle) surface interface was defined. It is strictly limited to surface modeling data and was implemented in almost all in house developed and purchased CAD-systems in the German car industry by the end of 1984. It is thus implemented in almost all major systems. Transmissions have been successfully accomplished between different computers and CAD-systems in different companies. The VDAFS also serves as an internal interface within companies between various systems or between particular modules

VDAFS is in the process of becoming a German DIN-standard. The German standardization effort for CAD interfaces is concentrated in the DIN NAM/TAP 96-4. This committee is working on the standardization of VDAFS, it also represents the German interests in the related international ISO working group, which is TC 184 WG 1.

An interface of some importance for CAD is the graphics metafile, it supports the transfer of graphic data i.e. of pictures or presentations in a standardized way. It serves as a first step to drive a distant graphical output device (plotter) if other means are not available.

1.4.7. Data Base Interface

The interface between CAD systems and the future CAD data base is even more crucial and demanding.

Data base or engineering data base in the context of CAD denominates the total field of:

- structuring CAD-data independently of given CAD-systems,
- integrating CAD-data into the corporate data base, providing for geometrical queries,
- safely archiving and managing all CAD-data of a corporation,
- providing access for all concerned to any combination of CAD and other data,
- providing all necessary standardized parts, including the respective design-rules, to the designer.

This represents a level of integration which has not been achieved anywhere today in larger companies designing and manufacturing complex products such as cars or planes. However, it underlines the importance of interfaces. A neutral interface format for CAD data is considered a necessary step before the neutral data base structure for CAD data can be defined.

The CAD-data as generated by today's CAD-systems is large in terms of volume. 200 kBytes is the typical storage space required for one version and is often created within a time frame of between some days and several weeks. A CAD design staff of 50 designers creating a new version every four days working 40 weeks per year will create a net volume of 0.5 GByte. Assuming a time space of ten years 5 Gbytes will have to be managed in a data base which will typically double the data volume to be handled to a total of 10 GBytes. In larger companies a tenfold volume increase will occur.

These estimates show data volumes and complexities of the data structures which far exceed the present capabilities of available database systems. Within these limitations the first step is towards a data dictionary concept whereby CAD data of the amorphous data type is accessed, archived and distributed by means of a key, i.e. part number and some additional attributes. With this, the meaningful communication of CAD data between different systems has to rely on CAD-interfaces for direct transfer. Communication channels and the interface formats have to be capable of handling the data volume shown above.

1.4.8. Interface Implementations

Many other special interfaces have been developed and are in use. They typically connect two CAD-systems and serve a special purpose and application. These interfaces are often of so little generality that, as soon as one of the systems connected changes its revision level, the interface has to be reworked. Most of these interfaces will eventually disappear because of the costly support required in the fast changing CAD-environment.

Starting with IGES Version 1 and with VDAFS the vendors of CAD-systems started to develop processors. Intermediate and not fully tested versions of partial IGES implementations then became available. Due to the clarity and simplicity of the specification VDAFS implementations were also developed within the German car industry. They worked satisfactorily for the same reasons and today carry the bulk of the transmitted surface data. In addition, VDAFS processors are in use to input colour shaded output and FEM-processors.

The present IGES processors suffer from the following limitations:

- The IGES subset implemented is not defined.
- Within this subset not all entities work in one or both directions.
- Documentation is insufficient.
- The user is seldom informed by a message if an entity fails, sometimes the execution stops without notice.
- Only the ISO drafting standard is the base, DIN is not taken care of.
- The implementors cannot be questioned, they are mostly hidden in the vendor's home plant in a distant country.

These limitations force the user to test each new version, which is a very cumbersome, time consuming task, requiring excellent knowledge of both CAD-systems. The quality of the IGES processors is slowly increasing, providing the only viable general CAD interface format. Figure 1.4.5 depicts the current status of IGES and VDAFS showing the currently available entities for some CAD-systems in use at VW. Figure 1.4.6 shows a concise test example which was developed for

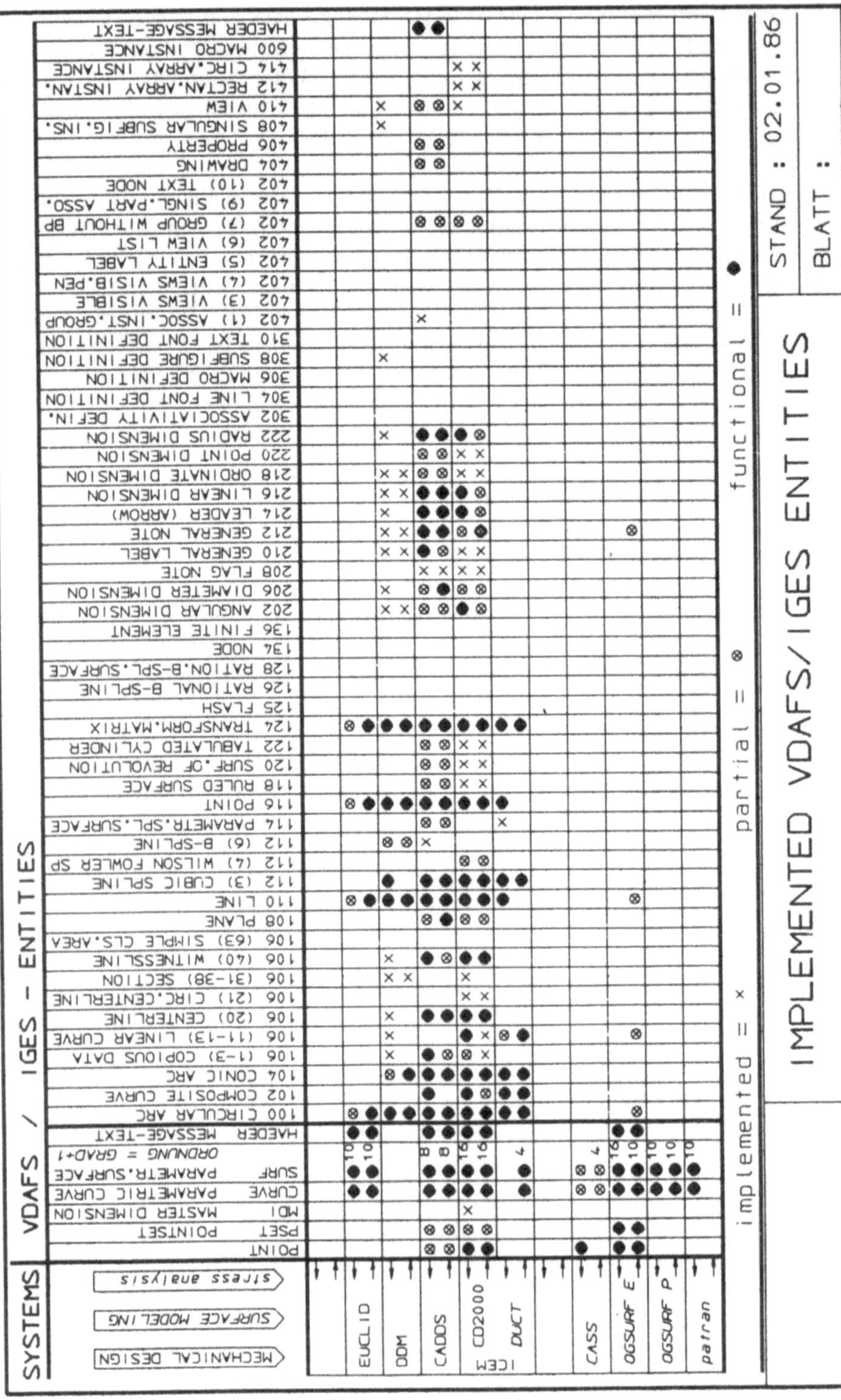

Fig. 1.4.5. Implemented VDAFS/IGES entities

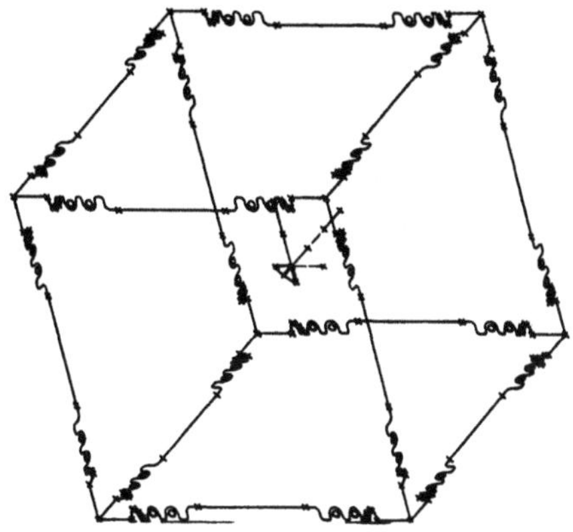

Fig. 1.4.6. IGES-test part

this purpose which has also been proposed for general use in the IGES community.

1.4.9 Conclusion

The available means of CAD-integration have been described. They provide the basis on which CAD-data is presently transferred between different systems and applications.

Graphic interface formats such as the metafile provide for drawings to be transported via communication lines to distant plotters. The transfer from CAD-systems to FEM and NC processors via appropriate interfaces is commonplace. IGES and VDAFS will become more important in this field.

In many cases the transfer of geometrical data between CAD-systems of the same or different types has been accomplished by special interfaces. Here IGES has already become the general interface for the exchange of geometrical and drawing data and will be even more so in the future. VDAFS is currently already in use within the German car industry and some of its suppliers.

The ultimate benefit of CAD applications in industry however will result from integration of the various systems. This includes analysis, NC-systems and processors and more importantly the corporate data structure, i.e. the commercial systems side. The CAD-interfaces are a prerequisite for this integration.

Chapter 2

Graphics Systems – Graphical Standards – GKS

2.1 Graphical Standards

G. Enderle

2.1.1 Introduction

In the area of Computer Graphics Systems, much activity in the last ten years has concentrated on the development of standard interfaces. Now the first project has attained the status of an International Standard: The Graphical Kernel System, GKS. But this first graphics standard is not an end point of the development, rather it has prompted a series of related projects. The goal is to create a family of compatible and consistent standard interfaces that covers the whole area of computer graphics. Keywords for the new projects are: 3D-GKS, PHIGS, CGM, CGI and WSI. These standards and their interrelation will be described in this contribution.

Computer graphics is in many cases one important aspect of application systems. For CAD systems, computer graphics components are needed for object presentation and for operator interactions. It is very desirable that standards in the CAD area be compatible with the graphics standards. The CAD product definition interfaces (like IGES) should in the long run be able to integrate information from graphics metafiles in a compatible and consistent way.

Another important application area is the handling of documents comprising both text and graphics. In this area, the upcoming standards handle graphics in accordance with the graphics standards.

2.1.2 The Graphical Kernel System – GKS

GKS is a standard for graphical application programmers. For example, if a programmer designs a Basic-program on a PC that draws piecharts, he can use GKS to do the graphics. He would need a GKS implementation integrated into the Basic language environment. For drawing the picture, the GKS output functions are needed. Another programmer, designing an interactive printed circuit layout program in FORTRAN could also use GKS. He would use output functions, picture segmentation function, and input functions. His GKS must be available as a set of FORTRAN subroutines.

Whereas for the Basic language, GKS is integrated in the form of additional statements, for most other languages GKS presents itself to the programmer in the form of a subroutine or procedure package. The original GKS standard (ISO 7942, [1]) is defined in a language independent way. For all important programming languages, a GKS representation that is compatible with the con-

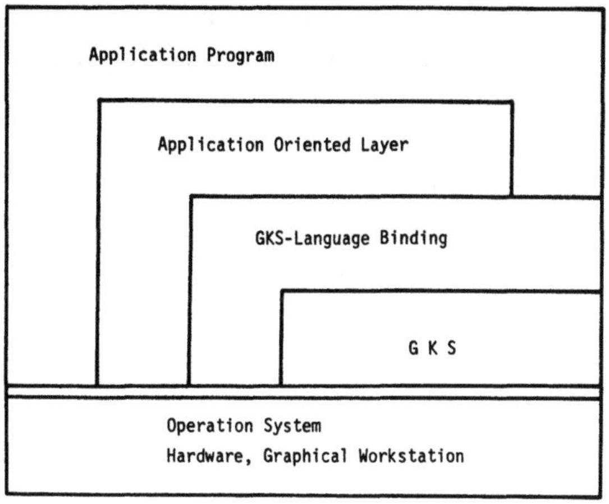

Fig. 2.1.1. Layer model of GKS

cepts of that language is defined. All these "language bindings" are parts of another standard (ISO 8651, [2]). With the language bindings, application specific subroutine packages and whole application systems can be designed (see Fig. 2.1.1).

Graphical systems were present long before GKS. The achievements of GKS compared to these systems are:

- Standard functionality. Many computer graphics experts from various nations reached a concensus on these functions after a long and sometimes controversial design and review process.
- Device independence. GKS addresses the whole range of graphical devices, from simple pen plotters to highly interactive workstations.
- Application independence. GKS offers access to graphics for a wide range of applications.
- Language independence. GKS is defined language independent but its functions can be accessed in the context of all major programming languages.
- Reference model. The GKS concepts are based on a consistent model for computer graphics.
- Computer Graphics education. GKS is a unique sound base for education in computer graphics concepts and systems.
- Standard terminology. In order to design and describe GKS, a standard computer graphics terminology (ISO 2382/13, [3]) had to be agreed on.

The functions of GKS allow for creating and presenting pictures, for structuring pictures, for high-level interaction with a human operator, for picture manipulation, for geometrical transformation and for storing and retrieving pictures. Detailed information on GKS can be found, e.g., in [4].

In 1985, GKS will be published as International Standard, but also as National Standard in the United States, in the UK, in France (in French translation), and in the Federal Republic of Germany (in German translation).

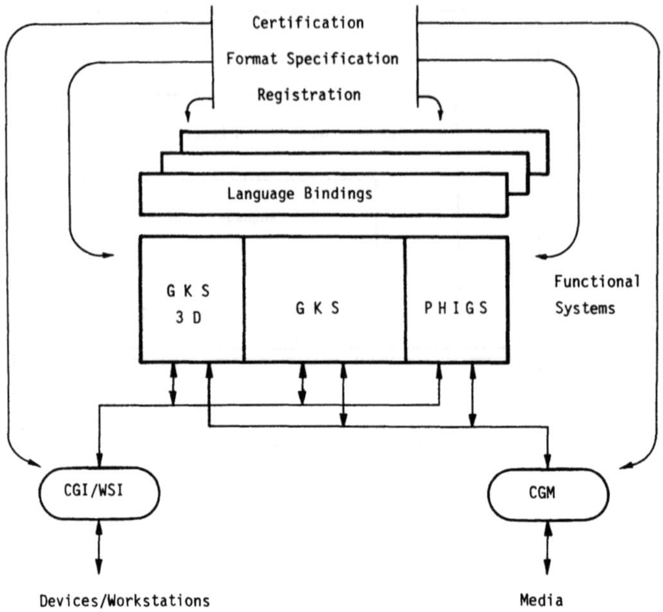

Fig. 2.1.2. Model for graphical standards

2.1.3 GKS and Other Graphics Standards

GKS is the basis for a methodology in computer graphics, and all new projects in this area are defined in a compatible way. Figure 2.1.2 shows GKS in the center of these new projects. In the functional area, two important extensions are specified: 3D-GKS, adding three-dimensional graphical functions, and PHIGS, offering a hierarchical picture structure for fast real-time 3D-transformations. All functional specifications need language bindings for various languages. All functional systems have interfaces with the devices (CGI and WSI) and with picture storing and transfer (CGM). Certification, formal specification, and registration are activities related to all graphics standards.

2.1.4 Language Bindings

To be used by an applications programmer, GKS functions have to be defined in terms of the concepts of a programming language. For languages that have a subroutine mechanism, the GKS function names have to be transformed into subroutine or procedure names obeying the conventions of the language. The GKS function parameters have to be mapped to parameters (and parameter types) available in the language.

As an example let us look at the GKS-function SET WORKSTATION VIEWPORT. It is specified in the GKS standard in the following way:

Table 2.1.1. GKS language bindings

Language	Status (1Q85)
FORTRAN	ISO DP 8651/1, DIS 2Q85
Pascal	ISO DP 8651/2, DIS 2Q85
Ada	ISO DP 8651/3, DIS 2Q85
C	Working draft [5]
Algol 68	Published proposal [6]
Basic	Binding is part of Basic Standard
Cobol	Unofficial draft
PL/1	Unofficial draft

SET WORKSTATION VIEWPORT

Parameters:
In workstation identifier N
In workstation viewport limits
XMIN XMAX, YMIN YMAC DC 4xR
("In" designates input parameters, "DC" means Device Coordinates, "N" stands for the GKS datatype "Name", "R" for the datatype "Real").

In the FORTRAN-Language binding, the same function is specified as follows:

SUBROUTINE GSWKVP (WKID, XMIN, XMAX, YMIN, YMAX)

Input Parameters:

INTEGER WKID	workstation identifier
REAL XMIN, XMAX, YMIN, YMAX	workstation viewport limits in device coordinates

(The GKS data type N has been mapped to INTEGER)

The same function in the Pascal binding:

```
procedure GSetWsViewport
(wsid : GTWsId; bound : GRbound);
```

The procedure used the PascalGKS data structures:

```
Coust GTWsId = INTEGER;
GRbound      = record
                 LeftBound, RightBound,
                 LowerBound, UpperBound : REAL;
               end;
```

In Table 2.1.1 the status of GKS language bindings is summarized (DP = Draft Proposal, DIS = Draft International Standard).

2.1.5 3D-GKS

GKS was specified as a two-dimensional (2D) graphics system. Many applications can be fully supported. However, for some application areas like CAD a

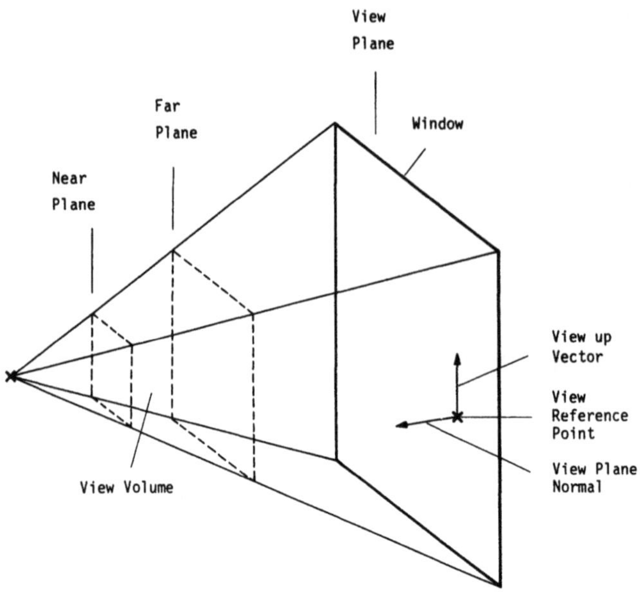

Fig. 2.1.3. GKS-3D viewing parameters

three-dimensional (3D) system is necessary. Such a 3D graphics system has been specified; it is called 3D-GKS [7]. In 1985 a DIS is expected.

3D-GKS is a consistent extension of 2D-GKS. No 2D functions are changed by this, 3D functions are a generalization of 2D functions. All 2D-GKS programs can be run in a 3D-GKS system, producing exactly the same results. The additional 3D-functions specify 3D output primitives, 3D transformations, the viewing transformation 3D → 2D, and 3D coordinate input. A hidden line/hidden surface mechanism will be included. Figure 2.1.3 shows the viewing parameters.

2.1.6 PHIGS

For some applications it is desirable to be able to support a hierarchical picture structure, and to manipulate the objects in this picture structure dynamically. Editing of objects and fast real time transformations are possible. PHIGS – the proposed "Programmer's Hierarchical Interactive Graphics System" [8], covers these most advanced concepts of computer graphics. PHIGS is a 3D system and the project is closely coordinated with the GKS and 3D-GKS projects. A stable draft can be expected within two years.

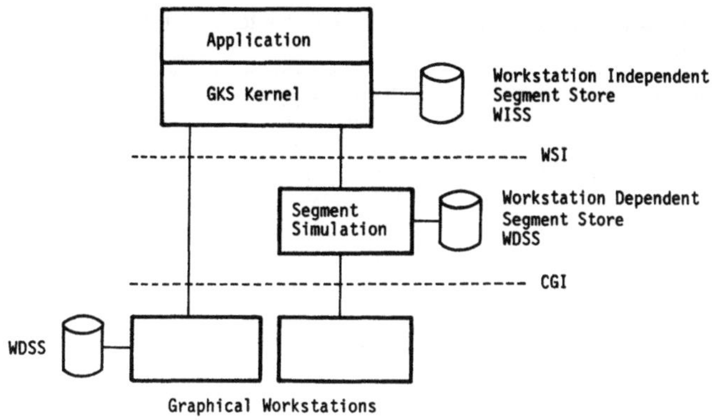

Fig. 2.1.4. Workstation interface and CGI

2.1.7 Metafiles and Device Interfaces

Graphics metafiles serve for storage and transfer of graphical information. Picture libraries can be built with metafiles, they also connect different graphics systems and devices, and they serve as picture transfer mechanisms in networks. GKS defines an interface with graphics metafiles and the format of a GKS protocol file, the GKS metafile or GKSM.

A subset of the GKS functions (GKS level – simple output) are included in the ISO Computer Graphics Metafile, CGM. The CGM functions can be represented by 3 different codings – a character coding using ISO 2022 code extension techniques, a clear text coding that is legible and editable by humans, and a binary coding. The CGM character coding will also be used for the CGI and within the CEPT picture coding standard [9].

Both the GKSM protocol file and the CGM picture file are compatible with GKS, their interface with GKS is clearly defined.

The GKS standard defines a unique interface for the application programmer. The mapping of GKS functions to device capabilities still has to be done by device drivers that often require substantial design efforts. A new project will standardize this interface between the graphics system (GKS, 3D-GKS, PHIGS) and the devices and workstations. This standard is called CGI: Computer Graphics – Interfaces for the Dialogue with Graphical Devices.

One main problem that has to be solved is the variety of devices to be addressed. Whereas a number of workstations offer complete GKS functionality in the workstation itself, other devices have no local intelligence at all. Therefore, the functions of CGI will be located at different levels. The highest level will duplicate exactly the GKS workstation functions. This subset of CGI is called Workstation Interface, WSI [10] (see Fig. 2.1.4). There are a number of workstations available on the marketplace that offer exactly the functions of WSI built into the workstation. This enables storing and manipulation of structured pictures on the workstation and fast interactions. Table 2.1.2 shows the status of CGM, CGI, and WSI.

Table 2.1.2. Status of metafile and device interface standards

Project	Status (1Q85)
CGM	
Part 1 – Character Coding	DP 8632/1 DIS 2Q85
Part 2 – Clear Text Coding	DP 8632/2 DIS 2Q85
Part 3 – Binary Coding	DP 8632/3
CGI	Working draft [11], work item in preparation
WSI	Working draft [10]
ECMA/CEPT GDV-PLPS	Draft SC2/WG8N106 [9]

2.1.8 Certification, Formal Specification, Registration

Certification procedures are defined within ISO and by several national standards bodies to test and certify the conformity of graphical standards (see the contribution by W. Hübner in Chap. 5 – Validation of Graphics Systems).

For the specification of standards, formal specification methods are under development which in the long run will replace or back up the more informal methods used up to now.

A registration authority for graphical standards has been set up at the U.S. National Bureau of Standards. Entities for which an exact definition has been left open in the graphics standards, will be registered, e.g. marker types, line types, character fonts, hatch styles.

2.1.9 Graphics and CAD

In a CAD system, the graphics part is responsible for presentation of objects and for the interaction. The graphics part can be realized by GKS. GKS controls the

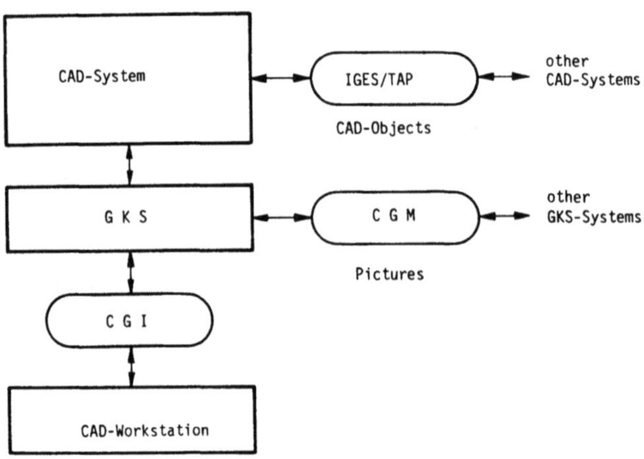

Fig. 2.1.5. CAD interfaces

workstations via the CGI interface. For storage of complete pictures, the CGM can be used (see Fig. 2.1.5).

A CAD system does not only deal with pictures (drawings), but handles and manages CAD design objects. Much of the object information is of geometric nature, but also nongeometric attributes like material data must be handled by the CAD system. Ideally, a complete description of a product (a camera, a gear box) is contained in a CAD system. This object description is at a higher, application specific level than graphics. If product definition information has to be stored or transferred, CAD interfaces are required like IGES or VDAFS. These are presented in great detail in other contributions to this book.

2.1.10 Graphics in Documents

There are a number of standards under development in the area of document processing and interchange. Documents comprise both (character) text and graphics. All projects use the appropriate graphics standards (most important GKS and CGM) for the inclusion of graphics in documents. Table 2.1.3 summarizes the status of the most important projects in this area.

Table 2.1.3. Document processing and interchange standards

Project	Status (1Q85)
ODA – Office Document Architecture	DP 8613/1–3
ODIF – Office Document Interchange Format	DP 8613/4 (= CCITT T.73)
CLPT – Computer languages for the Processing of Text Including SGML – Standard Generalized Markup Language	DP 1Q85

2.1.11 Outlook

GKS and the related graphics standards have created a reference model for computer graphics, a common educational approach and a common methodology. Graphical workstations offer GKS-functionality in hardware and firmware. More and more portable application systems are available.

A major impact can be foreseen in the areas of CAD/CAM and in document processing. Open systems interconnection in public digital networks and in digital private branch exchanges will integrate graphics, document handling, facsimile, database access, and other data processing.

Integrated Services Digital Networks (ISDN) will be in common use in many countries before the end of this decade. The standard graphics interfaces will be a prerequisite for integration in this area.

In the long term, animated raster graphics of high resolution will be possible in integrated networks (B-ISDN, broadband ISDN). The graphics standards must be able to cope with these new areas.

2.1.12 References

1. International Standardization Organization (ISO): Information Processing - Computer Graphics – Graphical Kernel System (GKS). ISO 7942 (1985)
2. International Standardization Organisation (ISO): Information Processing – Computer Graphics – Graphical Kernel System (GKS) Language Bindings. ISO DIS 8651 (1985)
3. International Standardization Organisation (ISO): Information Processing – Data Processing Vocabulary – Part XIII (Computer Graphics), ISO 2382/13 (1983)
4. Enderle G, Kansy K, Pfaff G: Computer Graphics Programming – GKS, the Graphics Standard. Springer, Berlin Heidelberg New York (1984)
5. Steinhart JE: A C Language Binding of GKS. ISO TC97/SC21/WG5-2 N247 (1984)
6. Martin RR, Anderson C: A Proposal for an Algol 68 Binding of GKS. Computer Graphics Forum 4, No 1 (1985)
7. International Standardization Organisation (ISO): Graphical Kernel System for three Dimensions (GKS-3D). ISO TC97/SC1/WG5-2 N277 (1984)
8. International Standardization Organisation (ISO): Information Processing – Computer Graphics – Programmer's Hierarchical Interactive System (PHIGS). ISO TC97/SC21/WG5-2 N305 (1985)
9. ECMA/CEPT/ISO: Graphics Virtual Device Presentation Layer Protocol Syntax (GVP-PLPS). ISO TC97/SC2/WG8 N106 (1984)
10. International Standardization Organisation (ISO): Information Processing – Computer Graphics – GKS Workstation Interface. ISO TC97/SC21/WG5-2 N238 (1984)
11. International Standardization Organisation (ISO): Information Processing – Computer Graphics – Interfaces for the Dialogue with Graphical Devices (CGI). IS0 TC97/SC21/WG5-2 (1985)

2.2 GKS and Intelligent Terminals

N. Kastner and G. Klebes

2.2.1 Introduction

Today almost all graphical devices are considered intelligent. Due to enormous hardware development graphical devices have become increasingly efficient. So XY-printers have developed into simple plotters with variable penpositioning, vector plotting and presentation of simple text. Some plotters include local memory for repetition of pictures and local programs to draw circles, arcs, axes, curves, programmable macros etc. The development of terminals has been comparable. Colour raster devices have developed from storage tube devices, terminals with local features have developed from simple plotting devices.

In considering the local capabilities of graphical devices we are not aiming at completeness, but at grouping into various fields of interest. Therefore it is no significant limitation to confine ourselves to intelligent terminals. However, a strict boundary will be drawn at graphical workstations, i.e. decentralised computers with integrated graphical capabilities, which can be plugged into networks. The philosophy of these units is entirely different. Therefore they will not be part of our considerations.

2.2.2 Intelligence of Terminals

What do we mean by the intelligence of terminals? We distinguish between two types of intelligence:

- functionality
- interface comfort.

Functionality includes the local capabilities of the graphical terminal. They influence the efficiency of application software and offer many advantages to the user.

Interface comfort is of primary importance to the complexity of the use of local capabilities. This is of special importance to the system designer, since the successful connection of a device to a graphical system essentially depends on it. Segmentation control is an example: a device with internal segment operations can be integrated into a graphical system more easily than a device whose control has to be organised externally. We will refer to this again later on.

In the following paragraph we want to discuss functionality in more detail. The local capabilities can be associated with the following areas:

- graphical output primitives
- local memory open to manipulation
- local transformations
- input capabilities
- raster-functions
- three-dimensional display.

As far as primitives are concerned it is worth mentioning all functions which exceed the simple graphical primitives, such as drawing of a vector, setting of a pixel and displaying of a character. These are – without aiming at completeness:

- rectangle
- circle and arc-polygon
- axes
- pie charts
- complex curves
- fill area
- graphical text
- raster display of pictures.

The local memory includes the possibility of storing graphical objects locally to manipulate them. Such picture elements are called segments. The following operations on segments are possible:

- set visible or invisible
- highlight
- make pickable
- zoom
- shift
- rotate
- copy
- rename
- delete.

Often several segments may be combined dynamically into groups and modified collectively. Sometimes it is possible to build hierarchical data structures. In many cases basic graphical elements used repeatedly may be defined locally. These may then be drawn without regenerating them.

Terminals often include separate vector and pixel storage. The resolution of the vector storage is normally higher than the resolution of the pixel storage via local transformation. By setting windows in the vector storage a detail may be selected for display. This detail will be mapped via transformation into pixel storage. This is a zooming operation.

Often it is possible to select an area in the pixel storage in which the graphical elements inside the window of the vector storage are mapped. This area is called the viewport. Clipping at the viewport boundaries is performed locally by the device. Some terminals may process up to 64 different local transformations. Related windows and viewports are defined and selected whenever needed.

Each terminal allows locator input and text input. Furthermore, input of other input classes, i.e. choice, pick and valuator input, is possible, occasionally via additional hardware. As a rule, the desired input is produced on request after a user action. On some devices there is the possibility of an input mode called sample-input, which reports the current state of the input device to the application program. On a very few devices it is possible to initiate an input of different input classes at the same time, where the actual input must be tested for its class membership and processed accordingly ("event input"). The input control is of great importance for interactivity. It facilitates the use of a system for the user.

Another important element of the input control is the echo type. The most common echo types are:

- crosshair cursor
- display of a digital representation of the actual input location
- rubberbanding, i.e. drawing of a line from a fixed point to the actual input-position
- segment dragging, i.e. shifting of picture segments according to the change of the input position.

Raster technology has produced a number of new functions called raster operations.

The vast proliferation of this class of devices and the novelty of its capabilities make a separate consideration of raster operations necessary. The most important functions are:

- dynamic change of colour lookup table
- setting of segment priority
- Boolean display operations
- splitting of bitplanes

With the possibility of dynamic changes of the colour lookup table, colour reaches a new quality.

On conventional devices the change of colour definition does not influence the primitives so far displayed. On raster devices change of the color lookup table can affect so far displayed primitives, e.g. parts of the picture may be deleted by setting their colour to the background colour.

The display priority defines the sequence of segment redrawing. This creates the visual impression of foreground and background.

Boolean operations define the combination of new graphical pixel information with information already displayed. The most common operations are:

- SET mode: existing information is replaced
- OR mode: the union is formed. This will cause an additive mixture of colours.
- XOR mode: the difference is formed, i.e. existing colour portions are deleted if they are also part of the new colour information, this results in a subtractive blending of colours.

Bitplane splitting means the splitting of existing bitplanes into various groups. Each group is differently mapped and controlled. This results in piled up display areas. A priority relation defines an ordering of the display areas, i.e. specifies which parts of overlapping areas are visible.

In future, three-dimensional display will become more and more important. At present some terminals with the following capabilities exist:

- processing of three-dimensional coordinates
- hidden line and hidden surface removal
- changing of perspective
- picture rotation and 3D segment transformation
- shading.

It is therefore clear that the development of local terminal intelligence is not yet complete.

Table 2.2.1 gives an incomplete overview of the intelligence of some devices.

2.2.3 GKS Driver Interfaces

GKS [1] is a device-, system- and implementation-independent interface between graphical application software and one or more graphical devices.

Between the application software and the GKS system there may be an application-orientated layer, e.g. a plot package. GKS is separated in a worksta-

Table 2.2.1

Terminal	Text			Bundle	Addr.	Clipping			
	Fill		Primitives	Seg.		Trafo			Remarks
Lexidata 8100S	+		circle, message	–	+	32	+	+	hierarchical data structures, bitplane splitting, cell def.
Somatech	+		circle, pattern	–	+	16	+	+	
Chromatics 4300	+		circle, rectangle, pattern, Bezier	–	+	16	+	+	div. character fonts
D-Scan	+		hatching	–	+	16	+	+	dragging, 64 segment levels, subsegments
Envision	+	stroke 45 deg.	circle, pattern, pie, rectangle	–	+	16	4		
TEK 4114	–	45 deg.		–	+	12	–	–	dragging
TEK 4107/4109	+	stroke, rot.		–	+	12	64	+	raster operations bitplane splitting
TEK 4115	+	stroke, rot.	rectangle	–	+	32	64	+	raster operations bitplane splitting (3D functions)
SIGMEX	+	string		+	+	16	64	+	GKS functionality
Seillac 7	+	rot.	circle, ellipse, cube	–	+	16	+	+	3D functions
Ramtek 7215	+	stroke	circle, cube, bar, ellipse	–	+	16	+	+	3D functions, floating point
Westward Graphics Manager			circle, ellipse	–	+	16	4	+	

tion independent and a workstation dependent part. The interface between these parts of GKS is, however, not defined by the GKS standard. But the existence of such an interface is implied by the demand for the existence of certain internal lists (GKS state lists, workstation state list, workstation description table), yet further information is not available.

The standardization of this internal interface has been started, but not yet been completed. The decision as to its shape and its location has to be made by the implementor. Possibilities for locating the interface will be discussed in more detail in Sect. 2.2.7.

2.2.4 Utilization of Local Intelligence by GKS

The question arises as to how many of the various local possibilities of the graphical devices can be used by GKS implementations. In GKS only the most necessary primitives are produced by individual functions. Additionally, there exists a general output function, "Generalized Drawing Primitive", for mapping of output primitives not specifically defined. By applying these generalized drawing primitives all device dependent intelligent functions mentioned in Sect. 2.2.2 can be used. The increase in local possibilities would make a definition of the most common GDPs useful.

Level 1 of GKS provides a workstation-dependent segment storage (WDSS). The local memory offers this possibility. As a rule GKS segment attributes and transformations are supported by terminals. But there are terminals which offer GKS functionality, either fully or partially, and there are others in which picture storage has to be organized by the host. As mentioned above interface comfort is important in this sphere, and in this case the implementation of a driver can become quite extensive. This especially concerns vector refresh terminals with display file processors.

GKS uses two steps to convert application coordinates into device coordinates. The normalization transformation maps the user coordinates onto normalized device coordinates. The workstation transformation maps normalized device coordinates onto device coordinates. The intelligent terminals have only one transformation possibility. This can be used for workstation transformation. The NDC-area is mapped on to the vector storage. The window in the vector storage corresponds to the workstation window; a viewport within the pixel storage corresponds to a workstation viewport.

Input possibilities of terminals can be mapped onto the appropriate functions without any problems. This applies to the input of primitive classes (locator, choice, pick etc.) as well as the operation mode (request, sample, or event input). The echo types are highly device dependent and not specified by GKS. GKS, however, offers the possibility of using existing echo types.

In raster operations GKS supports the change of colour lookup table, segment priority and pattern representation. The escape function can be used for further device-dependent functions.

GKS supports only a 2D-functionality. A 3D-GKS has been specified. The international standardization is in progress.

2.2.5 Problems: GKS versus Intelligent Terminals

The use of local intelligence of terminals via GKS causes problems in the following areas:

- coordinate range
- high quality text
- fill area
- segment manipulation
- input
- bundle technic

The terminals only process integer coordinates in the range from 12 to 32 bit resolution. When the workstation transformation is performed by the terminal, the NDC area must be mapped onto the address range of the terminal. This may lead to a considerable loss of precision. Coordinates which are not within the identification area will be processed not at all or incorrectly. Mapping the range of the extended NDC area $(-7, +7)$ in GKS to the addressing range is even more inaccurate.

All terminals with local transformations offer the possibility of local clipping at the viewport boundaries.

There are two steps to clipping in GKS: at viewport and at workstation viewport. The execution of the complete clipping procedure by the terminal produces partly incorrect pictures, i.e. if the viewport is part of the workstation window. As mentioned before, coordinates outside the addressing range cannot normally be processed, e.g. if the start and end points of lines are outside the clipping rectangle, the clipped part is not drawn but omitted.

Also, text whose starting point is outside the clipping rectangle is either clipped completely or in the wrong position.

The correct display of graphical text in GKS is not simple. Many geometrical attributes have to be considered:

- character height
- character up vector
- text path
- character spacing
- character expansion factor

None of the devices examined support all these attributes. Frequently the text definition is more simple. In these cases the attributes set in GKS must be adapted to the device definition by the host, e.g. consideration of text alignment when deciding on the starting point. But with adaptation alone not all possibilities can be realized, e.g. some terminals can only rotate text in steps of 45 or 90 degrees.

Another problem in correct text mapping is text precision, only a few terminals support all types of precision.

Complex polygon filling is included in GKS. The inline method, i.e. filling from an inside point to a specified boundary colour, does not fulfill these specifications. The clipping problem with regard to coordinates outside the address

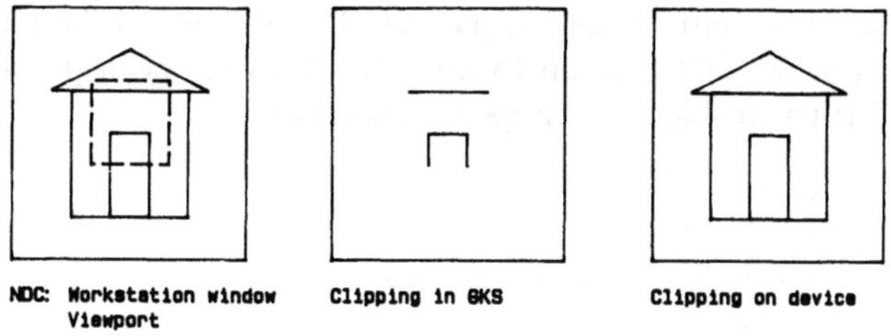

Fig. 2.2.1. Clipping: GKS-device

range has already been referred to. This has severe consequences as far as areas are concerned (see Fig. 2.2.1).

In a local transformation the segments are logically tied to the viewport which was current when the segment was created. Manipulation of segments, such as setting of attributes, transformation or deletion, is done only when the corresponding viewport is active. More than one viewport, however, cannot be active simultaneously. This is not sufficient for full GKS functionality, so the device driver of a GKS implementation has to provide a switching mechanism of viewports for segment manipulation.

There are also input problems related to viewports. Clipping at viewport boundaries often cannot be avoided, not even for the input. It may not even be possible to move the crosshair cursor over viewport boundaries. In some applications, e.g. if both graphic and menu areas are used, the use of several viewports is indispensable.

Besides the pair of coordinates, GKS provides the number of the transformation used as a return parameter in the locator input; these are not necessarily delivered by most devices. Furthermore only those segments can be picked which lie inside the active viewport, which is also a restriction on GKS.

In GKS attribute selection can be achieved via so-called bundles. In this case a predefined bundle of attributes is automatically selected via a bundle index. There is a bundle table for each primitive type, e.g. the colour is seperately selected for each primitive type, but most terminals can only distinguish between text colour and line colour.

There are further problems, e.g. GKS demands a picture regeneration for some functions (the so called implicit regeneration), which is not performed by most devices. However, we do not want to concentrate on a complete listing of problems which may be encountered in connecting intelligent terminals, but on a synopsis of the complexity of the problem.

2.2.6 Minimal GKS

With increasing local intelligence of terminals and the advancement of their functions to GKS, the idea has developed of integrating the entire GKS within the graphical device. A "Minimal-GKS", running on the host, simply compiles the calls and parameters from programming languages into a device format, e.g.

device-specific escape sequences. This minimizes the load of the host. But apart from the fact that up to now this has only been possible on one device, some further problems do appear concerning:

- inquiries
- error handling
- multi-workstation management
- metafile.

GKS allows inquiries as to system states, attribute settings, and workstation capabilities. This possibility does not exist in most devices, nor does GKS-style error handling. But the user program must be able to query errors in order to react correspondingly (i.e. exit from a data base system). In a minimal GKS this is either not possible or subject to limitations.

Minimal GKS is absolutely device-dependent. The plugging in of devices of other producers is hardly possible and forces the user to produce a specific program version for every device. This should be avoided by using GKS. It is also not possible to use more than one workstation simultaneously. Lastly the possibility of picture storing in metafiles does not exist.

Result: If a general device independent graphical system is needed, the processing cannot be moved totally to the graphical device.

2.2.7 Distribution of GKS in Kernel, Driver, Device and Utilities

The question of where to place the interface between the GKS kernel and the workstation driver must be considered. In principle the two following possibilities are conceivable:

- Interface as simple as possible
- Interface as comfortable as possible.

Figures 2.2.2 and 2.2.3 show these interfaces.

In the first case most of the operations have to be done by the kernel. Therefore it is a fairly simple interface: The drivers are relatively short and have a standardized design because only commands and data coming from the kernel have to be compiled into the code of the device. The disadvantage of this solution is, however, that the intelligence of the terminals cannot be used, because for any device, intelligent or not, the same actions (segment simulation, fill area simulation,...) are performed by the kernel, and the complex operations are converted into simpler ones. Therefore only a very small proportion of the capabilities of the device can really be used.

In the second case the kernel is kept very small and only operations which cannot be executed by any workstation are carried out (i.e. administration of the workstation-independent segment storage and the GKS state list, selection of workstations). The advantage is that the capabilities of intelligent terminals can be used more effectively by the conversion of more or less complex operations into the device specific-functions. If a device does not support all capabilities

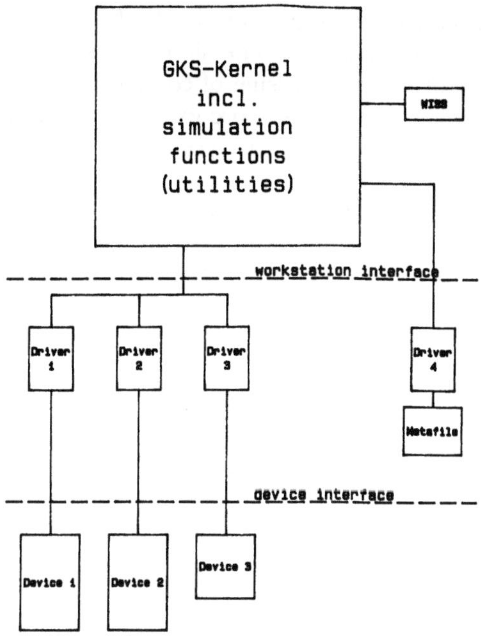

Fig. 2.2.2. Simple workstation interface

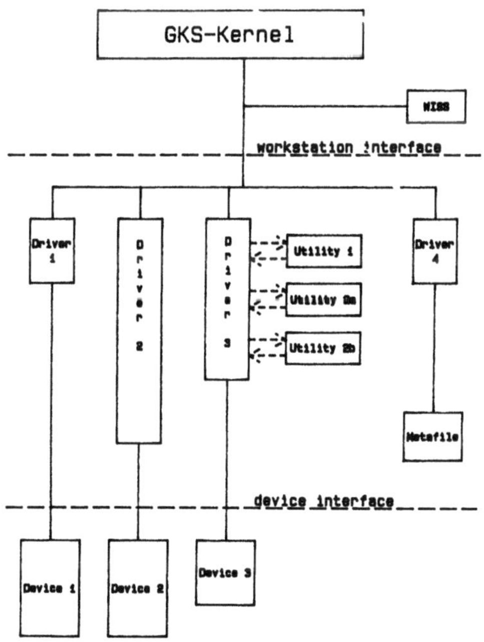

Fig. 2.2.3. Comfortable workstation interface

demanded by GKS (or by the kernel) then utilities must be provided which process the appropriate simulations. They are used directly by the driver and perform the processing of complex operations.

The drivers are more extensive than in the first case; the processing of the programs, however, is accelerated since fast hardware capabilities are used instead of the slow software simulations whenever possible.

The second alternative has been proposed by the ISO-working group. Independently an identical interface for the GKS 7.2 – implementation GRIBS II of S.E.P.P. has been designed and realized.

2.2.8 Reference

1. Graphical Kernel System (GKS), Version 7.2. ISO/DIS 7942 (1982)

2.3 Tektronix PLOT 10 GKS – Tailored for Customer's Needs

R. Putensen

2.3.1 Introduction

Tektronix has been setting graphics standards with hardware and software innovations for years. Already in the early Seventies Tektronix put a software tool on the market called PLOT 10 Terminal Control System.

Virtually all important graphic sofware designed during the last ten to twelve years is based on the PLOT 10 TCS Library. PLOT 10 is not only a term for the TCS Library but is also used by hardware competitors for the 4010 Terminal interface. Competitors like to avoid mentioning the name Tektronix when talking about compatibility of their terminals to Tektronix products and state PLOT 10 compatible instead of Tektronix 4010 Terminal compatible. But this is a misrepresentation. PLOT 10 is a trade mark of Tektronix Inc. for *all* host implemented software. At present, there are already several PLOT 10 packages available, such as

PLOT 10 Terminal Control System (TCS)
PLOT 10 Easy Graphing
PLOT 10 Interactive Graphics Library (IGL)
PLOT 10 TekniCAD

and our latest product in this family is

PLOT 10 Graphical Kernel System (GKS)

We are now among the first to have implemented the Graphical Kernel System, a new international graphics programming standard.

GKS is the culmination of over ten years of work carried on by several national organizations, all striving to develop a common framework to support host and device-independent graphics worldwide.

4000P70 PLOT 10 GKS brings the goal of software portability into focus. Implemented as a library of ANSI FORTRAN '77 graphics subroutines, PLOT 10 GKS is a development tool which an applications programmer can use to create graphics programs without regard for device specifics. Like the standard it supports, PLOT 10 GKS is based on Tektronix' years of experience and solid software engineering.

The source code is written in MORTRAN which stands for MOdular foRTRAN. The MORTRAN preprocessor, a development of the Computer-Research Group at the Stanford Linear Accelerator Center, Stanford, California, allows structured programming, inclusion of macros for tailoring and configuration of the GKS package. Feature switches can be set to include or exclude certain device drivers or metafile I/O. System constants, like the number of workstations or dynamic memory size, can be specified to tune the package for the most efficient use in a customer's given environment. The MORTRAN preprocessor and configurator is always part of the delivered software and generates ANSI FORTRAN '77 output. Many customers have also used the advantages of the MORTRAN processor for their own application program development.

2.3.2 Dynamic Memory Management

PLOT 10 GKS also incorporates Dynamic Memory Management. Since FORTRAN does not support dynamic data structures, sufficient memory space must be allocated (dimensioned) to allow storage for the maximum number of workstations with the maximum number of allowable input devices. This takes up a lot of memory that is not likely to be used, while the space available for the storage of segments, pattern arrays and character fonts may be very restricted and fragmented.

The Dynamic Memory Management System allows allocation and reuse of a memory pool. Memory not currently used for workstation variables can be used for segment storage, pattern arrays and character fonts. When the memory pool becomes full, the system copies parts of these data structures to a disk file in a "Smart" way based on the type of structure and its potential impact on system performance. This single view of storage is transparent to the programmer and user. Through the use of installation tools, PLOT 10 GKS can enable or disable this feature based on the requirements of the installation and the size of the memory pool. Also the disk overflow area can be independently configured. This offers the strength of a "virtual-like" function for non-virtual machines and the benefits of a non-paging, large-shared pool on virtual systems.

2.3.3 A New View of Workstations

PLOT 10 GKS adds new meaning to the concept of a graphics workstation. This was traditionally defined as a collection of hardware devices cabled together in some manner. The controlling software knew only one Window and Viewport and only one set of display attributes. PLOT 10 GKS supports a Window/Viewport on each workstation. And each workstation (defined as an active display or input device) can have its own "bundle" of display attributes such as linestyle, line color or character geometry, set to take advantage of specific device characteristics. The application program can dynamically assign input and output devices without having to reset display attributes.

2.3.4 A Standards Solution to Graphics Problems

The solution to the device dependence dilemma has been a long time coming. First came the de facto standards set by industry leaders, then formal standards

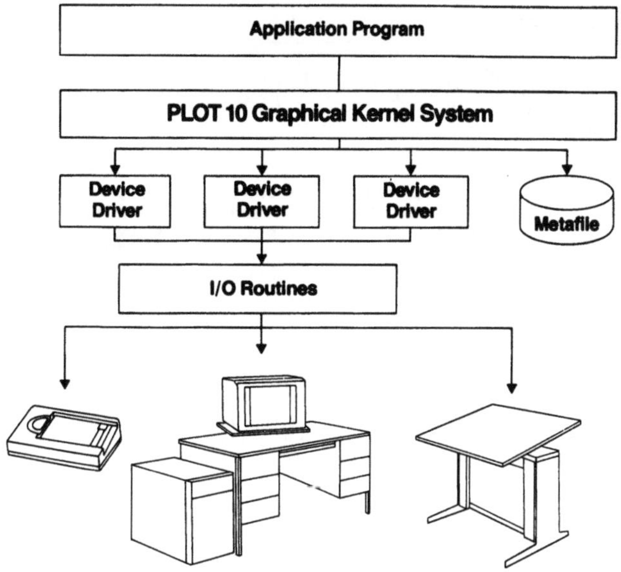

Fig. 2.3.1. GKS architecture features interchangeable device drivers and a metallic concept to achieve highly portable application programs

began to evolve. ISO and ANSI, after years of work, have produced GKS as a draft international programming standard. GKS allows graphics programs to be transported between different computer installations by providing a consistent interface to FORTRAN '77. This not only ensures program portability, it also means programmer portability. GKS gives the applications programmer a common graphics model and syntax (a specified set of subroutine call names) to speed up the programming task and increase productivity.

To the experienced graphics programmer, PLOT 10 GKS is a natural evolution of tools that requires only an orientation experience. To the new programmer, it is the foundation on which most graphics applications will be built.

2.3.5 Standardization Means Device Independence

PLOT 10 is packaged with device drivers for Tektronix terminals, plotters and digitizing tablets. Application can be written without concern for the physical attributes of a device because the specifics reside in these device-dependent software modules. The initial application investment is protected and a path is opened for upgrading or changing the system – when new equipment is added, it only requires new device drivers. In addition to providing support for the family of Tektronix hardware, PLOT 10 GKS will offer support for selected non-Tektronix devices.

A device driver model and its documentation will also be provided to offer the professional programmer a tool to develop drivers for non-Tektronix devices.

GKS LEVELS

Output Level \ Input Level	A	B	C
0	No graphic input. Minimal control. Predefined bundles only.	Request input. Mode setting. Initialize input device. No pick. No input priority.	Sample and Event input. (Not supported by FORTRAN '77)
1	Full output including full bundle concept. Multiple work-station concept. Graphic segment support. Metafile storage.	All of 0B above, plus Request Pick mode. Setting and Initialize for Pick.	Sample and Event input. (Not supported by FORTRAN '77)
2	All of 1A above, plus workstaton independent segment storage.	All of 1B above.	Sample and Event input. (Not supported by FORTRAN '77)

Fig. 2.3.2. 4000P70 PLOT 10 Graphical Kernel System is a full implementation of GKS Level 2B

PLOT 10GKS is a library of ANSI FORTRAN '77 graphics application subroutines. It conforms to the GKS Draft International Standard ISO/DIS 7942.

The host environment should have at least 500 K bytes of directly addressable or virtual memory, with random access disk storage of intermediate files available during installation. Adequate space for text stroke tables and the graphic segments created by the application program is also required.

2.4 Common Graphics Manager – Design Concepts

J. Bechlars

2.4.1 Introduction

Common Graphics Manager (CGM) is an implementation of the Draft International Standard Graphical Kernel System (GKS) of Level 2b/2c in FORTRAN 77. The design concepts which make CGM a strong versatile system are outlined below.

2.4.2 Concepts of GKS

The Graphical Kernel System GKS is the international Standard whereby application programs have access to graphics. It is accepted by the International Standard Organization ISO and many national organizations (ANSI, DIN, etc.) [1]. Language bindings for the usual programming languages ensure the portability of application programs using graphics.

The advantages of GKS are:

a) New graphical application software can be bought or developed independent of the pool of graphics devices.
b) New graphics devices can be installed independent of the pool of graphical application software.
c) Unique concepts allow a better training of graphical application programmers.

2.4.3 Further Standards

In addition to the application interface there was a demand for the storage and transport of pictures. The GKS metafile GKSM is an appendix – but not part of the standard. It contains a segment structure and is therefore suitable for further interactive manipulation. The Computer Graphics Metafile [2] is becoming a standard, it is suitable for GKS, but contains no segmentation and is not suitable for interactive manipulations.

In order to implement GKS in distributed systems as well as to ensure access to highly sophisticated graphics workstations there is a need for a standardized workstation Interface. DIN has developed a Workstation Interface WSI [3] for GKS. ANSI is developing a Computer Graphics Interface CGI (or Virtual Device Interface VDI) [4] for different graphic packages. At present the standards-setting community is among to combine WSI, CGI and CEPT [5].

2.4.4 Design Concepts

The GKS implementation Common Graphics Manager was designed in response to the need to produce a practical and efficient system with the following properties:

a) Maximum portability for the installation over a wide range of different computer types and operating systems.
b) Maximum flexibility in response to different user demands.
c) Maximum performance through the full use of graphic device capabilities.
d) "Real device independence" by simulation of all functions supported by GKS but not by the device.
e) Easy adaptation of new graphics devices.
f) Distributed architecture for the installation on computer networks and for the adaptation of programmable graphic devices.

2.4.5 Design Realization

a) Common Graphics Manager is completely written in ANSI FORTRAN 77 and conforms to the GKS FORTRAN language binding [6]. Preprocessors allow the setting of installation parameters and the generation of direct access files, which are tuned for a given word- and recordlength. Additionally the object code may be managed by the use of special loader features (Capsule Loading under NOS and NOS/BE on CDC). There exist over 100 installations from 16-Bit micro to the Cray (see Appendix a).
b) Dynamic memory management and pointer based table chaining allow the user an unlimited number of workstations, bundles, patterns and segments.
c) A driver skeleton exists for the easy generation of new device drivers. Driver programming allows the support of exotic device features via ESCAPE function. For a list of available device drivers see Appendix b.
d) A library of driver utilities allows the simulation of all functions not supported by the device. So area fill and 21 stroke precision fonts can be generated on all graphic devices. Zooming, picking segments and segment manipulations are possible on all graphic displays. Raster devices without own rasterization, for example electrostatic plotters, ink-jets, matrix- and laser-printers are supported by CGM Raster Package. In contrast to usual vector sorting algorithms not only line drawing, but also overlapping areas are supported.
e) New device drivers can be installed in the system by the use of a preprocessor.
f) The separation of the system into a GKS kernel, workstations and Raster Package allows the installation in a distributed system.

2.4.6 Conclusions

Common Graphics Manager was developed between 1980 and 1986 realizing several versions of the GKS standard at the computer center of the Freie Universität Berlin ZEDAT.

The distribution, support, installation and development of marketable enhancements has been undertaken by Graphische Systeme GmbH Berlin (GraS).

2.4.7 Appendix

a) Computers on which GKS-CGM (Level 2b) has been implemented:

Manufacturer	Computer type	Operating system
AEG	TR 440	BS 3
Control DAta	Cyber 17X	NOS BE; NOS
CRAY	1-M	COS
DEC	VAX 11-7XX	VMS; ULTRIX
	Microvax	VMS
	System 10	TOPS 10
Hewlett Packard	HP 1000 (900 A)	RTE-A
	HP 9000 (500)	UNIX
Honeywell Bull	System 6	G COS
IBM	370/XXXX	MVS
	3032	TSS
	4381	VM/CMS
PCS	CADMUS	UNIX
PRIME	X50 Serie	PRIMOS
SIEMENS	7XXX Serie	BS 2000; BS 3000; VM
Sperry (UNIVAC)	1100	OS 1100
various UNIX systems, e.g. FORCE, RIDGE, SUN		
Personal Computer		
FUJITSO	16 S	CPM 86
IBM	AT	PC DOS
METROLOGIE	BFM 186	MS DOS

b) Available Drivers

Terminals

DATAGRAPH	VTC 8000	ENVISION	2XX
	VTC 8001	HP	2623A
	VTC 8002		2648A
	VTC 8003		2627
DEC	VT100 Retro Graphics/Selanar	IBM	3279
		SIGMEX	61XX
	VT125	TEKTRONIX	40XX
	VT240		410X
	VT241		411X
D-Scan	1104	WESTWARD	32XX

In preparation:

RAMTEK	9460
GENISCO	G 62XX
PERICOM MONTEREY	2006

b) Available Drivers (continued)

Plotter

Pen Plotter (e.g. Calcomp, Benson, HP, Tewidata)

Electrostatic Plotter (e.g. Versatec 8224a, V80) incl. Raster Package[a]

Printer-Plotter incl. Raster Package[a]
Ink-Jet-Plotter incl. Raster Package[a]

[a] Vector-to-raster-converter

2.4.8 References

1. International Standard ISO 7942. Graphical Kernel System GKS, Functional Description, 1st edition (August 1985)
2. Computer Graphic Metafile for transfer and storage of picture description information. Functional description and encoding, Part 1, 2, 3, 4. ISO TC97/SC5/N881–N884 (July 1984)
3. The GKS-Workstation Interface, Vers. 1.0, DIN-AK 5.9.4 (August 1984)
4. Computer Graphics Interface, dpANS X3H3 84/85
5. CEPT Videotex Presentation Layer. Data Syntax
6. Draft International Standard 8651. GKS Language Bindings, part 1: FORTRAN (December 1985)

2.5 GKSGRAL – Software and Hardware Realizations of the Graphical Kernel System

N. Cullmann and G. Pfaff

2.5.1 Introduction

GKSGRAL is a full implementation of the graphical kernel system GKS, which is both an international ISO standard (ISO DIS 7942) [1] and accepted as several national standards, e.g., DIN, ANSI, BSI, AFNOR, NNI.

This first international standard offers capabilities for the creation and representation of two-dimensional pictures, handling input from graphical workstations, for structuring and manipulating pictures, and for storing and retrieving them.

The main objectives of the standard are

- portability of application programs between different GKS installations in differing computing environments
- unifying the concepts of graphics programming, and thus easing the programmer's training
- guiding hardware and system manufacturer when providing graphics capabilities.

Detailed information about GKS and graphics programming is found in [2].

The following report is intended to describe the GKSGRAL design and system structure, the interfaces and various modules, like the metafile input and output handler, the segment storage, the input component, etc.

The final section presents the GKSGRAL implementation in a specific hardware environment: the GKSGRAL Engine.

2.5.2 The GKSGRAL System Structure

The GKSGRAL implementation is a modular subroutine package with a well-defined internal structure and a set of interfaces that can be used for many configuration possibilities.

The GKSGRAL system can be subdivided into three layers:

- the GKSGRAL kernel
- the GKSGRAL workstation layer
- and the GKSGRAL device driver layer.

These layers are separated from each other by welldefined interfaces. These interfaces, the structure and the modules within the system structure are shown in Fig. 2.5.1.

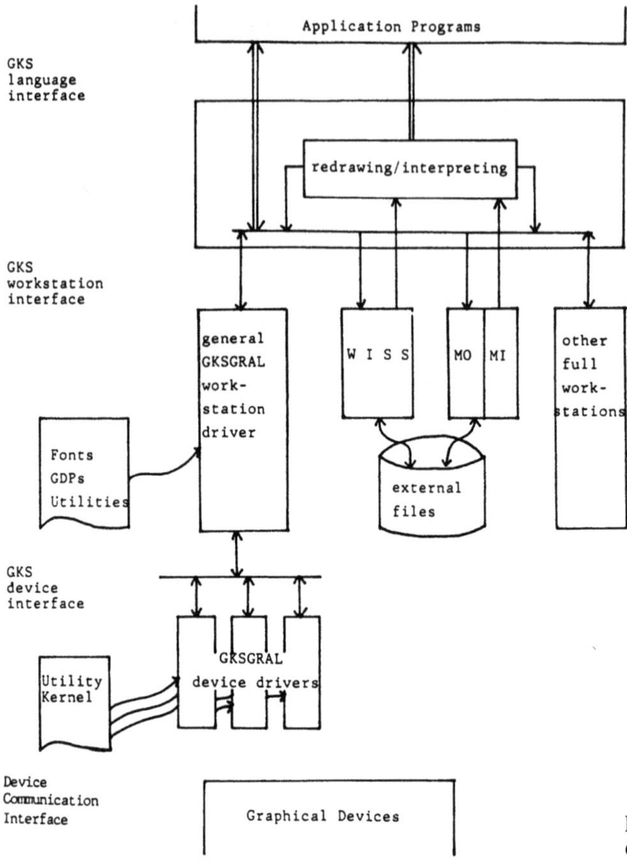

Fig. 2.5.1. Structure of the GKSGRAL implementation

2.5.2.1 The GKSGRAL Kernel

The GKSGRAL kernel has the following main tasks:

- it provides the standard FORTRAN interface with application programs. Other language interfaces as well as communication interfaces in distributed systems sit on top of the FORTRAN interface.
- keeping the GKS state list, handling most of the GKS error conditions and distributing commands to the single workstations.
- interpreting the GKS metafile input; associating, copying and inserting segments out of the segment storage workstation.
- redrawing segments on workstations which have no own segment storage or cannot fulfill all of the GKS dynamic modification functions.

2.5.2.2 The GKSGRAL Workstation Interface

The GKSGRAL kernel is separated from the workstation layer by the GKS workstation interface. For all full workstation drivers, this is implemented via one subroutine called GKWKLK (workstation link). Via this subroutine all workstation commands and the relevant data are exchanged between the GKSGRAL kernel and the workstation drivers. A description of the workstation interface is contained in the GKSGRAL-Installation Guide [3]. The workstation interface is used for fully equipped GKS workstations such as the IBM 5080 GKSGRAL workstation driver or the GKSGRAL – GKS workstation driver. The latter allows a separate GKS system to be used as a workstation of GKSGRAL.

Another workstation driver available is for the GKS metafile output. For more details of it, see Sect. 2.5.5. The metafile output workstation is connected via the subroutine GKMFOU from GKSGRAL.

The third workstation type connected at this interface is the workstation independent segment storage, which is also used as workstation dependent segment storages for workstations lacking this feature (see Sect. 2.5.6 for more details). The output part of this driver is headed by the subroutine GKSSOU.

Finally, the fourth workstation type is the general GKSGRAL workstation handler which simulates features that most existing low level graphics devices do not support. This module is described in Sect. 2.5.4.

2.5.2.3 The GKSGRAL Workstation Layer

The main task of the GKSGRAL workstation layer is to map the logical GKS workstation functions onto the existing peripheral device functions. For real graphical devices, this is a set of graphics commands. To facilitate the writing of new graphics device drivers, we separate the device-specific command coding from algorithmic computations. The latter, e.g., coordinate transformations, clipping and high quality text are performed within the workstation layer; the coding of a coordinate into characters is done within a device driver. The two parts (workstation/device drivers) are separated by a DI/DD-interface (separating the Device Independent from the Device Dependent parts). The DI/DD-interface varies according to each device's capabilities. It is close to the upcoming ISO-CGI definition. Its exact contents are described in [3].

For metafiles, the workstation layer maps the GKS functions to standard codings on sequential files with fixed record lengths and vice versa (see [3]).

For the WISS, an optimised portable solution is implemented that stores and retrieves GKS picture descriptions with the help of a memory resident working set and a direct access file (see [6]).

2.5.2.4 The GKSGRAL Device Interface

Similarly to the workstation interface, the GKSGRAL device interface is implemented via one subroutine named GKDDLK (device driver link). This exchanges command and data between GKSGRAL and device-drivers. As at the workstation interface, it is very easy to connect new device drivers to GKSGRAL. The commands and data possible are listed in [3].

2.5.2.5 The GKSGRAL Device Driver Layer

As already mentioned, GKSGRAL device drivers are designed to perform the device specific command and data coding and to communicate with the operator via the hardware. All device drivers must fulfill a certain set of functions and may contain an optional set of functions. The minimal required set of functions comprises the GKS output primitives in device coordinates, the relevant direct attributes, and a set of INQUIRY functions. To ease the work of providing the minimal functionality, there exists a device driver skeleton and simulation routines which may be needed (e.g., for hatching). By modifying this structure, the writing of new drivers may take less than a day. More details can be found in [3].

2.5.3 GKSGRAL Interfaces

The GKSGRAL system provides a set of interfaces which support well-defined exchangeable subsystems and system components, either in accordance with certain ISO standards or as defined by GTS/GRAL.

These interfaces are:

- the language interfaces (2.5.3.1)
- the metafile interfaces (2.5.3.2)
- the graphics device interface (2.5.3.3)
- symbol interfaces (2.5.3.4).

2.5.3.1 Language Interfaces

While the implementation is written in a portable FORTRAN subset, its application interface can be adjusted to various user languages. Language interfaces currently available are

- FORTRAN 77 (according to the ISO-GKS-FORTRAN language binding, DP – Jan. 85)
- FORTRAN 77 Subset (according to the ISO-GKS-FORTRAN language binding, DP – Jan. 85)
- FORTRAN IV (derived from the FORTRAN 77 Subset binding)
- PASCAL (according to the ISO-GKS-PASCAL language binding, DP – Jan. 85).

Other language bindings will be available as soon as the relevant standard is be defined. Candidates close to this status are ADA and C.

The language bindings are described in the GKSGRAL User Manual [4].

2.5.3.2 Metafile Interfaces

The GKSGRAL system comprises metafile handlers that can read and write the following metafile formats:

- GKS-Metafile: Clear Text Coding in all variants
- GKS-Metafile: Binary Coding (computer dependent)

The GKS-Metafile is described in appendix E of the GKS ISO standard and in the GKSGRAL User Manual [4].

– CGM: character coding

The Computer Graphics Metafile, which is currently an ISO draft proposal is close to the GKS-Metafile Level 0a standard. A separate CGM workstation is available in the GKSGRAL implementation.

2.5.3.3 Graphical Device Interfaces

GKSGRAL supports two such interfaces, i.e., the GKS workstation interface and the GKSGRAL device driver interface. The first interface corresponds to the DIN proposal submitted to ISO in the context of the CGI (VDI) definition. The GKSGRAL device interface provides great flexibility ranging from the level of the CGM contents up to the GKS workstation interface contents. This interface will thus be used to support any upcomming CGI-ISO standard.

2.5.3.4 Symbol Interfaces

GKSGRAL defines a special internal interface for the representation of graphical symbols such as character, markers and icons. This allows any user to define his specific symbol set and connect it to the GKSGRAL system. Existing symbol definitions can be linked to GKSGRAL if a format converter is used to map from the existing to the GKSGRAL symbol format. More information can be found in the GKSGRAL symbol editor product description [5].

GTS/GRAL also provides an interactive product called symbol editor [5]. This is based on GKS functions only. After the user has edited his specific symbol set this is stored in the special GKSGRAL symbol representation format. An escape function is provided, which allows the font definitions to be loaded into the system and used via implementation dependent attribute values.

2.5.4 The GKSGRAL Workstation Handler

The GKSGRAL system contains a special set of subroutines which perform the tasks a GKS workstation is intended to do. This solution was chosen in order to avoid the duplication of work and code for each new workstation driver. The GKSGRAL workstation handler controls those functions which are common to all drivers. It is however flexible enough to pass the performance of workstation functions to a device driver, if this reports the capacity for performing them. Examples of workstation functions are:

a) keeping the workstation state list, the description table and the bundle tables, the colour and pattern tables.

b) performing the coordinate transformations from WC to DC (from WC to NDC, if the driver contains the workstation transformation).
c) clipping all primitives at the clipping rectangle (viewport and workstation window; at the viewport resp. NDC only, if the driver contains workstation transformation).
d) resolving stroke precision text to lines, areas and curves for fonts/precisions which the driver is not able to fulfill.
e) resolving generalized drawing primitives which the driver cannot perform.
f) redrawing single segments or all segments, if a dynamic modification is not accepted by the driver. This is done in connection with the redrawing capability of the GKSGRAL kernel and the WISS.
g) sending the output buffer command at appropriate times, if the device contains a picture buffer.
h) handling all inquiries to the workstation state list, description tables and bundle tables, the colour and pattern tables.

In order to inform the workstation handler about the functions of a device driver, its description is passed at open workstation time. Each device driver contains functions to report its facilities.

The workstation handler is able to handle any number of workstations simultaneously. In order to optimise memory requirements, the maximum number of simultaneously available workstations can be adjusted at compilation time.

It is possible to configure a GKSGRAL system to omit the workstation handler.

2.5.5 The GKSGRAL Metafile Handler

GKSGRAL implements the GKS metafile in all defined formats, ranging from binary coding to clear text coding. An extra function is provided to the user to specify the desired format.

When passing metafiles into the GKS (interpreting), GKSGRAL also offers the possibility of processing metafiles with different formats. By using metafile output and input simultaneously, metafiles can also be converted between different formats. In this way, files from other GKS installations can be interpreted without any problem.

One particular advantage offered by the GKSGRAL is the generation of metafile-oriented plot files with a reduced range of functions, e.g. without segmentation and only using static attributes such as line type and line width. Via special metafile drivers, GKSGRAL reduces the functions of the GKS to these simple functions. Thus, plot files for post-processors can be generated which do not have the full GKS functionality. Metafiles at a higher GKS level can also be converted into lower-level plot files.

Looking at the internal structure, the GKSGRAL metafile output driver has one entry routine called GKMFOU. This routine uses some 10 subroutines to write metafile information in the various formats.

The metafile input driver also has one entry routine, called GKMFIN, which is used by the various GKS metafile input functions. This routine is responsible for interpreting all the different metafile formats.

2.5.6 The GKSGRAL Segment Storage Handler

The GKSGRAL segment storage is implemented by means of the GKSGRAL storage module. Let us first describe this module:

2.5.6.1 Purpose

The GKSGRAL storage module is a set of subroutines which handles the storing and retrieving of a varying amount of data. Since FORTRAN systems do not allow for dynamic storage management, this GKSGRAL module was implemented to provide a portable means of handling the varying requirements of GKS data storage.

2.5.6.2 The Storage Module Interface

The GKSGRAL storage module interface consists of two elements: firstly, the data record structure and secondly, the operations on the storage module. The data record structure (key, data) simply consists of the tuple where key is a pair of key1, key2 and data is

iv: a single integer value
ia: an integer array of arbitrary length
(rx, ry): two real arrays of arbitrary equal length

The operations on the storage module are

a) INITIALISE: initialise the GKSGRAL storage module
b) INSERT: insert a new record into the storage module
c) GET: retrieve a record (and its data) from the storage module
d) REPLACE: replace the data of an existing record in the storage module
e) RENAME: rename a record (or a range of records)
f) DELETE: delete a record (or a range of records)

2.5.6.3 Storage Module Structure

The storage module is divided into a memory-resident and an external file part. The size of each part can be adjusted at compilation time according to application needs and the particular computer and operating system characteristics given.

Basically, the storage module is designed to obtain a number of variable size data records. The data records are stored in so-called data pages, the according keys in so-called key pages. Key pages contain the keys of all records sorted in increasing order. For the key of each record, a pointer to a data page address is stored which indicates the beginning of the relevant data. Data pages contain the data of all records in sequential order. Thus, if new records are inserted, the corresponding keys are inserted at their appropriate place within the key pages, the corresponding data are stored after the last actual address used in the data pages.

To speed up insertion and retrieval access, a key page administration is kept in the memory, which contains the key range of each key page. If new records are inserted between two existing ones, all higher keys have to be moved by one entry. A mechanism is implemented to restrict this data shifting to two key pages at most.

Key and data pages have a fixed, user adjustable size, PLEN. A total of MAXPST pages can be kept in the memory at any time. The number of key pages is limited to MAXKP, which is also adjustable by the user.

The storage module implements a LRU algorithm to write the key or data pages least recently used to an external file and load new required pages into the memory.

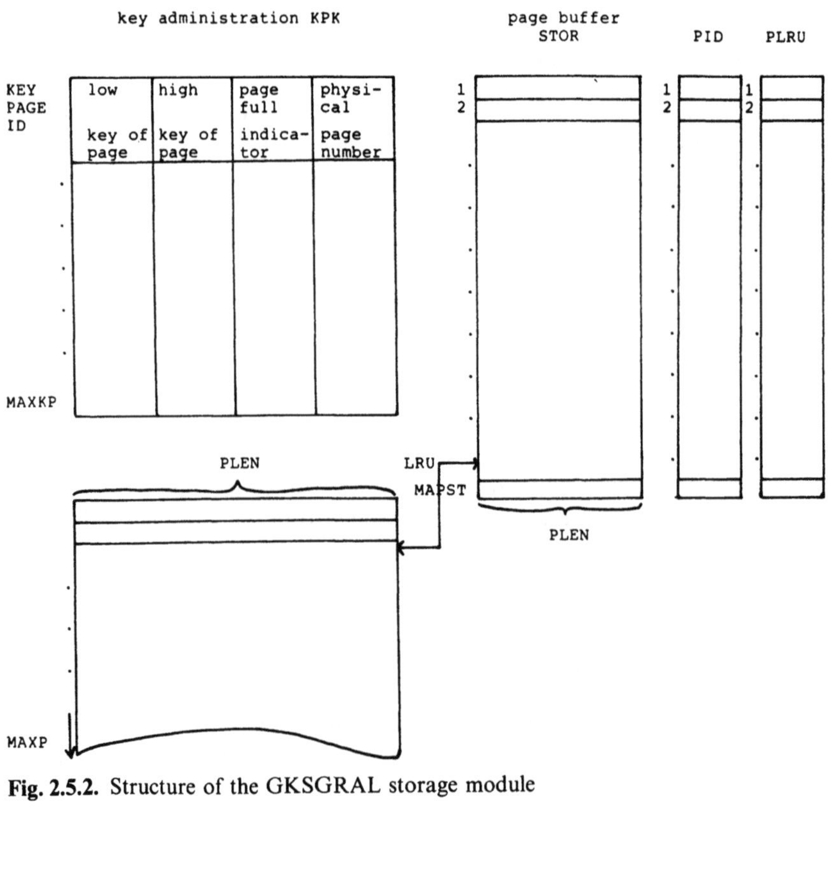

Fig. 2.5.2. Structure of the GKSGRAL storage module

Thus, a large amount of data can be handled, while providing for maximum data availability.
Figure 2.5.2 gives an overview of the storage module structure.

2.5.6.4 Integration of the WISS into GKSGRAL

The output part of the GKS segment storage handler is headed by the subroutine GKSSOU. This accepts all workstation commands and data and stores them in the GKSGRAL storage module.

Segments are stored as a list of records where the first key represents the segment name and the subsequent keys identify the primitives or attribute records. The GKSGRAL segment storage stores all primitives in world coordinates in order to allow the concatenation of all transformations into one matrix.

The input part of the GKSGRAL WISS is implemented by several routines:

- GKDISG is used to redraw a segment on one or several workstations as part of the implicit regeneration of a whole picture or a single segment, as part of segment association, copying, redrawing or updating.
- GKINSG is used to insert a segment into the currently open segment.

2.5.7 GKSGRAL Input

The input part of GKSGRAL is divided into three modules above the device interface and one module below it. The three modules above are:

a) The Request Input Module
This module comprises the INITIALISE, the SET MODE, the corresponding INQUIRE and the REQUEST functions. These functions perform the error handling, data conversions like unpacking the data record, string into integer conversion, etc., and the simulation of non-supported logical input devices like calculating a segment name from a position for a PICK device, or transforming points from DC into WC for LOCATOR and STROKE devices. All data are passed via GKDDLK to the device drivers.

b) The Sample Input Module
This module only contains the SAMPLE functions. Error checking is performed, the input data are sampled via the device interface and transformed (or mapped) to the world coordinate level.

c) The Event Input Module
This module implements the GET functions, the AWAIT and FLUSH functions and one INQUIRE function. It also contains the current event report. The event queue is kept in the device input handler. When calling the AWAIT function, the DC event reports are aquired via the device interface then transformed (or mapped) to the world coordinate level, and stored as current event report.

d) The Device Input Handler Module
This set of routines is situated below the GKDDLK interface. It keeps the current logical DC input device measure values and the DC input queue (one for all

connected devices). It is also responsible for mapping the physical input values into logical DC values, and for performing the echo, if this is not done by the input handler of the physical input devices.

The input handler can be realised in three ways, depending on the operating system facilities:

1) it can be called asynchronously by an interrupt routine (e.g., in MS-DOS)
2) it can run as a separate task together with the device drivers (e.g., on PDP's, VAXes)
3) it performs only when an AWAIT function or a REQUEST function is pending, i.e., only when the application program is waiting for an input. This realisation allows several input devices to be handled simultaneously (if the application program enables a number of input devices and waits for the input from any one of these). However, it does not inplement true asynchronous input handling, i.e., input devices can only be handled and echo is only performed, when the application programm calls REQUEST or AWAIT-EVENT functions.

2.5.8 GKSGRAL Configuration Possibilities

The GKSGRAL system is designed in a most flexible way. First of all, it is written in a special preprocessor language using conditional code. This follows generation of GKSGRAL FORTRAN objects

- in FORTRAN 77
- in FORTRAN 77 Subset
- in FORTRAN IV
- with and without TRACE facility
- with and without a workstation interface
- with and without the GKSGRAL workstation handler
- in the GKS levels 0b, 2b and 2c

While this configuration is created before delivering the GKSGRAL system, other configuration possibilities are left open. These can be created by the customer receiving the FORTRAN code. Customer configuration possibilities include

- adjusting the GKSGRAL storage modul
- adjusting GKSGRAL buffers
- adjusting GKSGRAL state lists
- adding and removing character fonts
- adding and removing device and workstation drivers
- replacing GKSGRAL modules by dummy modules

How to configure the system is described in the GKSGRAL installation guide [3].

2.5.9 GKSGRAL Installations

GKSGRAL can be installed on different computers and operating systems by adapting

- a set of parameters describing data representation characteristics (at most 5 variables)
- logical unit numbers and file handling operations
- a set of communication routines for data exchange with graphics devices (5 routines)
- a set of character handling routines (4 routines)
- a set of frequently used, computation-intensive routines

GKSGRAL is now available for equipment of more than 25 different manufacturers, for more than 20 different operating systems, and in more than 200 installations with end users. The precise list of currently available computer interfaces is available in [6].

2.5.10 GKSGRAL Device Drivers

GKSGRAL communicates with graphics devices via GKSGRAL device drivers. These all have a common internal structure derived from a skeleton driver. The design allows a new device driver to be built very easily. The skeleton driver supports devices which themselves have very low graphics intelligence. This driver is adapted by replacing the various graphics simulation or emulation parts by device-specific code pieces which utilize the available device functionality.

GKSGRAL drivers therefore use all the graphics intelligence offered by the particular devices as long as this fits into the GKS concepts. For example, local display lists are used as device dependent segment storages, hardware zooming is used for the GKS workstation transformations and built-in prompting and echoing functions are used as GKS prompt/echo types.

The skeleton driver is also supplied to users for derivation of their own device drivers.

The device drivers currently available support more than 25 manufacturers with more than 80 models; they are listed in the GKSGRAL device driver list [7].

2.5.11. The GKSGRAL Engine

Following the availability of GKSGRAL on a number of computer-types, and drivers for nearly all graphical devices, the Graphical Kernel System has now been made available in a GKS-specific machine by GTS/GRAL: the GKSGRAL ENGINE.

2.5.11.1 Functionality

The GKSGRAL Engine presents a host- and device-independent firmware-realisation of the complete GKS standard:

GKS functions are accepted and processed via the host-interface. User-actions are processed locally; input results are passed on to the host via GKS input functions.

In the GKSGRAL Engine complete graphical processing takes place according to GKS 7.4 including the segment handling.

Drivers, selected by the user, serve different graphic-devices via serial or parallel interfaces. Suitable monitors can be directly accessed via RGB-interfaces.

2.5.11.2 Advantages

The GKSGRAL Engine relieves the application-computer and thereby essentially increases the efficiency of the complete system.

This increase in efficiency benefits host-computers as well as small workstation computers, especially in multi-user-mode.

Interface routines are available for the application computer so that application-programs can be executed without alteration on a GKS software installation as well as with the GKSGRAL Engine.

2.5.11.3 Software/Firmware

GKSGRAL, the GKS implementation of GTS/GRAL, forms the basic part of the GKSGRAL Engine.

Included are a number of simulation-routines for device-features which are not available on the peripherals, as well as a number of text fonts.

An interpreter accepts the commands and data coming from the host, decodes them and distributes them to the corresponding GKS functions.

Output parameters are coded and returned to the host.

As long as the OPEN-GKS-command has not been received, the interpreter passes on all messages coming from the host to the serial interface device. Messages coming from there are also passed on to the host. This enables a direct communication between graphics terminal and application-computer, bypassing the GKSGRAL Engine.

The below end of the GKSGRAL implementation consists of the device driver linkage routine, which invokes the different GKS-device drivers.

The communication with the host, as well as with all graphical devices, is finally established by an interrupt routine which also handles spooler-functions to plotters.

2.5.11.4 Hardware

The hardware of the GKSGRAL Engine consists of a VME-BUS-system with Motorola 68000-Processor, 512 KB RAM, 128 KB EPROM, Winchester and Floppy.

The basic configuration contains, besides the host-interface (RS 232C, V24), two further serial interfaces for terminal and plotter.

VME-BUS-platines with graphic processors are available for the direct access of colour monitors.

2.5.11.5 Extensions

Besides extensions of interface-boards, the floppy disk drive offers the possibility of producing and reading GKS-metafiles.

The Winchester disk drive allows for extensive data logging directly on the GKSGRAL Engine; this imposes an additional reduction of the software load on the application computer.

2.5.12 References

1. GKS-Draft International Standard. ISO DIS 7942 (January 1985)
2. Enderle G, Kansy K, Pfaff G: Computer Graphics Programming. GKS – The Graphics Standard. Springer, Berlin, Heidelberg, New York, Tokyo (1984)
3. GKSGRAL – Installation Guide
4. GKSGRAL – User Manual
5. The GKSGRAL Symbol Editor
6. GKSGRAL – Computer Interfaces
7. GKSGRAL – Device Drivers

Chapter 3

Initial Graphics Exchange Specifications

Implementation, Experience

3.1 Product Data Exchange; Design and Implementation of IGES Processors

U. Weissflog

3.1.1 Abstract

The Initial Graphics Exchange Specification (IGES) was introduced in 1981 as an american (ANSI) standard for the exchange of product data between dissimilar CAD/CAM systems. Since then, vendors and users of CAD/CAM systems have designed and implemented IGES translators. When these translators were actually used in translation processes many problems surfaced. These problems were created by both the IGES standard itself and the translators. This paper describes both, (1) the attempts of various national and international standards groups (such as NBS in the USA or DIN in Germany) to improve the existing standard and define an ISO standard and (2) a design concept for IGES translators that solves many of the implementation problems.

The creation of one international product data exchange standard is the common goal of the various national standard groups in the International Standards Organization (ISO). Because of the well known deficiencies of the current IGES standard a twofold approach seems to emerge. One, to correct the existing IGES to make it practically applicable and the other to define a new standard that goes far beyond the scope of the existing IGES. The state of these activities is described and the different national positions are explained.

The design described in this paper is based on IGES 2.0. It allows for the successful exchange of subsets of product data even with the deficiencies of the existing IGES. Central to the design is the restructuring of the original IGES file into the Internal IGES Files (IIF). Instead of IIF record descriptions, a subroutine package (the IIF Interface) provides access to IIF. The design divides the IGES translation into two phases, the conversion between IGES and IIF (Edit phase), and the entity translation between IIF and the target CAD/CAM system (Exchange phase). This design allows implementation of IGES translators for different CAD/CAM systems with a reduced programming effort. Allowing end-users to control entity mappings in the Exchange phase, the design adds flexibility to the translation process.

3.1.2 Introduction

Since the late 1970's, technical committees in various nations have been seeking a solution to the problem of exchanging product data between dissimilar CAD/CAM systems. One solution, the definition of a neutral exchange file, seems to

Table 3.1.1. Product data exchange proposals

Name	Country	Organisation	Proposed by	Status	Year	XLT
Y14.26M–1981	USA	IGES/ANSI	ANSI	Standard	1981	Yes
IGES Vers. 2.0	USA	NBS	IGES	Spec.	1983	Yes
IGES Vers. 3.0	USA	NBS	IGES	Spec.	1985	No
SET Vers. 1.0	France	AS	AS	Spec.	1984	Yes
SET Vers. 1.1	France	AFNOR	AS	Prop.	1986	No
VDAFS	Germany	DIN	VDA	Standard	1983	Yes
TAP	Germany	DIN	NAM96.4	Pos.PPR	1984	No
PDDI	USA	NBS	U.S.A.F.	Prop.	1984	No
PDES	USA	BS	IGES	Prop.	1984	No
STEP	int.	ISO	all	Prop.	Future	No

XLT = Translators available (Yes/No)

have been generally accepted. It is the basis for most standardization activities in the various countries. The proposals discussed by ISO/TC184/SC [1] up to the end of 1984, their originators and whether translators are available can be seen in Table 3.1.1.

Y14.26M–1981	U.S. ANSI [2] standard published in 1981 for the exchange of product definition data.
IGES 2.0	U.S. NBS [3] update of IGES 1.0 published in 1983.
IGES 2.1	U.S. NBS update of IGES 2.0 which will be available in 1985.
SET 1.0	Specification for the exchange of product data from AeroSpatiale in France. The english translation of the SET 1.0 document was published 1984.
VDAFS	Proposed german DIN [4] standard created by VDA [5] and VDMA [6]. The document was first published 1983.
TAP	DIN position paper on Transport and Archiving of Product data prepared by NAM96.4 [7].
PDDI	U.S. Air Force effort for Product Definition Data Interface (PDDI).
PDES	Effort coming out of the IGES community, intended to meet the requirements for a Product Data Exchange Standard (PDES).
STEP	The international effort by ISO/TC184/SC trying to combine the different national activities in one international Standard for the Exchange of Product Model Data (STEP).

[1] International Standards Organization/Technical Committee 184/Sub-Committee 4
[2] American National Standards Institute
[3] National Bureau of Standards
[4] Deutsche Industrie Norm
[5] Verband der Automobilindustrie
[6] Verband Deutscher Maschinen- und Anlagenbau e.V.
[7] Normenausschuß Maschinenbau, Sub-group 96.4

ANSI published *ANSI Y14.26M – 1981* [1] in September 1981 as a standard for the exchange of graphical and structural data between dissimilar CAD/CAM systems [2, 3, 4]. This ANSI standard, more commonly known under the name *IGES*, was the first national standard published in the field of product data exchange. Because of flaws in the standard, communication problems, and poorly designed translators, IGES was criticized from various groups in and outside the US. This criticism resulted in two different philosophies for dealing with IGES: One accepting IGES as a working base and another disapproving of IGES completely. Between 1981 and the end of 1984 work was done following both philosophies resulting in the various proposals listed in Table 3.1.1.

Translators exist for IGES 1.0 and 2.0, SET 1.0 and VDAFS. Only IGES translators have an international distribution, SET and VDAFS translators are available in France and Germany. The principles of translator design described in the following sections are generally applicable, although only the design of IGES translators is described.

3.1.3 IGES: Overview

Since *IGES* was published, translators based on the standard have been implemented both by CAD/CAM system vendors and users of corporate CAD/CAM systems. When these translators were used in production and test environments many problems surfaced. Flaws existed not only as deficiencies of the IGES translators, but also within the IGES standard itself. Figure 3.1.1 shows the concept of IGES and Fig. 3.1.2 the conceptual design of an IGES Translator.

Problems with IGES relate to its large file size, file organization, and the entity set. Problems with IGES translators have been misinterpretations of the standard, programming errors, and implementations of different IGES entity subsets.

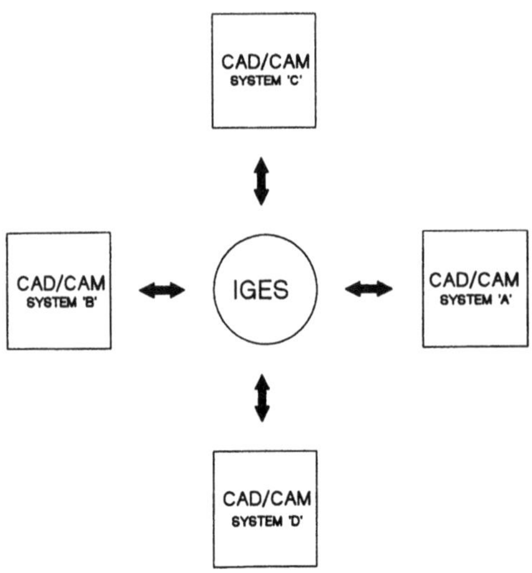

Fig. 3.1.1. IGES concept

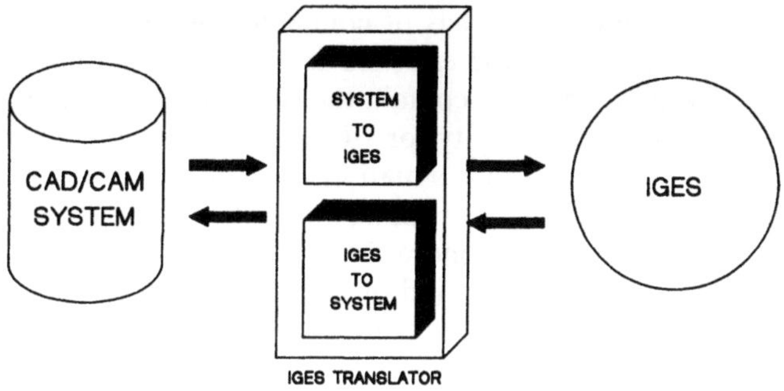

Fig. 3.1.2. IGES translator concept

The design described in this paper is based on the reorganization of the IGES file into a new file organisation (the Internal IGES Files (IIF)) and an associated program interface (the IIF Interface). The reorganization of the IGES file into the Internal IGES Files eliminates most of the problems related to the format of the original IGES file. The functions to reorganize the IGES file are separated from those related to the entity translation.

The IFF Interface provides convenient access to IGES entities for the programmer of an IGES translator. It makes the job of writing IGES translators easier because

- it contains procedures to retrieve and store all IGES entities defined in IGES Version 2
- it creates pointer and status information, which specify entity relations and dependencies automatically upon user request
- and it allows direct access to the data

The IBM IGES Processor [5] is an IGES Translator that utilizes the IIF Interface to exchange data between IGES and the CADAM [8] system [6]. This translator is an example of the capabilities of IIF and the IIF Interface.

3.1.4 IGES: Intrinsic Problems

The same conditions that justify the establishment of a graphics exchange standard are the source of a number of serious intrinsic problems that must either be overcome or dealt with by an IGES translator. The following sections discuss some of these problems in more detail.

3.1.4.1 IGES Entity Set

IGES itself embodies a set of entities that, presumably, establishes a standard for exchanging graphical data. The CAD/CAM system from which data has to be

[8] CADAM, Registered Trademark of CADAM Inc.

translated into IGES, has of course its own set of entities. Consequently, the following situations can exist: IGES contains an entity for which a specific CAD/CAM system does not contain the equivalent entity, and a specific CAD/CAM system contains an entity for which no IGES entity exists. An IGES translator might either ignore such situations, and not translate the entity, or it might deal with the situation by translating the entity into a similar one that closely approximates the original. If more then one approximation is possible the translator should allow for some kind of user control to select the approximation that is most appropriate for the specific translation. The IGES Rational B-Spline entities cause these problems because some CAD/CAM systems do not contain these entities.

Furthermore, a specific CAD/CAM system and IGES may define the same type of entity in quite different ways. Such variations can cause problems if one of the definitions is less complete than the other. In such cases, differences will occur among the representation of a specific entity in the originating system, in IGES, and within the receiving system. Examples of this problem occur frequently with dimension and text entities [7].

3.1.4.2 IGES Format

Another problem with IGES relates to two conflicting forces IGES has to reconcile:

- IGES entity definitions must accommodate complex structures and relationships so that complex CAD/CAM models can be exchanged successfully between diverse CAD/CAM systems: IGES, therefore, requires considerable complexity
- The IGES file format, because it must be processable by a wide range of different computer systems, can use only data formats and data management methods known by these systems: IGES, therefore, requires a certain simplicity.

IGES uses a sequential file organization with fixed length records to satisfy the simplicity requirement and a physical pointer system to represent model complexity. The IGES file itself is organized into sections. Information about the entities is stored in the Directory Entry (DE) and Parameter Data (PD) sections. Information about the origin of the file and the model that it contains is found in the global section. A start section stores man-readable information and a terminate section contains information about the file itself. Despite the modular design, the IGES format embodies a number of persistent problems, among them;

- data redundancy in the DE and PD sections
  (results in large file sizes and in excessive processing times for IGES translators),
- the conflict between the file organization (sequential) and the pointer system (direct access)
  (results in multiple processing or internal restructuring of the IGES file, again contributing to excessive processing times for IGES translators).

3.1.4.3 IGES Translators

IGES translators are the source of another set of problems when dealing with IGES files. These problems are related to the implemented entity set and the programming and design quality of a specific translator.

CAD/CAM systems generally do not provide a description of the physical data and file layout for their entity sets. An interface program will normally access the database or the file system of the CAD/CAM system. The entity set provided by this interface does not always match the entity set of the CAD/CAM system itself. Furthermore, a specific release of an IGES translator may have only a certain number of entities implemented. The designer of an IGES translator needs to consider the entity sets:

- IGES Entity Set
- CAD/CAM System Entity Set
  - Interface Entity Set
    - Implementation Entity Set

The current generation of IGES translators is characterized by relatively small implementation entity sets. Based on a survey done by Booz-Allen & Hamilton Inc. [8] in 1983 only 3 IGES geometric entities (point, line and circle) were commonly supported among the translators in the survey.

Another problem is the different design and programming quality of IGES translators currently available, which results in error prone IGES files. This is due to:

- vagueness in certain areas of the standard itself
- non-existence of complex and realistic test cases
- lack of minimum requirements for the translator itself

Any data exchange between two dissimilar CAD/CAM systems requires two IGES translators. One, the pre-processor, translates the CAD/CAM model into an IGES file. The other, the post-processor, translates the IGES file into a CAD/CAM model. The success and quality of any IGES translation depends on the quality of both translators. The more uniform the translators are, with respect to their entity sets, the better the translations will be.

3.1.5 Design of an IGES Translator

The design described in the following sections separates the functions related to data management and structure from those related to entity translation. These are referred to as the edit and exchange phases. Central to the design are the Internal IGES Files (IIF) which store IGES definitions in a different format from the original IGES file. IIF are associated with the IIF Interface [9] which allows a program to read from and write to IIF in a uniform way. IIF and IIF Interface take advantage of the data management methods that are available within an IBM/370 or 43xx environment. IIF Interface contains read and write routines which are callable from most higher level programming languages including

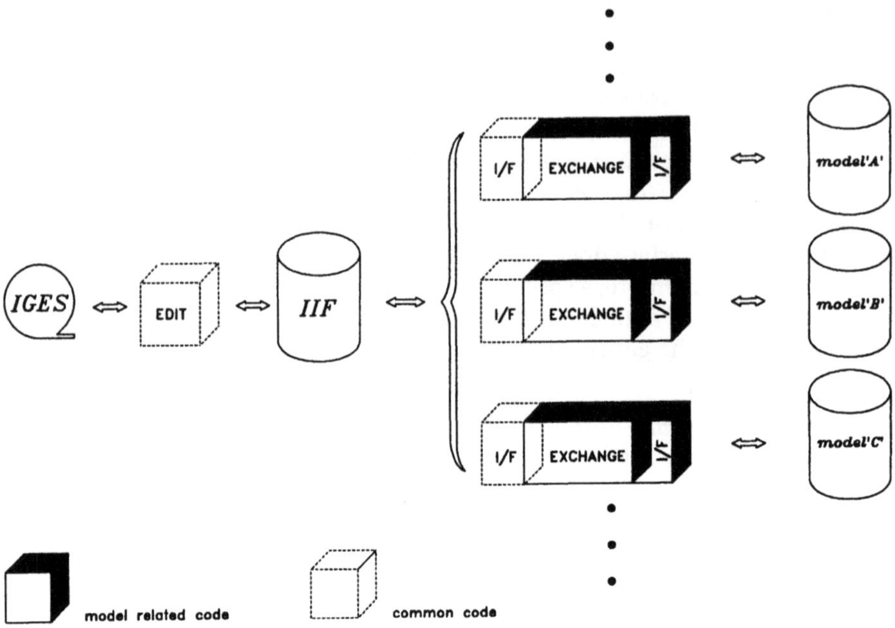

Fig. 3.1.3. Design overview

FORTRAN, Pascal, and PL/1. Thus they simplify the task of writing IGES translators. Figure 3.1.3 displays an overview of this design.

3.1.5.1 Internal IGES Files (IIF)

The physical format of the Internal IGES Files (IIF) is different from that of the original IGES file, but it contains the same logical data. The five sections of the IGES file are reorganized into four new files.

- The Directory and Parameter Data (DPD) file combines the information from the DE and PD sections of the IGES file.
- The DPD Continuation file contains additional information that does not fit in the fixed records of the DPD file described above.
- The global file contains information from the GLOBAL and START sections of the original IGES file.
- The text file contains all text information from the START, DE, and PD sections of the original IGES file. Pointers to the text file are found in the other three files.

The reorganization of the original IGES file solves some of the problems related to the IGES format because IIF store data in binary format, allow for direct access processing, and reduce the amount of redundant information within the DE and PD sections.

3.1.5.2 IIF Interface

The IIF Interface consists of a set of routines to retrieve data from and store data in IIF. It is based on the following design objectives:

- Program independence from the physical file layouts.
- Simplified processing of entity relations.

IIF Interface contains all routines necessary to

- control the sequence in which entities are processed
- retrieve or write entity specific data
- build or retrieve structural information
- provide information about the processing status

IIF Interface routines use a parameter sequence which is identical to the field sequence in the IGES DE and PD sections. The interface uses stacks to build each entity and its relations before it is written to IIF or passed to the calling program.

3.1.5.3 Functions of the EDIT Phase

The Edit phase contains functions to convert an IGES file into IIF and to convert IIF back into an IGES file. For a specific system environment this phase needs to be implemented only once. The convertion from IGES to IIF includes

- transfer of the IGES file into the IIF environment
- data conversion from ASCII to EBCDIC
- checking the formal correctness of the IGES file
- restructuring of the IGES sections into IIF

The conversion from IIF to IGES includes

- reformatting of IIF into IGES sections
- user control for data precision in the IGES file
- data conversion from EBCDIC to ASCII
- transfer of the IGES file to tape or disk

3.1.5.4 Functions of the EXCHANGE Phase

The exchange phase contains functions to translate IGES entities between IIF and a specific CAD/CAM system. Each individual CAD/CAM system needs a separate implementation of this phase. The three basic functions of this phase are

- data storage in and data retrieval from IIF (through the use of IIF Interface),
- individual entity translation between IIF and the CAD/CAM system,
- data storage in and data retrieval from the CAD/CAM system.

To enhance the usability of this phase, two additional functions are provided

- user decisions
- error reports

Figure 3.1.4 shows implementation of this design in the IBM IGES Processor.

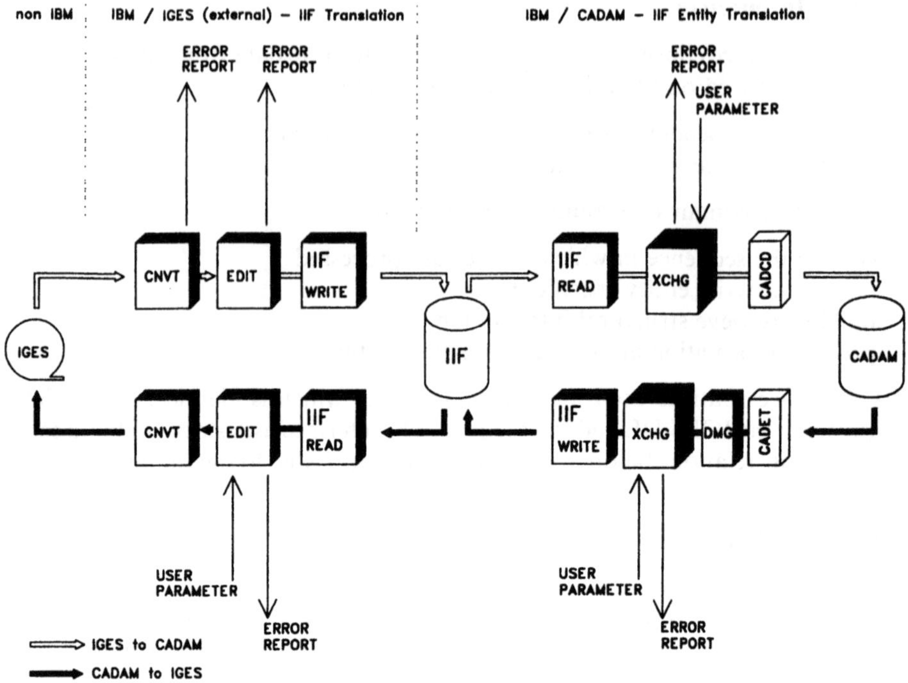

Fig. 3.1.4. IBM IGES Processor

User decisions allow translator users to select one specific approximation from a range of approximations in cases of entire translations with more than one possible approximation. These decisions are stored in a separate file called the translation profile.

Error reports inform the user about the type of error that occured, and where in the original IGES file the faulty entity was found. This information can then be used either to correct the original IGES file with the help of a text editor, or to send the IGES file and the error reports back to the originating system.

3.1.6 Summary

IGES is becoming accepted in the United States and in Europe by both the user and the CAD/CAM vendor community. Despite counter proposals, IGES has established itself as the leading standard for the exchange of graphical data. With IGES Version 2 (published by NBS[9] [10]) many of the intial problems of IGES have been solved. This version provides sufficient definitions for the exchange of drawing data, wireframe and surface models.

[9] U.S. Department of commerce, National Bureau of Standards

But, despite the positive results that have been obtained, many problems still remain. As more entities are added to IGES, the inadequacies of the basic IGES structure will become more apparent. These inadequacies need to be resolved next and will require a restructuring of the IGES standard itself. The proposals discussed by ISO/TC184/SC4 already include corrections and new ideas based on the experience with IGES. It is the goal of this committee to define one new international standard. But until this happens IGES is the only realistic method available.

The design that has been discussed in this paper, specifically the IIF Interface and the User Decisions, has significantly improved the quality of the IGES translations. Furthermore, with the help of the IIF Interface, the development time for an IGES translator has been drastically reduced.

3.1.7 References

1. Digital Representation for Communication of Product Definition Data, ANSI Y14.26M-1981. The American Society of Mechanical Engineers (1981)
2. Lewis JW, Kennicott PR: Designing IGES Processors. General Electric, USA (1980)
3. Liewald MH: Intersystem Data Transfer Via IGES. Boeing Commercial Airplane Company, Seattle, USA (September 1981)
4. Smith BM: IGES, A Key Interface Specification for CAD/CAM Systems Integration. National Bureau of Standards, USA (1982)
5. Initial Graphics Exchange Specification (IGES) CAD/CAM Processor, Program Description/Operations Manual, IBM Publication Number SH20-5630, IBM (1983)
6. Computer-Graphics Augmented Design and Manufacturing System, User Training Manual, IBM Form Number SH20-2035-3
7. Weissflog U: Experience in Design and Implementation of an IGES Processor. IBM, Los Angeles, USA (1983)
8. Product Definition Data Interface, Task I – Evaluation and Verification of ANSI Y14.26M Standard, IGES Committee Presentation, Booz-Allen & Hamilton Inc., USA (October 1983)
9. IIF Interface Library, User's Guide and Program Reference, IBM Publication Number SH20-6236, IBM (1984)
10. Initial Graphics Exchange Specification (IGES), Version 2.0, U.S. Department of Commerce, National Bureau of Standards, Washington, DC 20234, USA (February 1983)

3.2 Experience Gained Using the IGES Interface for CAD/CAM Data Transfer

D. Trippner

3.2.1 Introduction

3.2.1.1 CAE Use in Product Development

CAE (computer aided engineering) systems are currently used for the performance of specific tasks in almost all engineering areas of modern industry.

Depending on the various technical problems which have to be solved during the individual product development stages, such as construction, calculation or testing, a variety of different EDP aids are currently used, enabling the engineer to accomplish these tasks efficiently. The following application-specific CAE systems can be listed:

- CAD (Fig. 3.2.1)
  - Systems for 2D diagrammatic representations and technical drawings
  - Systems for handling 3D objects for mechanical construction
  - Systems for the construction and smoothing of free form surfaces
- CAM
  - Systems for the creation and preprocessing of NC data
- Calculation Systems
  - FEM systems
  - Simulation systems
  - Systems for aerodynamic testing

A substantial increase in productivity and quality results from the possibility of the integrated use of CAE systems, when, by linking design steps, multiple access to construction data already created can be effected [3].

In addition to linking different CAD systems in the construction and design phase, the provision of CAD data for further use in FEM and CAM systems for the calculation and production phases is likewise of economic importance (Fig. 3.2.2).

A first attempt at the integrated use of CAE systems for product development was undertaken by Boeing with the CIIN (Boeing's CAD/CAM Integrated Information Network Standard Format). This CAD/CAM interface definition was the starting point for the *IGES INTERFACE* (Initial Graphics Exchange Specification), which was established as the American standard ANSI Y14.26M in 1981. In the last few years, it has been implemented as a universal CAD interface by almost all CAD system suppliers in the form of IGES pre- and postprocessors with different quality levels.

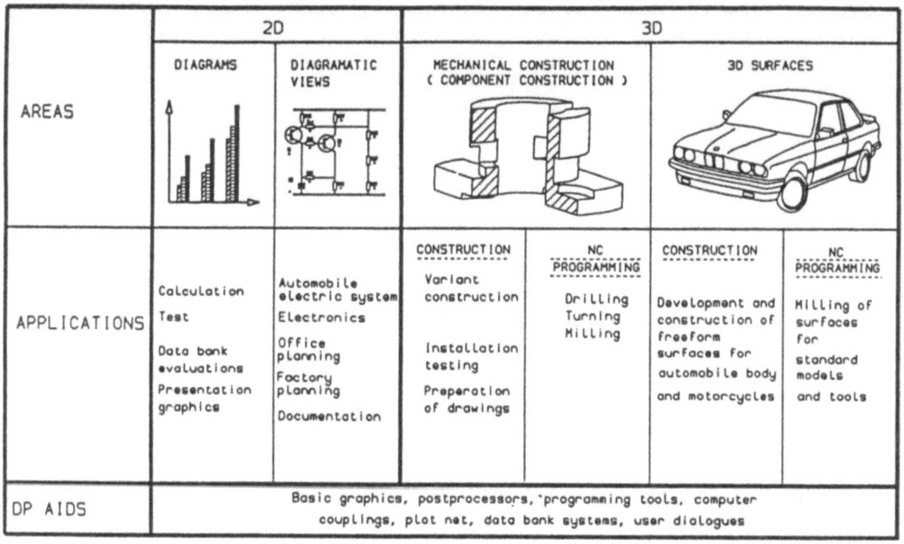

Fig. 3.2.1. CAD/CAM application areas

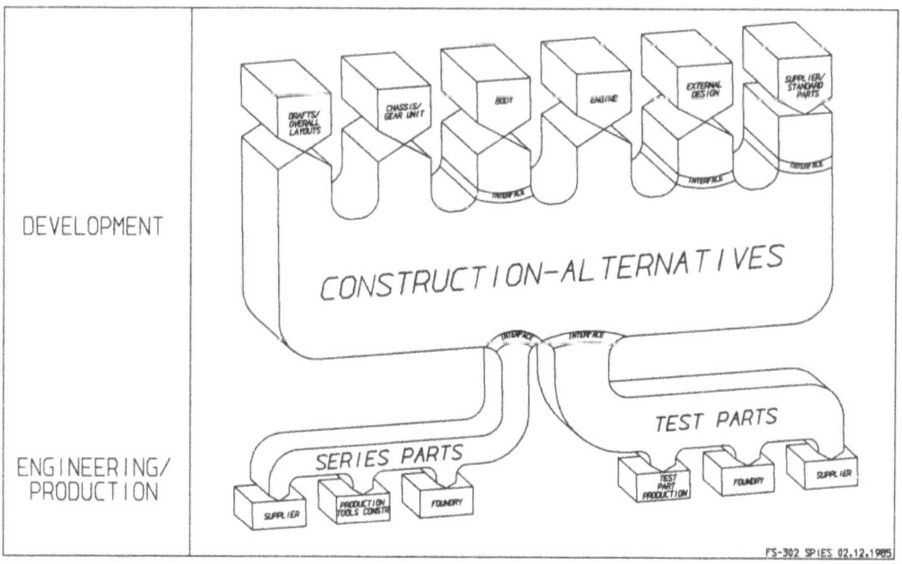

Fig. 3.2.2. Data flows – the construction of components and production tools

The concept is based on the idea of converting internal CAD construction data via a system-specific preprocessor into a neutral data format. This system-neutral data can then be further converted into the data format of another CAD system via a postprocessor (Fig. 3.2.3).

The advantage of this concept is that, in contrast to a direct coupling of n systems, n* (n−3) fewer pre- and postprocessors have to be implemented. In

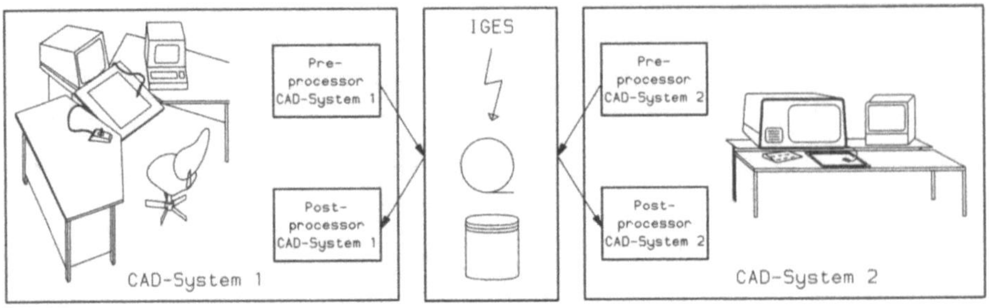

Fig. 3.2.3. Data exchange between CAD-systems via IGES

practice, this means that for a company with data exchange between, for instance 9 different (supplier and in-house) CAD systems, 54 fewer pre- and postprocessors will have to be developed and maintained. When considering the development work needed for pre- and postprocessors, it immediately becomes clear how important the standardized data exchange format is.

IGES was originally designed for the exchange of CAD engineering drawings, simple 3D wire frame and surface models. In version 1.0, which conforms to the ANSI standard, 34 different entity types with 41 different subtypes are defined.

The entity types can be classified as

- Geometry
- Annotation
- Structure

In subsequent versions, the standard was extended by basic entities for FEM and electrical systems.

This extended entity volume has, as yet, however, hardly been implemented by systems suppliers so that it can be assumed you are talking about a subset of the IGES entities of version 1.0, when talking about IGES pre- and postprocessors.

The data format established by the IGES file is a sequential text file with a fixed record length of 80 characters (punch card format) in ASCII code.

The transfer file is divided into 5 sections:

- Start Section
- Global Section
- Directory Entry Section
- Parameter Data Section
- Terminate Section

The Start Section can contain a prologue to the file, which is intended for the receiver. In the Global Section, information about formats, source system, originator, etc. is stored in a fixed order.

The actual component or drawing data is contained in the DE and PD Sections, whereby the element type-independent data is filed in the DE Section and the element type-dependent parameters in the PD Section.

3.2.2 Areas of Applications for the IGES Interface at BMW

In the case of computer-aided product development, the data flow via the IGES interface at present takes place mainly between CAD systems of different origin, but also between CAD systems and calculation systems, and between CAD and CAM systems.

3.2.2.1 Data Exchange Between CAD Systems

The CAD product data exchange takes place between suppliers and BMW as well as between different technical areas within BMW.

The application spectrum covers the exchange of data at the following model levels:

- Technical drawing/diagrammatic representations
- 3D wire frame model
- 3D surface model

Depending on the extent to which the CAD systems involved are to be utilized and operated, the transfer can take place both within a model level as well as between different model levels. Typical applications examples are:

- Adopting supplier's 3D wire frame and surface models for installation tests
- Making technical drawings for production based on 3D wire frame and surface models
- Constructing 3D wire frame and surface models based on 2D drawings
- Graphical documentation for assembly and marketing on the basis of 2D drawings, 3D wire frame and surface models
- Construction of production tools on the basis of the component geometry
- Use of the transmitted geometric data for motion simulation

3.2.2.2 Data Exchange Between CAD and CAM Systems

Today product data exchange via the IGES interface between different CAD and CAM systems is restricted mainly to the transfer of geometric data. Due to the limited entity volume of the IGES specification, especially in the area of free-form

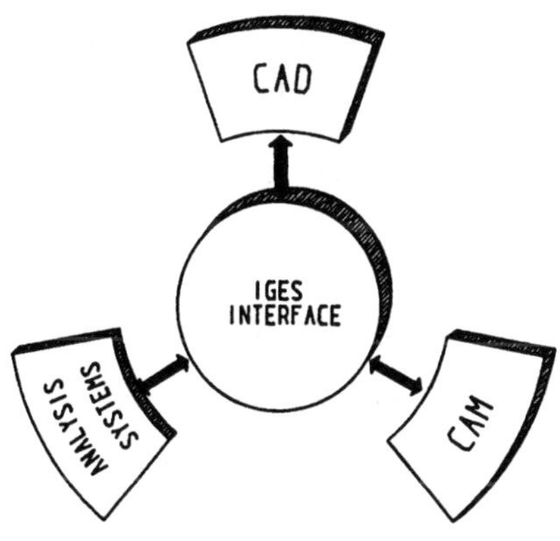

Fig. 3.2.4. Application field of the IGES interface at BMW

geometry, data transmission at present takes place from CAD systems in the Mechanical Construction development area to 2-axis NC production processes in the Production Tools and Test Parts production area.

With the aid of a coupling module, the transmitted component geometry can be transformed interactively into NC programming system language statements. It is necessary to add missing geometric, delete superfluous geometric, and add necessary technological information, such as material data, cutting speed, etc.

The following NC production procedures can be handled, using the NC language statements created:

- Drilling
- 2-axis milling
- oxy-acetylene cutting
- Nibbling
- Wire eroding

3.2.2.3 Data Exchange Between CAD and Calculation Systems

An important phase during the development of a new product is the prediction, definition and verification of the physical characteristics of the product or parts of the product using different calculation methods [1]. In the case of the product development of a vehicle, emphasis is laid on the following 3 technical calculation applications:

- FEM
- Aerodynamics
- Simulation

Many of the various calculation systems are based on a more or less idealized and complex component geometry.

In addition to the possibilities of creating this component geometry via coordinates or the digitalization of technical drawings, there is the possibility of transmitting the component geometry created in a CAD system via a standard interface to the calculation system.

This can be achieved today via the IGES interface, since the first IGES postprocessors are also available from suppliers of calculation systems.

As in the case of the coupling between CAD and CAM systems, further processing of the geometry either in the CAD or in the calculation system will normally be done as well. This further processing mainly consists in the idealization of the geometric model. i.e. deletion of unimportant drill-holes and roundings or subsequent construction of neutral fibers.

The structuring of the geometry that is required for calculation, such as the preparation of a FEM network, is then carried out in the calculation phase.

3.2.3 Basic Problems in the Field of CAD Data Transfer

3.2.3.1 CAD System Variety

About 250 different CAD systems are offered on the market worldwide [5]. These can vary considerably with regard to

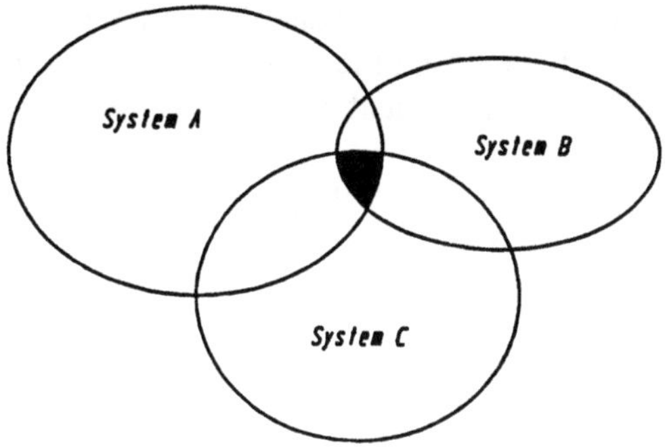

Fig. 3.2.5. Common model data of different CAE systems

		CD/2000 ENTITIES	CADDS 4X ENTITIES	CODEM 2D ENTITIES	CABLOS 2D ENTITIES	CADCAPL 2D ENTITIES	SUPERTAB ENTITIES
Defined by IGES Version 2.0	GEOMETRY	POINT	POINT	POINT	POINT	POINT	
		LINE	LINE	LINE	LINE	LINE	LINE
		CIRCLE 3D	CIRCLE 3D	CIRCLE	CIRCLE	CIRCLE	CIRCLE
		GENERAL CONIC		ELLIPSE	CONIC 2D		
		SPLINE 2D	SPLINE 2D	SPLINE	SPLINE 2D		
		SPLINE 3D	SPLINE 3D				SPLINE 3D
		PLANE	PLANE				
		SURFACE OF REVOLUTION	SURFACE OF REVOLUTION				
							B SPLINE SURFACE
		TABULATED CYLINDER	TABULATED CYLINDER				
		COPIUS DATA	COPIUS DATA				
	ANNOTATION	LINEAR DIMENSION	LINEAR DIMENSION	LINEAR DIMENSION			
		CIRCULAR DIMENSION	CIRCULAR DIMENSION				
		LABEL	LABEL	LABEL			
		DIAMETER	DIAMETER	DIAMETER			
		ANGULAR DIMENSION	ANGULAR DIMENSION	ANGULAR DIMENSION			
		NOTE	NOTE	NOTE	NOTE		
		CENTERLINE	CENTERLINE				
		CROSS HATCHING	CROSS HATCHING				
	STRUCTURE	COMPOSITE CURVE				COMPOSITE CURVE	
		GROUP					
		RECTANGULAR ARRAY					
		CIRCULAR ARRAY					
		VIEWLAYOUT					
					SUBFIGURE		

Fig. 3.2.6

- Model philosophy (e.g. CSG or Boundary Representation)
- Volume and selection of application-specific entities
- Data structures
- Data contents
- Data and storage formats
- Accuracy

The above-mentioned differences are reflected in the amount, the form and the quality of the information stored. This constitutes the basic problem of data exchange between CAD systems, which can only be solved by standardization of the systems.

When considering the variety of information that can theoretically be stored by each system, only the data volume common to all systems is exchangeable (Fig. 3.2.5).

In practice this means that in a company, in which data exchange must, for instance, take place between 6 different CAE systems (Fig. 3.2.6) with a total of

59 different entity type definitions, the common data volume consists of 2 entities, that is the line and the circle. And even in the case of these 2 element types, there are system-dependent differences in terms of dimensions, data structure and data accuracy.

This example clearly shows that using the common data volume of all the relevant CAE systems to obtain a system-neutral data base – in this case the line and the circle – is not a very helpful approach.

This rather negative result is modified, however, by the fact that in the case of linking only 2 systems for specific applications, the common data volume available is often sufficient to make possible an economic and efficient data exchange.

3.2.3.2 IGES Interface Definitions

Besides the basic problems in the field of data transfer resulting from the variety of systems, the concept of a standard CAD interface definition has also had considerable influence on the success or failure of product date exchange, as well as the quality of processors used.

For the productive use of a CAD interface, it is therefore important to know which basic capabilities and/or shortcomings are inherent in the interface definition itself.

For this reason a comprehensive analysis of the IGES specification was carried out by the DIN working committee DIN NAM 96.4, which is concerned with the drawing up of a German CAD interface standard [6].

The result of this analysis can be summarized as follows:

- The applicability of IGES is, because of its history, better tailored to the CAD systems of the 70's than to others.
- The present spectrum of IGES entities is designed to concentrate on the transfer of technical drawings, 3D wire frame models as well as on initial attempts at 3D surface models.
- The possibilities of showing annotation of technical drawings are restricted to the ANSI drawing standards; furthermore, important dimension and symbol elements are missing.
- The annotation entities allow a graphically exact reproduction of the dimensional picture as it exists in the transmitting system. The functionality of the annotation, i.e. the possibility of modifying the annotation received in latter applications with usual drafting modification functions, is not guaranteed for want of additional information.
- The present data format is unnecessarily complicated and voluminous, which results in extended processing times and large transfer files.
- For some geometric entities unsuitable representational forms are chosen, which in limiting cases can lead to numerical problems (e.g. circles).
- In many cases entity definitions are redundant or inaccurate.

In spite of these, in some cases rather serious, shortcomings, IGES can currently be used economically for certain applications.

3.2.3.3 IGES Processors

In view of the often poor results of data transfer via the IGES interface, the mistake is frequently made to attribute this to the IGES specification alone. Systematic tests of different processors have shown, however, that the quality of the processors, which differs from one system supplier to the other, often remains at the lowest level [7].

The reason for this often lies in the system supplier having little interest in supplying the CAD user with a highly developed product, with which a system change can be performed at any time, and also in the overall structure of the IGES standard.

The lack of an IGES level structure, like the GKS, makes it possible for the system supplier to maintain that there is an IGES interface to his CAD system, even if it covers only such entities as points, lines and circles.

This statement is confirmed by a study [7] carried out in the USA which revealed that the IGES processors of 12 well-known CAD systems tested covered an average of only 27% of the entity volume available in IGES Version 1.0.

Aside from this, there are a number of other problems to be confronted when using IGES processors.

These can in part be traced back to both unfavourable and inaccurate IGES specification and to poor implementation. They can be summarized as follows:

- In pre- and postprocessing it often happens that there is a complete conversion break-off without the user receiving the appropriate error messages. This leads to the non-transferability of all the data. Error handling, as in the case of compilers, is necessary here.
- Many processors do not allow the user to carry out systematic conversion via control possibilities, such as dialogue or control file.
  Experience has shown that it is often desirable to select only specific data items, such as levels, entities or subtypes of entities for conversion, or to display these in another more application-specific form.
  Examples would be the breaking down of splines of a higher degree to a lower degree, or the transformation of annotation into pure geometry with text.
- Some postprocesssors, when processing IGES data files, assume that these are syntactically and semantically correct without having checked this in whole or in part as a separate step. This leads either to the aforementioned break-off of the processor run or, which can be even more fatal for the user, to wrong results in the receiving system.
- Another important aid for the user, which is not offered by most IGES postprocessors, is information about the transfer file processed. For production applications it is important to know which data contents are transmitted, which are approximated, and which are not transformed.

3.2.3.4 Transfer Media

A further problem which may occur with regard to data exchange is the transfer of the IGES data created with the help of the transfer medium available.

The following methods of data transfer are possible:

- direct computer coupling
- remote data transfer
- magnetic tape, data cassette or floppy

In practice, however, the direct computer coupling in the case of inhouse exchange, as well as the transfer of data on magnetic tape in the case of exchange with suppliers, are of major importance. Unlike the direct computer coupling, where the transmitting and receiving systems are always known, the exchange using magnetic tapes keeps creating difficulties.

The data format prescribed by IGES Recommended Practices [8], i.e., a 9-track tape with 1600 bpi, 7-bit ASCII code, (8th bit = zero), unlabeled, 80 character fixed length records, 10 records per block with single end-of-file mark for each IGES file as well as with multiple end-of-file marks for the end of the tape, is often not observed, which complicates reading unnecessarily.

These difficulties can, however, be prevented when appropriate arrangements are made with the producer and/or receiver of the tape.

3.2.4 Example of Practical Use

The following example illustrates the possibilities, as well as the difficulties, involved in using the IGES interface in data transfer. Of particular interest here is the amount of transferable and non-transferable data, the editing steps neccessary, the processing time of the processors and the cost involved, as well as the size of the files to be transferred.

The part shown in Fig. 3.2.7 is a 3D wire frame and surface model of a motor for an electric window mechanism from the supplying industry. The part received on tape had an IGES data size of about 2 MBytes and contained 1479 entities.

The IGES file contained the following entities:

- 26 Transformation matrices
- 812 Lines
- 6 Points
- 434 Circles
- 104 Parametric splines
- 1 Ruled surfaces
- 1 Surface of revolution
- 36 Copious data
- 36 Planes
- 6 Views
- 1 Drawing
- 16 User defined properties

The processing time for the postprocessor amounted to 254 CPU seconds, the generated file had a size of about 1 MByte.

Figure 3.2.8 shows the transferred model of the motor for the electric window mechanism immediately after it was read into the receiving system.

During the conversion, the following entities were lost:

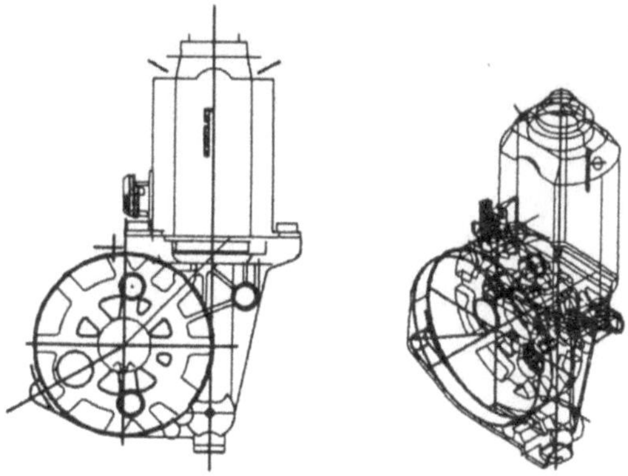

Fig. 3.2.7

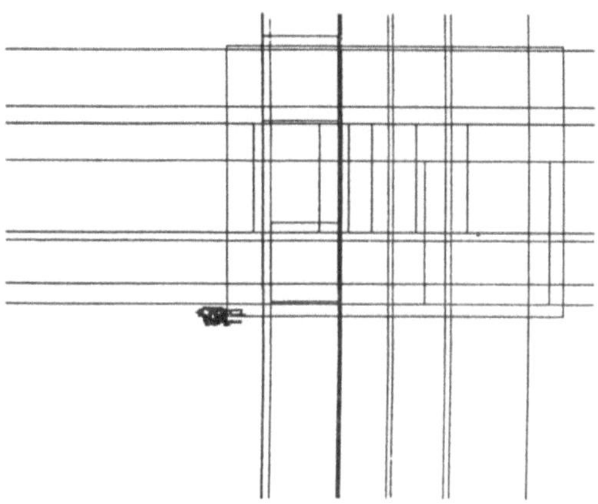

Fig. 3.2.8

- 6 Views
- 1 Drawing
- 16 Properties

The transfer of the 36 plane entities filed in the IGES file was performed incorrectly. The incorrect planes are the horizontal and vertical lines in Fig. 3.2.8 protruding from the electric window mechanism.

After elimination of the planes in the receiving system, the geometry model shown in Fig. 3.2.9 is available for further use in installation testing or other applications.

The time required for reading in, conversion and editing was about 1 hour for this example.

Depending on the computer type and the unit of account, the costs for postprocessing in this example are between DM 100,– and DM 1.000,–. When comparing the costs and the processing times involved with the costs and the amount of time required for a reconstruction, the economic advantage of a CAD data interface becomes clear immediately.

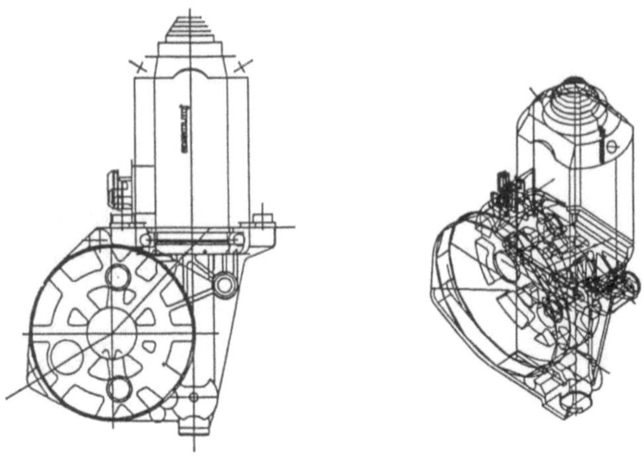

Fig. 3.2.9

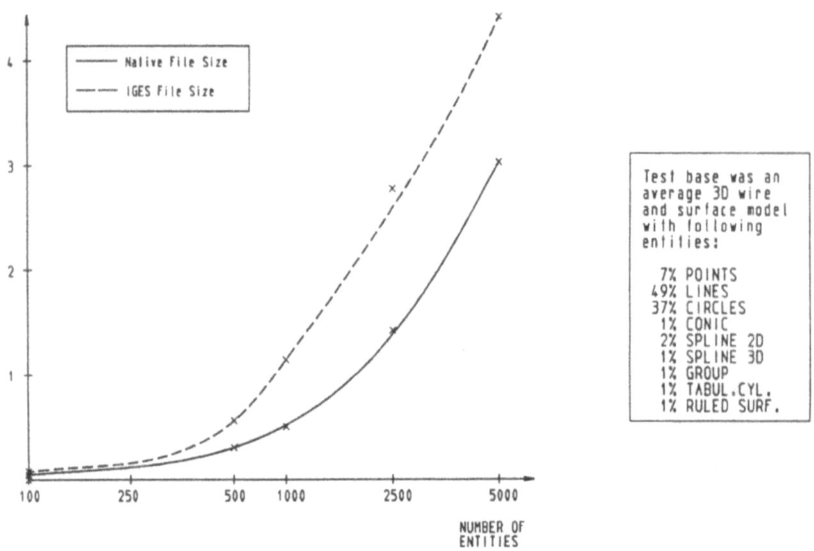

Fig. 3.2.10. Comparison of IGES and native file sizes

Independent of this example, Figs. 3.2.10 to 3.2.12 show the relevant practical data relating to processing times, of the storage locations needed and processing costs calculated on the basis of a geometric model with an average number of elements.

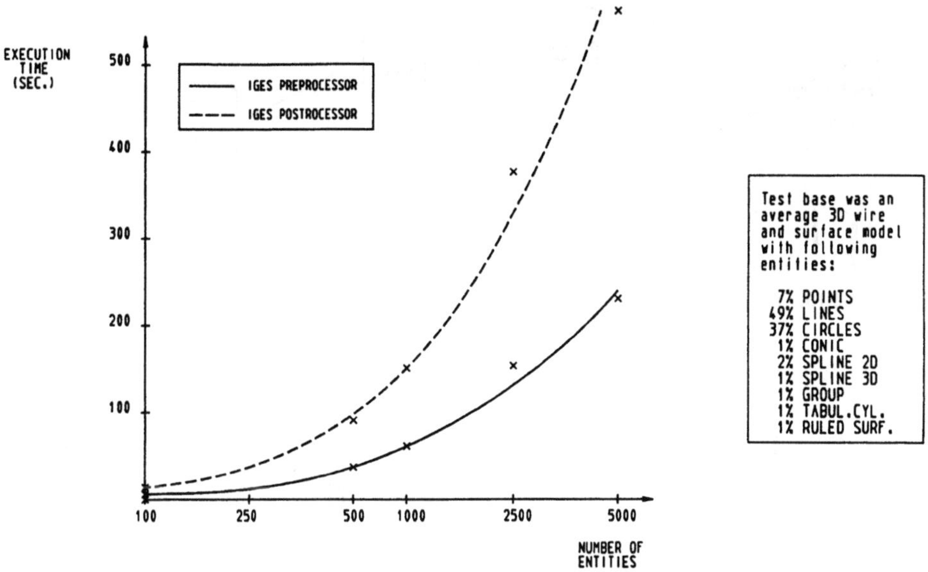

Fig. 3.2.11. Comparison of IGES pre- and post-processor execution time. Tested with a 5 MIPS and 1 megaword memory computer

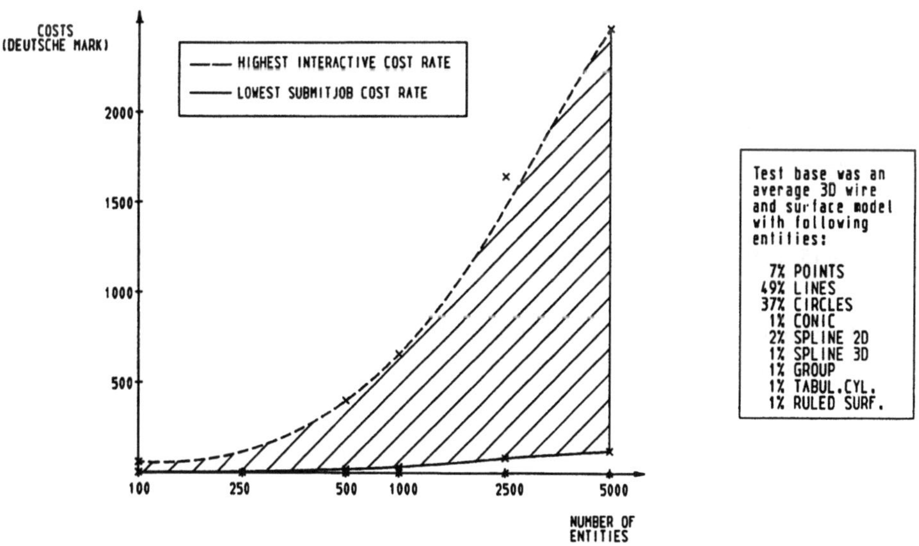

Fig. 3.2.12. Costs of IGES pre- and postprocessing

3.2.5 Verification of IGES Processors from the User's Point of View

The missing level structure in the IGES specification, but also the non-existence of a neutral validation institution, are the reasons why the user is often left in the dark about the real performance of the IGES processor for his CAD system.

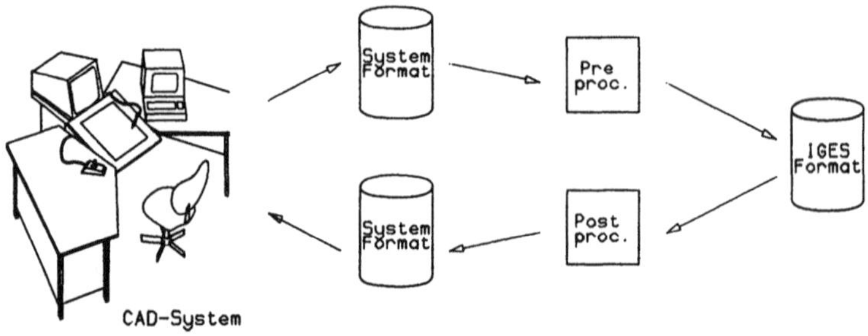

Fig. 3.2.13. The cycle test

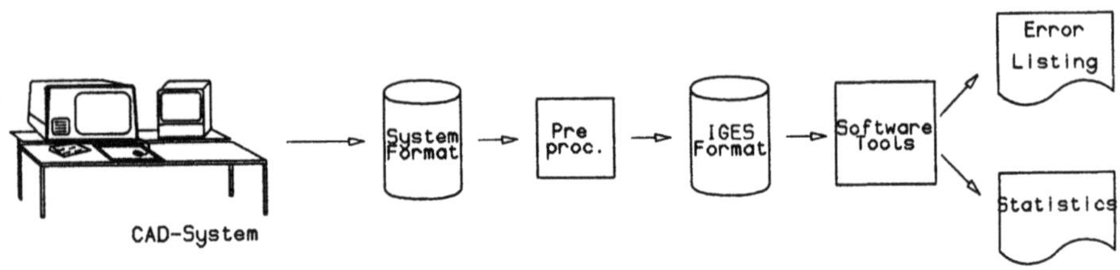

Fig. 3.2.14. Inter-system test

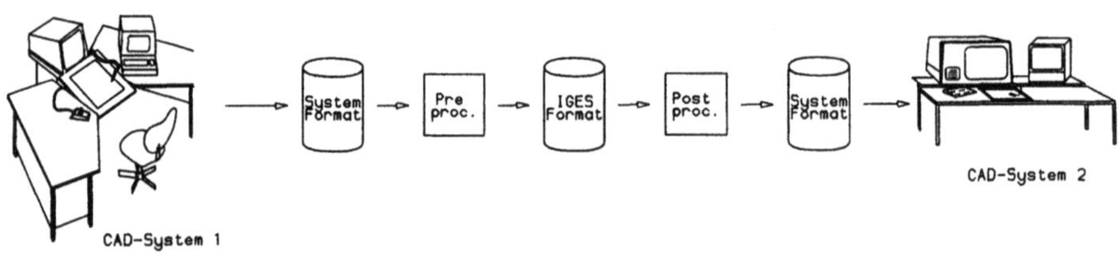

Fig. 3.2.15. Software tools

For routine use of the IGES interface for data exchange between 2 systems however, exact knowledge of the quality and quantity of the exchangeable data volume is absolutely essential. The user is therefore forced to determine the properties and the performance level of the processors involved in the data exchange by carrying out the appropriate tests. The test methods available are:

a) The cycle test, Fig. 3.2.13, is the simplest test method, with which a quick general view of the entities supported by the processors can be obtained by translating the CAD data into the IGES format by the preprocessor and by retranslating it again into the system-specific format with the aid of the postprocessor of the same system.
For a systematic examination, it would be advisable to use a synthetic test part similar to the test matrices shown in Fig. 3.2.16 and Fig. 3.2.17. The disadvantage of this test method is that in the case of errors and/or non-translation of the entities, it cannot be clearly determined whether the fault lies with the pre- or with the postprocessor.

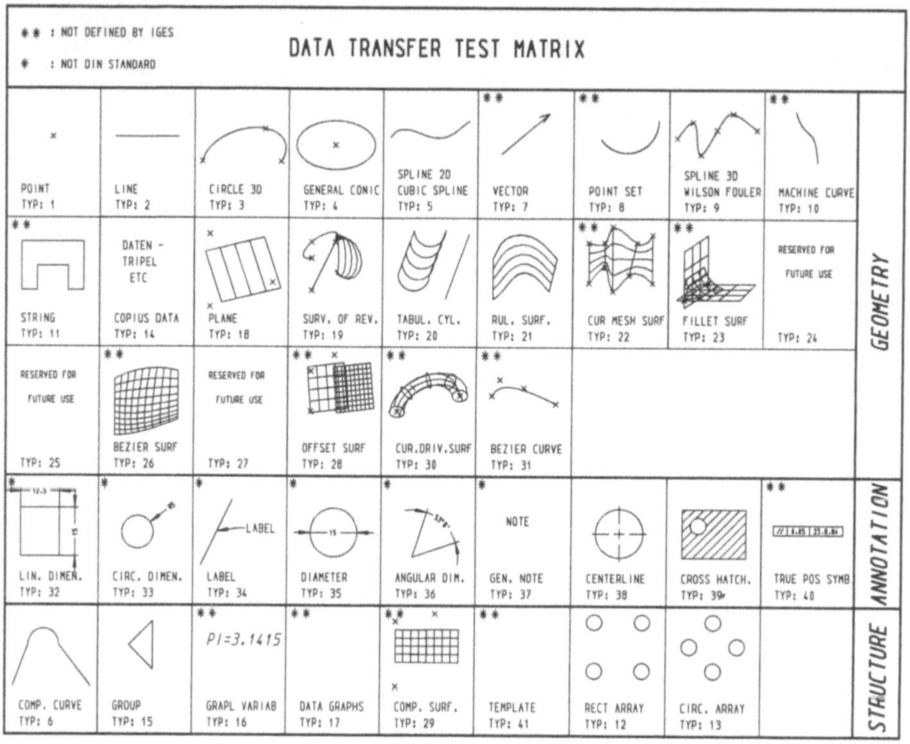

Fig. 3.2.16. IGES pre- and postprocessor test in CD/2000 defined entities

b) In the case of the inter-system test (Fig. 3.2.14) the situation is similar. During the transfer test it cannot be determined which of the two processors is responsible for possible bottlenecks.
This test is, however, of great importance with respect to determining the exchangeable data volume between the CAD systems used. The use of synthetic test parts, analogous to the cycle test, is advisable here as well.
For the systematic testing of the preprocessor, a combination of cycle and inter-system tests, as well as the use of software tools to check the syntactic and semantic correctness of the IGES file is necessary (Fig. 3.2.15). In the case of simple files, this can be done by hand; this, however, is very time consuming and costly and, furthermore, requires that the user has a detailed knowledge of the IGES specification. Software tools for checking IGES files are not yet available on the European market; there are independent developments by industry and universities, however, which are currently used for the verification of preprocessors.

c) Checking of postprocessors requires correct (system-neutral) IGES test data, which must be converted by the postprocessor and compared with the preset data in the CAD system. An IGES Test Library was set up at great expense at the National Bureau of Standards (NBS) in the USA, especially for this test method. This test library, however, comprises only a subset of the entities specified in the Standard and is therefore only of limited use.

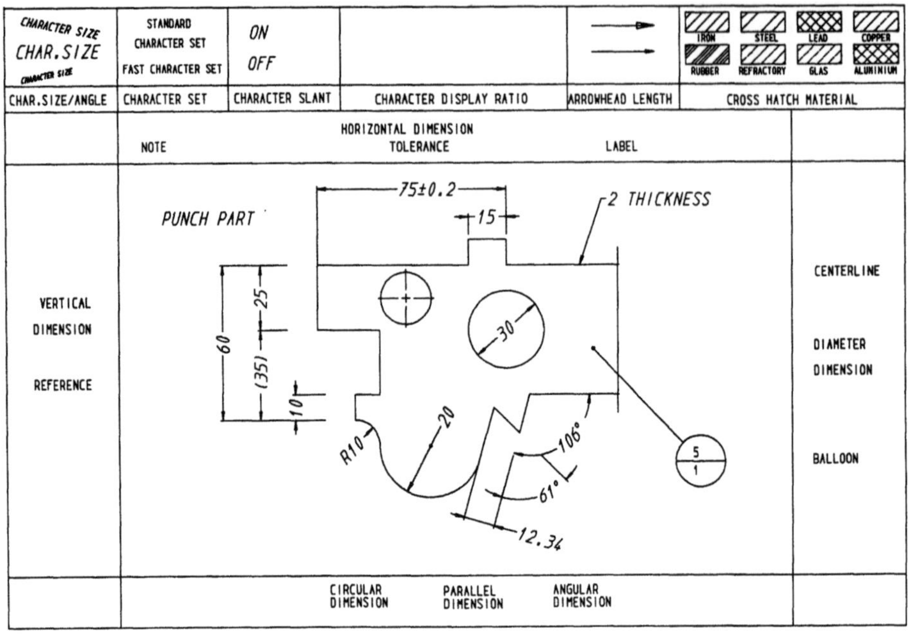

Fig. 3.2.17. Drafting test-matrix

3.2.6 Summary

The experience of the IGES interface during the 2 years of practical use at BMW can be summarized as follows:

- The current use of the IGES interface is already past the test phase.
- When using the IGES interface for the coupling of certain systems and appropriate applications, considerable economic effects can be obtained.
- Nevertheless, the IGES specification still needs considerable improvement.
- The quality of IGES processors available on the market varies enormously, but is, on average, unsatisfactory.

3.2.7 References

1. Schuster R, Trippner D: Anforderungen an eine Schnittstelle zur Übertragung produktdefinierender Daten zwischen verschiedenen CAD/CAM-Systemen. GI-Jahrestagung 1984, Braunschweig
2. Tröndle K: Datenaustausch zwischen verschiedenen Systemen. VDI Bildungswerk BW 6301, September 1984
3. Digital Representation for Communication of Product Definition. Data Chapter I–IV. ANSI Y14.26M 1981, USA
4. Vöge E: Zum Einsatz rechnergestützter Verfahren in der Produktentwicklung. GI-Jahrestagung 1984, Braunschweig
5. Schuster R: Rechnergestützte Konstruktion. CAD-Informationsaufbreitung für CAM. BMW AG, 1982

6. Anderl R, Glatz R, Nowacki H, Schuster R, Trippner D, Tröndle K: IGES Review and Proposed Extensions. DIN NAM 96.4/2–83
7. Product Definition Data Interface. Task-I-Evaluation and Verification of ANSI Y14.26M., Standard 18.10.83. Booz-Allen and Hamilton Inc.
8. Recommended Practice. NBS, IGES, TEST, Evaluate & Support Committee
9. Schuster R, Trippner D, Glatz R: Was geschieht bei der CAD/CAM Schnittstellennormung. CAD/CAM, Februar 1985

Chapter 4

VDAFS

Functionalities, Approximation Methods, Implementation, Experience

4.1 VDAFS – A Pragmatic Interface for the Exchange of Sculptured Surface Data

W. Renz

4.1.1 History

In 1982 the Association of the German Automotive Manufacturers and their suppliers, VDA (Verband der Automobilindustrie), created a new committee, called the VDA-CAD/CAM Committee.

The primary goal was to discover or, if necessary, to develop a data format for exchanging sculptured surface data between the automotive manufacturers and their suppliers. The pragmatic aspect is already obvious. The area of application of this format was restricted to a field of industrial cooperation where a lot of benefits could be achieved. This field covers the transition from car body design to design and NC-milling of models and dies. Digital representation and communication of sculptured surfaces is much faster and cheaper than reliance on drawings alone and leads to higher quality of the resulting product.

At the end of 1982, the VDA-CAD/CAM-Committee founded a working group "Geometric Interface", which developed VDAFS (VDA-Flächenschnittstelle) in cooperation with the TH Darmstadt, Fachbereich "Graphisch-interaktive Systeme" [2].

VDAFS was published in July 1983 [3]. Initial implementations have been working since the beginning of 1984. Furthermore VDAFS is going to be published as a German National Standard within the first quarter of 1985 (DIN 66301).

It is important to note carefully what VDAFS does and does not do:

- *VDAFS is no substitute* for a general international standard (as further developments of IGES is expected to be).
- *VDAFS is a pragmatic solution* within a special field of application which has just become operational. We hope that VDAFS will influence the process of defining well structured, easy to handle international standards.

4.1.2 Pragmatic Goals

When beginning to define VDAFS two outstanding questions had to be answered:

a) Which geometrical elements must be included?
b) Which general properties are expected?

4.1.2.1 Geometrical Elements

It was decided, that the VDAFS-Interface should include the following geometrical entities in three-dimensional space:

- Point
- Sequence of points
- Sequence of points and vectors (for NC-milling)
- Piecewise polynomial curves
- Piecewise polynomial surfaces (as a rectangular array of patches)

4.1.2.2 General Properties

The following properties (in decreasing order of priority) have been declared desirable:

- ease of implementation
- sequential structure
- small volume of data
- easy to read
- easy to handle (edit)

Table 4.1.1

```
(1)                                                                (72)   (80)

VDA001 = HEADER/7                                                      00000000
************************************************************************ 00000010
FILE NAME        : EXAM01                                              00000020
CONTACT PARTNER: VERBAND DER AUTOMOBILINDUSTRIE E.V.                   00000030
                 POSTFACH 170563                                       00000040
                 D-6000 FRANKFURT 17                                   00000050
                 Tel.: 0611/757 01                                     00000060
************************************************************************ 00000070
$$ TEST DATA TO DEMONSTRATE VDAFS                                      00000080
$$ ********************************************************************* 00000090
$$              GEOMETRICAL DATA FOR PUNCHES                           00000100
SET01   = BEGINSET                                                     00000110
P0001   = POINT /100., 200., 300.                                      00000120
PS001   = PSET   /20, 1., 0., 0., 2., 0., 0., 3., 0., 0., ... , 20., 0., 0.  00000130
MDI01   = MDI    /20, 1., 0., 0., 0., 0., 1., 2., 0., 0., 0., 0., 1., ...    00000200
CRV01   = CURVE/2, 0., 1., 2., 2, 10., 10., 0., 10., 0., 0.,           00000300
                  4, 20., 10., 5., 5., 10., 0., −9., −1., 0., 0., 0., 0.     00000310
SRF01   = SURF   /2, 2, 0., 1., 2., 0., 1., 2., 3, 3, ...              00000400
SET01   = ENDSET                                                       00000500
$$                                                                     00000510
$$              GEOMETRICAL DATA FOR DIE CAST                          00000520
SET02   = BEGINSET                                                     00000530
P0001   = POINT/0., 0., 0.                                             00000540
SRF02   = SURF   /1, 1, 0., 1., 0., 1., 12, 12, ...                    00000550
SET02   = ENDSET                                                       00001000
VDA001 = END                                                           00001010
```

4.1.2.3 Remarks

It is obvious that the restriction to such a small number of geometrical elements is a good precondition for the attainment of the properties in 4.1.2.2. On the other hand the limitations of VDAFS are clear: Special geometrical elements such as circles, conics, surfaces of revolution and others are *not available*. These elements have to be approximated by polynomial elements when using VDAFS. Furthermore, it is not possible to use VDAFS as an interface for two dimensional drawings including dimensioning.

4.1.3 Example

Let us now turn from practical to theoretical aspects of VDAFS by considering an example (see Table 4.1.1)

4.1.4 Syntax and Rules

4.1.4.1 General Rules

Let us point out the most important conventions and rules:

- A VDAFS-File consists of records, each with 80 characters, in ASCII Code.
- Integers and real numbers are written in free format.
- The delimiter is the comma. A continuation line is recognized if the last non-blank character of the preceding line in colums 1–72 is a comma.
- Comment lines must be marked at the beginning by "$$".
- The general syntax rule for geometric elements is as follows:

name = command word / parameter

  As this syntax is similar to APT statements, interpretation is easy and familiar to a lot of users.
- Command words are written in capital letters, names which have the function of labels consist of capital letters (A–Z) and digits (0–9). The first character must be a letter. A name consists of 1 to 8 characters.

4.1.4.2 Geometrical Elements

The command words for the geometrical elements listed in 4.1.2.1 are

- POINT for points
- PSET for point sequences
- MDI for point vector sequences
- CURVE for piecewise polynomial curves and
- SURF for piecewise polynomial surfaces

The first parameter after the command word PSET (MDI) is the *number* of triples (sextuples) of coordinates. The following parameters are the coordinates themselves (see Sect. 4.1.3 Example).

Let us have a more detailed look at the entity CURVE. The first parameter is the *number of segments* (n), followed by the $(n+1)$ *global parameters* ($par_1, \ldots, par_{n+1}$). Then the *first segment* is described completely: the first parameter gives the *order* (iord) of the polynomial function, followed by the polynomial coefficients $((ax_i)_{i=0,\,iord-1}, (ay_i)_{i=0,\,iord-1}, (az_i)_{i=0,\,iord-1})$ sorted according to increasing power of monomial basic functions.

All coefficients are related to a local parameter (u), which runs from 0. to 1. for each segment and which is the linear transformation of the global parameter (par) running from par_1 to par_2 within the first segment. ($u = (par - par_1)/(par_2 - par_1)$ for $par_1 \leqq par \leqq par_2$). All segments are described in this way.

Thus the element CURVE, which is named CRVO1 in the example 4.1.3, consists of two segments. The first one is linear, starting at (10., 0., 0.) and ending at (20., 10., 0.). The coordinate functions for the second segment are of order 4 (i.e. cubic functions) with

$$x(u) = 20. + 10. * u + 5. * u^2 + 5. * u^3$$
$$y(u) = 10. + 0. * u - 9. * u^2 - 1. * u^3$$
$$z(u) = 0.$$

and $0. \leqq u \leqq 1.$

The entity SURF is the natural generalization of the entity CURVE. In Sect. 4.1.3. the first entity SURF, named SRF01, consists of 2 * 2 patches with normalized parameters in both directions (0., 1., 2.). The first patch is of order (3, 3) (i.e. biquadratic). For more details see [3].

The main properties of the entities CURVE and SURF are:

- Each segment (patch) may have its own polynomial order. For each patch the order in u-direction may be different from the order in v-direction.
  These are the most important properties of curve and surface representation within VDAFS.
- As each segment (patch) is defined independently from the others, segments (patches) may or may not join smoothly. Thus VDAFS surfaces may have edges along the boundaries of patches.
- It is no problem to transform other surface representations (with other basic functions) such as COONS, BEZIER, B-SPLINE into monomial representations.

4.1.4.3 Non-Geometrical Elements

The non-geometrical elements within VDAFS are Header, Trailer, Comments and Structuring (see Sect. 4.1.3 EXAMPLE).

The header was introduced to transmit information such as sending firm, file name, validation date of the file, contact partner, etc.

Table 4.1.2

	IGES	IGES, Chapter 5	Internal proposal which is now called VDAFS
Number and type of elements which are necessary to define a interface, covering 4.1.2.1	7 entities	1 entity 4 structures 11 relations	5 entities
Time necessary for programming and implementation of the interface-software in relative units	2–5	3–7	1
Volume of data in relative units	2–5	1.5–7	1
Editing possibilities, ease of reading	Very bad	Bad	Satisfactory

The structuring element is very simple, because it allows only a single level set structuring.

4.1.5 Really Pragmatic?

4.1.5.1 Why Not IGES?

When the VDA-Working-Group "Geometrical Interface" started discussions, there were three different proposals, which had to be checked against the goals, stated in Sect. 4.1.2.

a) A Subset of "IGES" [1]
b) A subset of "IGES", as described in Chap. 5 of [1]
c) A proposal of a German automobile manufacturer, which was the prototype for VDAFS.

Let us note that a) is the IGES interface, realized in a lot of CAD/CAM-systems. b) is a proposal, very different from a) in structure and syntax.

The decision within the VDA Working Group was easily made having looked at Table 4.1.2 (due to P. Rewald [2]). The internal proposal, which is now called VDAFS, needs the smallest number of elements to cover 4.1.2.1, the shortest time for programming and implementation and less space for data storage than the others.

4.1.5.2 VDAFS – State of the Art

In 1984 all German automobile manufacturers and some of their suppliers were already working with VDAFS. Programming and implementation can be done in a short time, about 4 to 6 weeks for a qualified person. A lot of vendors of turnkey CAD/CAM-systems are implementing this interface or have announced their intention to do so.

In addition the VDA CAD/CAM-committee created a Working Group "Test", which is going to define official test data. These test data files will establish an effective instrument for validating all current and future implementations of VDAFS. To achieve a "VDAFS-certificate" it will be necessary to read and to rewrite the test data correctly. This will guarantee that implementations of VDAFS are reliable interfaces.

In the author's opinion these facts are strong enough to eliminate the question mark in the title of this section.

4.1.6 Further Developments

It is not the intention of the "fathers of VDAFS" to develop this interface and broaden it up to a general interface for geometrical data. Consequently all further developments should be restricted to that field of application which is described by the name VDAFS itself (i.e. interface for surfaces). Therefore we look forward to suitable pragmatic solutions to the following problems:

- Representation of bounded surfaces, which are *not necessarily* a rectangular matrix of patches.
- Representation of topological properties, which will allow the transmission of a combination of surfaces.

Nevertheless *the actual range of VDAFS will remain valid as a pragmatic kernel* of the interface.

4.1.7 References

1. Digital Representation for Communication of Product Definition Data. ANSI Y14.26M-1981 (1982)
2. Rehwald P: IGES-Schnittstelle für die Oberflächenbeschreibung in der Automobilindustrie. TH Darmstadt, GRIS 83-1 (1983)
3. VDA-Flächenschnittstelle (VDAFS), Version 1.0. Verband der Automobilindustrie e.V. (VDA) (1983)

4.2 Approximation Methods Used in the Exchange of Geometric Information via the VDA/VDMA Surface Interface

H. Nowacki and L. Dannenberg

4.2.1 Introduction

The exchange of geometric information between different CAD systems has become a matter of increasing practical importance. Many industrial organizations are using several CAD modelling systems side by side or exchanging geometric data with their vendors and subcontractors. Thus the data need to be converted from one representation to another because each modelling system has its own distinct type of internal geometry representation. The most effective approach to communication between several heterogeneous CAD systems is based on providing a neutral external representation of the geometric model, that is, a standardized form of modeller interface.

This need has been also recognized by the automotive industry in Germany, particularly for the exchange of curve and surface definitions of automobile parts. Their association, the VDA (Association of the Automobile Industry), has developed a neutral interface format, primarily for the exchange of surface data. These developments, which were later cosponsored by the VDMA (German Association of Mechanical and Process Plant Design Industries), have resulted in the draft of a German national standard, called VDA/VDMA Surface Interface [1].

This interface differs from other proposed modelling interfaces in that it supports only the communication of freeform curve and surface data with associated comments, but no other geometric or non-geometric entities, not even conic sections (circle, ellipse, ...) or quadric surfaces (cylinder, cone, ellipsoid, ...). Therefore, it is limited to representations by parametric polynomials, but this covers the great majority of free-form CAD modelling systems. It includes, in particular, Bézier, B-Spline, and Coons tensor product types of surfaces and corresponding curves.

Whenever two modelling systems possess polynomial representations with the same maximum polynomial degree, the conversion can be performed directly by straightforward matrix multiplication. In practice, there is much variation in the maximum degree supported in individual systems, ranging between degrees 3 and 20. In going from a high degree representation into systems of more limited degree capability it is necessary to make an approximate conversion, reducing the degree and – for compensation – decreasing the mesh spacing in the surface subdivision. Going from low to high degrees requires the opposite transformation.

The general aim in making these approximate conversions is to maintain a high degree of accuracy, that is, to minimize the loss of geometric information.

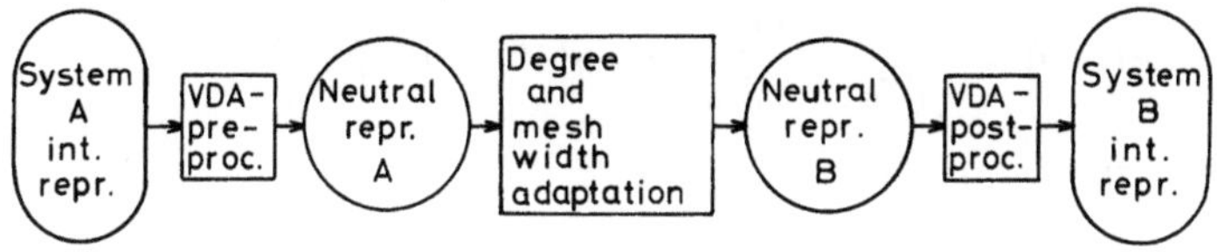

Fig. 4.2.1. Conversion of geometric representations via VDA-FS

The present paper, which is based on an investigation sponsored by the VDA, describes a method for approximate polynomial curve and surface conversions based on a combination of interpolation and least squares approximation.

4.2.2 The VDA-VDMA Surface Interface

Figure 4.2.1 shows the process of conversion for geometric representations using the VDA/VDMA Surface Interface, abbreviated by VDA-FS. The internal representation of the originating system A is first converted into the neutral VDA format by means of a preprocessor. If the receiving system B requires different polynomial degrees and mesh spacings, then an approximation is performed which results in a new neutral format to be read by the system B postprocessor.

The VDA-FS neutral file format is a standard 80 ASCII character record in free format. Its principal contents are CURVE and SURFACE entities. These are defined as follows.

– *CURVE*:

A "CURVE" is a set of segments with natural parametric polynomial (monomial) representation. Each segment is of the form:

$$\boldsymbol{r}(u) = \sum_{j=0}^{K_{\mathrm{ORD}}-1} \boldsymbol{a}_j u^j, \; u \in [0, 1]$$

The corresponding file format for a complete curve is

name = CURVE/n, $(n+1) * [\text{par}]$, $n * [K_{\mathrm{ORD}}, K_{\mathrm{ORD}} * [a_x], \ldots]$

where n = number of segments,
par = global parameter values at segment boundaries,
K_{ORD} = order number of particular segment,
$a_x, \ldots$ = polynomial coefficients in segment.

– *SURFACE*:

A "Surface" consists of a regular mesh of (nps * npt) parametric polynomial patches, each of arbitrary orders J_{ORD} and K_{ORD}:

$$\boldsymbol{r}(u, v) = \sum_{k=0}^{\mathrm{KORD}-1} \sum_{j=0}^{\mathrm{JORD}-1} \boldsymbol{a}_{jk} u^j v^k, \; u, v \in [0, 1]$$

The file format for a SURFACE is

name = SURF/nps, npt,
(nps + 1) * [pars], (npt + 1) * [part], ...

where nps, npt = number of patches in s- and t-directions,
pars, part = global parameter values at knots in s- and t-directions, respectively.

4.2.3 Approximation Methods

4.2.3.1 Goals

The principal goal in transferring curve and surface data from one CAD system to another is the best possible accuracy in shape agreement between original and resulting representations, since very tight error tolerances are usually specified for practical manufacturing applications. We must thus seek to minimize approximation errors. This is done by two counteracting measures, namely adjustment of degrees and mesh spacings. The following situations may be distinguished:

Case A: "Reduction of degree and mesh spacing".
This case pertains to the conversion of high order to low order polynomial representations with shrinking mesh widths.

Case B: "Elevation of degree and mesh spacing".
Conversion in the opposite direction.

Case C: "Degree reduction and/or mesh spacing increase".
This situation may arise if after a degree reduction it is possible to economize on the number of patches without exceeding prescribed error bounds. However, this case may be treated as a combination of cases A and B.

The objectives of the approximation processes are more specifically:

Case A:

1. Reduce the polynomial degrees (M, N) of a given patch to desired values (m, n) for a set of new patches.
2. Minimize the relevant errors between old patch and new patches.
3. Optimize the new patch pattern to achieve "uniform maximum errors".
4. Ensure desired continuity $(C^0, C^1, \ldots)$ at old – and new – patch boundaries.

Case B:

1. Raise polynomial degrees (m_i, n_j) of given patches (i, j) to desired value (M, N) of single resulting patch.
2. Minimize the relevant errors.
3. Maintain any existing intentional discontinuities.
4. Ensure accuracy and continuity at old – and new – patch boundaries.

Both problem formulations amount to an approximation problem with constraints. The condition that the resulting approximate surfaces must remain continuous at the boundaries of the original surface is imposed to avoid discontinuities being introduced accidentally between neighboring patches. This necessitates the adoption of an interpolation approach at the boundaries, placing constraints on offsets and pertinent derivatives there. As a result of this the approximation will meet tighter tolerances at the boundaries than in the interior of each patch.

The following error types are relevant:

Offset Error:

$$\Delta \boldsymbol{p}(u, v) = \boldsymbol{p}(u(\tilde{u}), v(\tilde{v})) - \boldsymbol{r}(\tilde{u}, \tilde{v})$$

where $\boldsymbol{p}$ = given surface,
$\boldsymbol{r}$ = approximating surface,
u, v = local coordinates, given patch,
$\tilde{u}, \tilde{v}$ = local coordinates, new patch.

Integral of Square Error:

$$Q = \int_{\tilde{u}=0}^{1} \int_{\tilde{v}=0}^{1} (\Delta \boldsymbol{p})^2 \, d\tilde{u} \, d\tilde{v} = \min.$$

Normal vector error:

$$E^{(1)} = 1 - \cos\gamma = 1 - \frac{\boldsymbol{n}^T \cdot \boldsymbol{n}'}{|\boldsymbol{n}|\,|\boldsymbol{n}'|}$$

where $\boldsymbol{n}(\tilde{u}, \tilde{v})$ = normal vector, given patch,
$\boldsymbol{n}'(\tilde{u}, \tilde{v})$ = normal vector, new patch,
γ = angle between old and new normal vectors.

Curvature Error:

Several types of curvature errors may be used as a reference: Gaussian curvature, mean curvature, principal curvatures.

4.2.3.2 Degree Reduction

In case A a degree reduction is accompanied by the introduction of a finer mesh subdivision (Fig. 4.2.2). The original patch $\boldsymbol{p}(u, v)$, the desired new polynomial

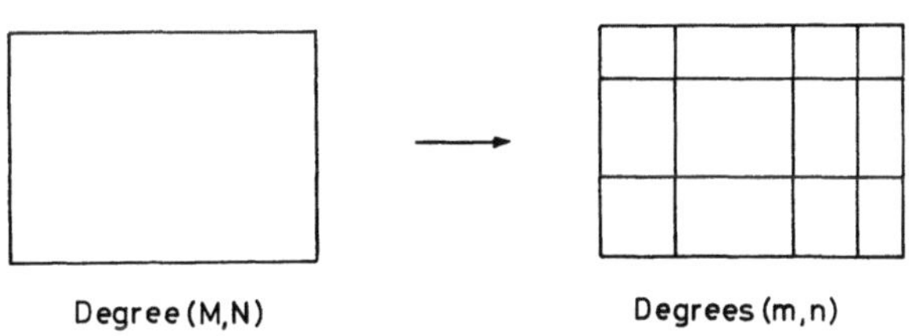

Fig. 4.2.2. Approximate conversion with degree reduction

degrees (m, n), error tolerances and desired continuity conditions at the boundaries are given.

To find the new patch equations the following approximation procedure is applied:

A1. Find a new subdivision with uniform maximum errors.
A2. Find equations of new patch boundary curves, using a combination of Hermite interpolation and least squares approximation.
A3. Find remaining coefficients of each patch.
A4. Check for all error types.
A5. Iterate on subdivision as necessary.

Step A1: New Subdivision

In order to find a new subdivision so that the maximum errors in all patches are made as uniform as possible, a special procedure is developed. It is based on a similar scheme proposed by de Boor [2, 3] and applied by Hölzle [4] for the subdivision of curves.

In Hölzle's procedure the given polynomial $\boldsymbol{p}(t)$, degree N, is approximated by a set of piecewise polynomials $\boldsymbol{r}_1, \ldots, \boldsymbol{r}_k$, each of odd degree n, within an error tolerance ε. The desired continuity at the new knots is $C^{(i_c)}$. Equating given and new polynomials at the knots of each new interval $t_{i-1} \leqq t \leqq t_i$ up to the desired continuous derivative s, a Hermite interpolation is set up:

$$\left.\begin{aligned} \boldsymbol{r}^{(s)}(t_{i-1}) &= \boldsymbol{p}^{(s)}(t_{i-1}) \\ \boldsymbol{r}^{(s)}(t_i) &= \boldsymbol{p}^{(s)}(t_i) \end{aligned}\right\} \begin{aligned} &i = 1, \ldots, k, \\ &s = 0, \ldots, i_c, \\ &i_c \leq (n-1)/2. \end{aligned}$$

The offset error in this interval i is defined as:

$$\delta_i = \max\{|\boldsymbol{p}(t) - \boldsymbol{r}_i(t)|,\ t \in [t_{i-1}, t_i]\}.$$

This expression has an upper bound estimate according to de Boor:

$$\delta_i \leq \max\{|\boldsymbol{p}^{(n+1)}(t)|\} \times \frac{((t - t_{i-1})(t_i - t))^{\frac{n+1}{2}}}{(n+1)!}$$

By further approximation

$$\delta_i \approx \alpha_i = \frac{1}{2^{n+1}(n+1)!}\left(\int_{t_{i-1}}^{t_i} |\boldsymbol{p}^{(n+1)}(t)|^{\frac{1}{1+n}}\, dt\right)^{n+1}.$$

This error grows cumulatively between the lower and upper boundary of the original curve interval. The cumulative error is based on the integral of the $(n+1)$st derivative of $\boldsymbol{p}(t)$ as follows:

$$g(t) = \int_{t_0}^{t} |\boldsymbol{p}^{(n+1)}(s)|^{\frac{1}{1+n}}\, ds.$$

This error estimate for the whole interval is compared with the error tolerance ε, and the number of subintervals is chosen so that all $\alpha_i \leq \varepsilon$. Further the knots t_i are placed so that all α_i are equal.

To apply an analogous procedure to surfaces, a sufficiently dense set of isoparameter lines is calculated in each parameter direction. The definition of $g(t)$ is modified so as to include that contribution $\boldsymbol{p}^{n+1}(s)$ from any isoline which for any given s yields the maximum contribution to the integral.

Although the error estimate is only an approximation, the procedure has in practice resulted in quite acceptably uniform errors.

Step A2: Treatment of Boundary Curves

The original boundary curve in each subinterval is mapped onto an interval of unit length

$$\boldsymbol{p}_i(t) = \boldsymbol{t}^T \cdot \boldsymbol{B}^{(i)},\ t \in [0, 1],$$
$$\boldsymbol{t}^T = [1, t, t^2, \ldots, t^N]$$

This curve segment is first approximated by Hermite interpolation:

$$\boldsymbol{r}_i(t) = \boldsymbol{t}^T \cdot \boldsymbol{M}_H \cdot \boldsymbol{A}_H^{(i)}$$

where

$\boldsymbol{M}_H$ = Hermitian basc matrix
$\boldsymbol{A}_H^{(i)} = \boldsymbol{C}^{(i)} + \boldsymbol{D}^{(i)}$ = geometry matrix, segment i

The matric $\boldsymbol{C}^{(i)}$ contains offsets and derivatives at interval ends obtained directly by Hermite interpolation up to the desired continuity i_c. If the approximating function has any remaining free coefficients by virtue of $n > 2\,(i_c + 1)$, they are included in $\boldsymbol{D}^{(i)}$ and are determined by least squares approximation.

The square error integral

$$Q_i = \int_{t=0}^{1} (\Delta \boldsymbol{p}_i(t))^2\, dt$$

with

$$\Delta \boldsymbol{p}_i(t) = \boldsymbol{p}_i(t) - \boldsymbol{t}^T \cdot \boldsymbol{M}_H \cdot (\boldsymbol{C}^{(i)} + \boldsymbol{D}^{(i)})$$

is minimized with respect to all coefficients $D_k \neq 0$ contained in $\boldsymbol{D}^{(i)}$. This yields the unknown D_k.

Step A3: Remaining Coefficients of Patch

After defining the boundary curves and hence all offsets and pure parametric derivatives at the patch corners, only the mixed derivatives of the tensor product patches remain to be determined. The given patch

$$\boldsymbol{p}^T(u, v) = \boldsymbol{u}^T \cdot \boldsymbol{G} \cdot \boldsymbol{v}$$
$$\boldsymbol{u}^T = [1, u, u^2, \ldots, u^M]$$
$$\boldsymbol{v}^T = [1, v, v^2, \ldots, v^N]$$
$$\boldsymbol{G} = \text{geometry matrix (given).}$$

The approximating subpatch is

$$\boldsymbol{r}_{ij}(\tilde{u}, \tilde{v}) = \tilde{\boldsymbol{u}}^T \cdot \boldsymbol{M}_H \cdot \boldsymbol{G}_{ij}^H \cdot \boldsymbol{N}_H^T \cdot \tilde{\boldsymbol{v}} \qquad \tilde{\boldsymbol{u}}, \tilde{\boldsymbol{v}} \in [0, 1]$$

$\boldsymbol{G}_{ij}^H = \boldsymbol{C}_{ij} + \boldsymbol{D}_{ij}$ = Hermitian geometry matrix, subpatch i, j.

$\boldsymbol{C}_{ij}$ = matrix of boundary curve coefficients

$\boldsymbol{D}_{ij}$ = matrix of mixed derivatives, unknown.

Hence $\boldsymbol{G}_{ij}^H = \boldsymbol{C}_{ij} + \boldsymbol{D}_{ij} =$

$$= \begin{bmatrix} C_{00} & C_{01} \dots C_{0n} \\ C_{10} & C_{11} \dots C_{1n} \\ C_{20} & C_{21} \quad \boxed{} \\ \dots\dots\dots & \boxed{0} \\ C_{m0} & C_{m1} \end{bmatrix} + \begin{bmatrix} 0 & 0 & \dots\dots\dots\dots & 0 \\ 0 & 0 & \dots\dots\dots\dots & 0 \\ 0 & 0 & D_{22} \dots & D_{2n} \\ \dots & & \dots\dots\dots\dots & \\ 0 & 0 & D_{m2} \dots & D_{mn} \end{bmatrix}$$

The square error integral

$$Q_{ij} = \int_{\tilde{u}=0}^{1} \int_{\tilde{v}=0}^{1} (\Delta \boldsymbol{p})^2 \, d\tilde{u} \, d\tilde{v}$$

with

$$\Delta \boldsymbol{p}(\tilde{u}, \tilde{v}) = \boldsymbol{p}(\tilde{u}, \tilde{v}) - \tilde{\boldsymbol{u}}^T \boldsymbol{M}_H (\boldsymbol{C}_{ij} + \boldsymbol{D}_{ij}) \boldsymbol{N}_H^T \tilde{\boldsymbol{v}}$$

is minimized with respect to all nonzero coefficients D_{kl} contained in $\boldsymbol{D}_{ij}$. This yields the D_{kl}.

Steps A4 and A5: Error Checking and Iteration
The curve and surface approximation obtained in steps A1 to A2 was controlled entirely by offset error requirements. Normal vector and curvature errors must now be examined by spotchecking the results at sufficient density. If any of these errors are exceeded, the procedure must be repeated after lowering the offset error tolerances accordingly, which will cause the mesh spacing to be reduced further. This adjustment may be applied iteratively if necessary.

4.2.3.3 Degree Elevation

For case B the objective is degree elevation in a set of given patches of individual degrees (m_i, n_j) to uniform degree (M, N). This results either in a single new patch or in a few subpatches in the event that intentional discontinuities existed at the original patch boundaries in the interior of the surface (Fig. 4.2.3). In other words, all intentional discontinuities are maintained as patch boundaries to prevent accidental removal of these features.

The given information consists of the original patch equations, error tolerances, desired new degrees (M, N), and continuity requirements.

The solution method resembles case A in most respects because a similar approximation problem with constraints must be solved. A combination of Hermitian interpolation and least squares approximation is used again. Only the

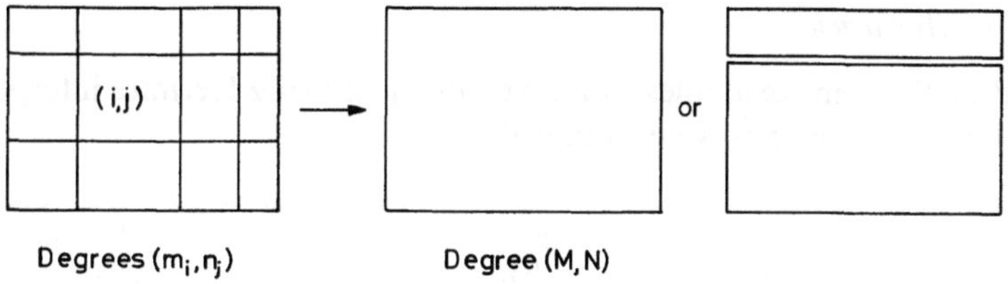

Fig. 4.2.3. Approximate conversion with degree elevation

subdivision step is different, requiring identification of intentional discontinuities.

The solution procedure is based on the following steps:

B1. Identify intentional discontinuities and find new subdivision.
B2. Find equations of new patch boundaries, combining Hermite interpolation and least squares approximation.
B3. Find remaining patch coefficients.
B4. Check for all error types.
B5. Iterate on problem formulation whenever necessary.

4.2.3.4 Results

The work on this project is still in progress, so only tentative numerical results have been obtained. The results obtained for case A are rather complete and demonstrate the viability of the method. Case B is still being tested, but current results do suggest that the approach works equally well for this purpose.

The experience with case A can be illustrated by a few examples with three different test surfaces. Here the given polynomial representations were reduced in degree from given values $(M, N) = (9, 5)$, $(6, 6)$, and $(18, 18)$, respectively, to bicubic and biquintic surfaces. The following results may be of interest:

a) Number of Approximating Patches Required to Meet Error Tolerances

Approxim. polynomial degree	Error tolerance (mm)	Number of patches for given surfaces of degrees		
		$M \times N = 9 \times 5$	$M \times N = 6 \times 6$	$M \times N = 18 \times 18$
$m \times n = 3 \times 3$	0.01	8×4	8×7	23×23
$m \times n = 3 \times 3$	0.1	5×4	5×4	13×13
$m \times n = 5 \times 5$	0.01	3×1	3×2	10×10
$m \times n = 5 \times 5$	0.1	2×1	2×2	7×7

These results were obtained merely by Hermite interpolation. Subsequent least squares approximation considerably reduces the errors, often by almost one order of magnitude. This suggests that the number of patches cited above, which was based on the Hölzle estimate, is rather on the safe side.

b) Accuracies

For the same examples as above, also just using Hermite interpolation, the following accuracies were obtained:

Given polyn. degree	Error tolerance (mm)	Approx. polyn. degree	Actual offset at boundary (mm)	Maximum offset is interior (mm)	Errors angle of normal (degrees)
9 × 5	0.01	3 × 3	0.0034	0.0045	0.02
	0.1	3 × 3	0.032	0.046	0.07
	0.01	5 × 5	0.0029	0.0016	0.004
6 × 6	0.01	3 × 3	0.0080	0.0140	0.03
	0.01	5 × 5	0.0034	0.0038	0.003
	0.1	5 × 5	0.014	0.017	0.02
18 × 18	0.01	5 × 5	0.0055	0.0072	0.007
	0.1	5 × 5	0.054	0.068	0.04

c) Error Distribution

Figure 4.2.4 shows the distribution of errors for the case of a single patch of degrees $(M, N) = (6, 6)$ having been approximated by $2 \times 2 = 4$ patches of degrees $(m, n) = (3, 3)$. The greatest errors in this case are -2.4 mm in the interior and $-1{,}6$ mm at the boundaries. Most errors are negative which is why subsequent least squares approximation by higher degree polynomials is apt to reduce these errors substantially.

4.2.4 Conclusions

An approximation method for conversion of polynomial surface representations from higher to lower degrees and vice versa was developed. The method is based

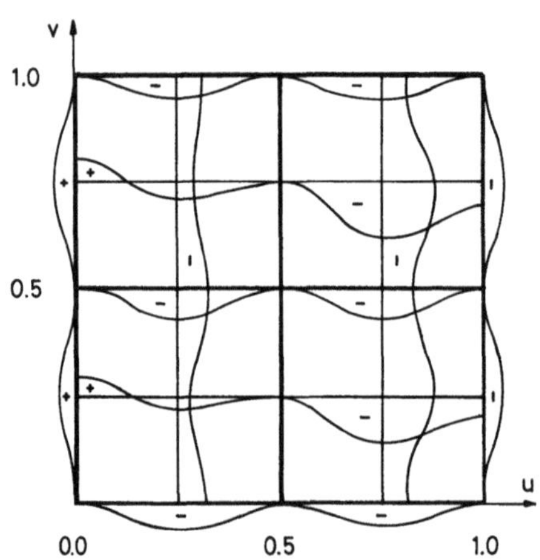

Fig. 4.2.4. Error distribution in approximating surface

on Hermite interpolation combined with least squares approximation. While the interpolation alone is sufficient to ensure high accuracies within the limits of the desired tolerances, the subsequent approximation has been successful in achieving further significant error reductions.

Acknowledgements. This work was sponsored by the Verband der Automobilhersteller (VDA) and initiated and supported by its Working Group "Geometric Interface". The authors wish to acknowledge their gratitude to the members of this group for their encouragement, support, and many helpful suggestions. They also wish to thank the students assisting in the implementation of the software system, Messrs. Lachmann, Volber and Zimmermann.

4.2.5 References

1. Anon: Format for the Exchange of Geometric Information (VDA/VDMA-FS), German Standard (DIN 66301). Beuth-Verlag, Berlin (1986)
2. de Boor C: A Practical Guide to Splines. Springer, Berlin, Heidelberg, New York (1978)
3. Conte SD, de Boor C: Elementary Numerical Analysis, 2nd edn. McGraw-Hill, New York (1972)
4. Hölzle GE: Knot Placement for Piecewise Polynomial Approximation of Curves, Computer-Aided Design. Butterworth, Guildford, U.K. (1983)

4.3 A Tentative Implementation of VDAFS

D. Hopert and T. Weissbarth

4.3.1 A Short Description of VDAFS

VDAFS is an interface between CAD/CAM-systems which are currently in use in the German automotive industry. The concept of this interface centers around the idea of transmitting certain geometric entities. The types of curves and surfaces permitted have a representation in which each curve segment is a polynomial segment and each surface patch is a tensor-product-polynomial patch; that is the k-th curve segment is defined as

$$c_k(u) = \sum_{i=0}^{m_k} \boldsymbol{a}_i^k \, u^i \tag{1}$$

and the (k,l)-patch is defined as

$$p_{kl}(u, v) = \sum_{i=0}^{m_k} \sum_{j=0}^{n_l} \boldsymbol{b}_{ij}^{kl} \, u^i \, v^j \tag{2}$$

where $0 \leqq u, v \leqq 1$ and $\boldsymbol{a}_i^k$, $\boldsymbol{b}_{ij}^{kl}$ are points in 3-D space. A curve $\boldsymbol{c}(s)$ is a collection of K curve segments. The parameter interval $[O, S]$ is divided into K partitions $O = s_o < s_1 \ldots < s_K = S$ such that $\boldsymbol{c}_k$ is defined over $[s_{k-1}, s_k]$ and the local parameter u is computed as

$$u = \frac{s - s_{k-1}}{s_k - s_{k-1}} \tag{3}$$

A surface $\boldsymbol{p}(s, t)$ is similarly defined as a collection of $K \times L$ patches over the parameter space $[O, S] \times [O, T]$ with the partitions $O = s_o < s_1 \ldots < s_K = S$, $O = t_o < t_1 \ldots < t_L = T$.

In addition to these curve and surface types, single points in 3-D space and series of single points are allowed by the interface. A point-vector series where a vector is attached to each point in the series can also be transmitted.

Some non-geometric information is included to allow identification of the data (header section) and to group entities into sets (BEGIN SET, END SET).

This interface can be used to transmit data between CAD/CAM-systems where geometry definition is (in part) based on polynomials, that is where Bézier curves and Bézier surfaces are used. The format for each entity is of the type

name = MWD [/parameters]

where the major word (MWD) stands for the different entity types (see Fig. 4.3.1).

```
EXAMPLE-HEADER/5
$*
$*     THIS IS AN EXAMPLE FOR A VDA FILE CREATED BY THE
$*
$*     PROGRAM *TVDA* R1.0 FROM AN IPARTD FILE.
$*
$$   POLYGON POINTS OF TWO BOUNDARY CURVES
$$
POINTS-BEGINSET
PNT1-POINT/0.17430750000E+03,0.10028464286E+03,0.0
PNT2-POINT/0.19499035714E+03,0.10790464286E+03,0.0
PNT3-POINT/0.22474464286E+03,0.10717892857E+03,0.0
PNT4-POINT/0.24252464286E+03,0.95204642857E+02,0.0
PNT5-POINT/0.17031607143E+03,0.16269607143E+03,0.0
PNT6-POINT/0.19680464286E+03,0.17793607143E+03,0.0
PNT7-POINT/0.23526750000E+03,0.17539607143E+03,0.0
PNT8-POINT/0.26175607143E+03,0.16233321429E+03,0.0
POINTS-ENDSET
$$
$$
$$   BOUNDARY CURVES OF THE SURFACE
$$
CURVES-BEGINSET
CUR1-CURVE/1,0.0,1.0,4,
          0.17430750000E+03,0.62048571429E+02,0.27214285714E+02,
          -.21045714286E+02,
          0.10028464286E+03,0.22860000000E+02,-.25037142857E+02,
          -.29028571429E+01,
          0.0                 ,0.0                 ,0.0                 ,
          0.0
CUR2-CURVE/1,0.0,1.0,4,
          0.17031607143E+03,0.79465714286E+02,0.35922857143E+02,
          -.23948571429E+02,
          0.16269607143E+03,0.45720000000E+02,-.53340000000E+02,
          0.72571428571E+01,
          0.0                 ,0.0                 ,0.0                 ,
          0.0
CURVES-ENDSET
$$
$$
$$   SURFACE
$$
SURFACE-BEGINSET
SUR1-SURF/1,1,0.0,1.0,0.0,1.0,4,2,
          0.17430750000E+03,0.62048571429E+02,0.27214285714E+02,
          -.21045714286E+02,-.39914285714E+01,0.17417142857E+02,
          0.87085714286E+01,-.29028571429E+01,
          0.10028464286E+03,0.22860000000E+02,-.25037142857E+02,
          -.29028571429E+01,0.62411428571E+02,0.22860000000E+02,
          -.28302857143E+02,0.10160000000E+02,
          0.0                 ,0.0                 ,0.0                 ,
          0.0                 ,0.0                 ,0.0                 ,
          0.0                 ,0.0
SURFACE-ENDSET
$$
$$
EXAMPLE-END
```

Fig. 4.3.1. Example of VDA-file with different entity types

4.3.2 Implementation

Control Data offers a wide range of CAE-applications such as the mechanical design packages ICEM DDN, ICEM DUCT and the finite-element-mesh generator PATRAN/G. These packages include Bézier curves and surfaces (for DUCT this is only true for curves). An interface besides IGES using VDAFS was desirable. Some of these systems already had an interface to the outside world called independent part files, or neutral data files, etc.

The VDA-interface was realized by creating a stand alone program called TVDA (Transform VDA files) which processes the VDA file and transforms its contents into neutral data file format according to user specifications, or creates a VDA file from the neutral data file (see Fig. 4.3.2). The advantage of this approach is threefold:

- CAE applications are not modified
- processing of the VDA file (syntax checking etc.) is done in one program
- only one program has to be maintained

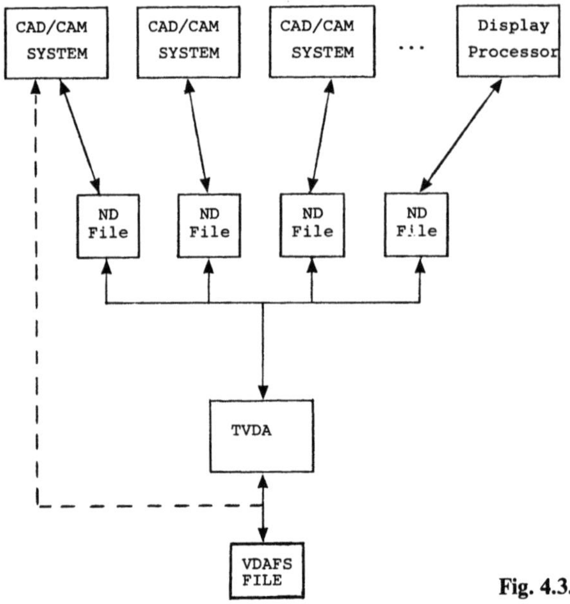

Fig. 4.3.2. Data flow for TVDA

```
*FROM,CD/2000
*TO,VDA
*PART=NEW
*SHEET=1
*/
EXAMPLE=HEADER/5
**
**    THIS IS AN EXAMPLE FOR A VDA FILE CREATED BY THE
**
**    PROGRAM *TVDA* R1.0 FROM AN IPARTD FILE.
**
$$  POLYGON POINTS OF TWO BOUNDARY CURVES
$$
POINTS=BEGINSET
*SELECT,POINT
POINTS=ENDSET
$$
$$
$$  BOUNDARY CURVES OF THE SURFACE
$$
CURVES=BEGINSET
*SELECT,PCURVE
CURVES=ENDSET
$$
$$
$$  SURFACE
$$
SURFACE=BEGINSET
*SELECT,PSURF
SURFACE=ENDSET
$$
$$
EXAMPLE=END
```

Fig. 4.3.3. Directive file

When using TVDA it must be specified what kind of transformations are to be performed:

ICEM DDN ↔ VDA
ICEM DUCT ↔ VDA
PATRAN/G ↔ VDA

This is accomplished by introducing a directive file which also contains information on which entities are to be selected for the transformations. A wide series of directives can be supplied to drive the TVDA-program (see Fig. 4.3.3). The directives are used to select or skip specified entities or entity ranges. Directives also control the TVDA-program to perform a certain type of transformation, for example, a curve that actually represents a series of straight lines can be transformed into a series of entities of entity type LINE when creating an independent data file for ICEM DDN.

When creating a VDA file, header information and comments imbedded in the directive file are transmitted to the VDA file in VDA file format.

Optionally listings can be produced to monitor the transformation. Since VDA files may contain erroneous data an error recovery parameter allows one to skip this data and proceed with the next entity selected.

Recently a transformation option was included that directs the TVDA program to produce a bilinear approximation to surfaces (up to a given tolerance) presented in VDA-file format. One patch of this bilinear approximation is determined by its four corner points which lie on the surface. This information is used to drive a display processor for generating shaded pictures.

4.3.3 Usage

The TVDA-program is widely used at our customers' sites. A typical situation seems to be that one particular part is created using certain techniques available in one system and that the geometry is later passed on to another system to continue with geometry definition or modification, to use drafting capabilities and so forth. Figs. 4.3.4 and 4.3.5 give two examples of geometrical parts passed

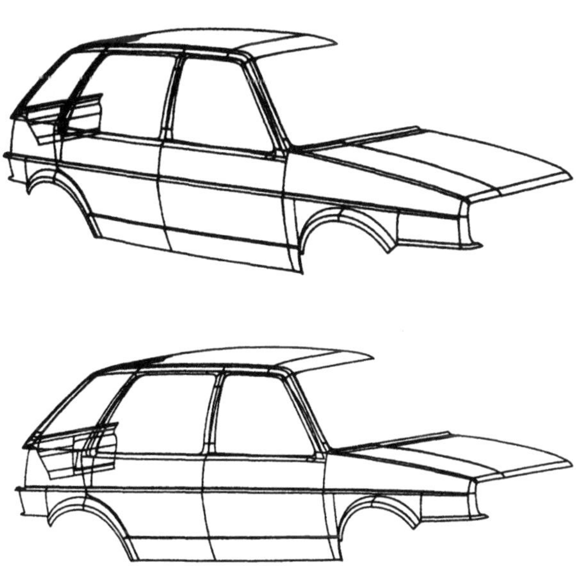

Fig. 4.3.4. Car body (VWSURF/ICEM DDN) (By courtesy of VW-AG, PKW-Konstruction)

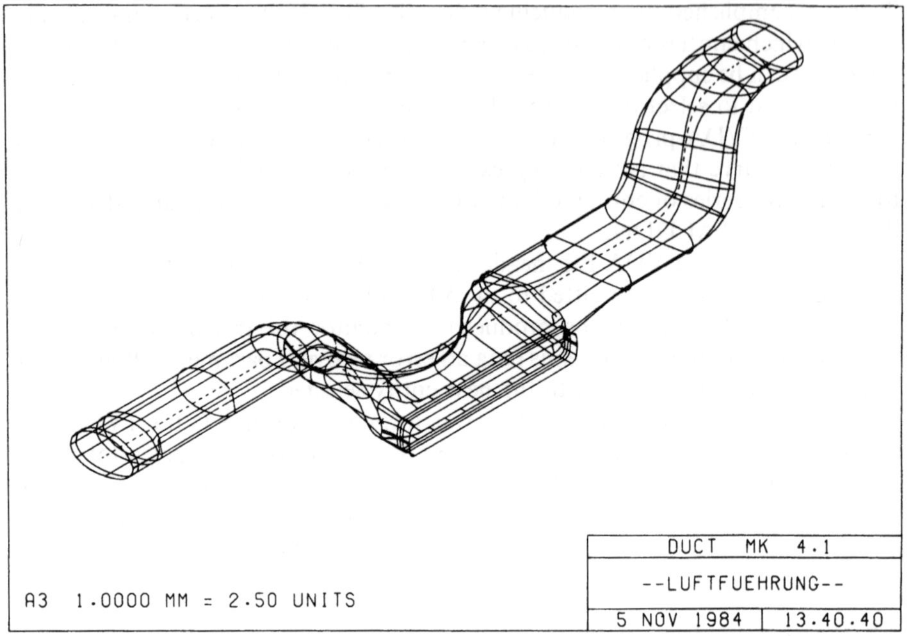

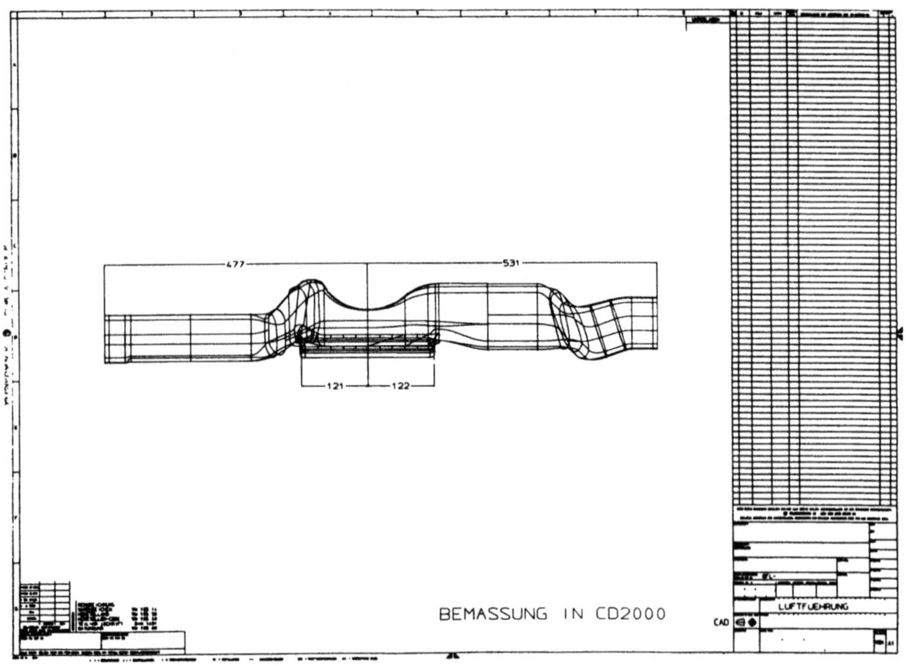

Fig. 4.3.5. Air duct (ICEM DUCT/ICEM DDN) (By courtesy of VW-AG Forschung)

on to different systems using the VDAFS. Fig. 4.3.4 depicts the outer car body created by the system VWSURF, a CAD/CAM-system in use at VW. The surfaces are modelled using least-squares-approximation techniques. For further interior design they are passed on to ICEM DDN.

Figure 4.3.5 illustrates the use of the package DUCT to create an "air duct". In this system Bézier curves consisting of cubic segments are used to model a 3-D curve called spine. Several planar cubic Bézier curve cross-sections which are attached to the spine at segment boundaries normal to the spine form a curve net. A certain blending technique is used to create the patches between the curve net. The resulting patches, however, have no exact polynomial representation. To pass them on to the VDAFS a least-squares-approximation is used to approximate each patch constraining the polynomial patch to interpolate the boundaries (which are Bézier curves) and the tangents across the boundaries. This is accomplished within the TVDA program.

At customers' sites data have been exchanged using VDAFS between ICEM DDN and DUCT, PATRAN/G, VWSURF, EUCLID, CATIA, SYSTRID.

4.3.4 Problems

Two types of problems come up when implementing and using VDAFS, one that is external to the definition of the VDAFS and one that is inherent in the definition.

Curve segments and surface patches are defined by formulas (1) and (2). The numbers m_k, n_k are called the degree of the segment or the patch. Different systems allow different maximal degrees. To pass data from one system to another it may be necessary to reduce the degree of the entity. One method is to prescribe derivatives at both ends of the curve segment. If the segment $c_k(u)$ is represented with Bernstein basis functions

$$c_k(u) = \sum_{i=0}^{m_k} A_i^k \binom{m_k}{i} u^i (1-u)^{m_k - i} \tag{4}$$

then a recursive algorithm can be used to determine a curve segment $c_k(u)$ where the degree is $m_k - 1$ (see [3]). Another method is to use constrained approximation techniques. Both methods will in general change the curve segment so that degree reduction and subdivision has to be used. Subdivision is a process where one segment is split into two at the midpoint $u = 0{,}5$ (see Fig. 4.3.6).

To reduce the degree of a patch the technique for curves is applied to rows and columns of the matrix formed by the B_{ij}^{kl} of formula (5).

$$p_{kl}(u, v) = \sum_{i=0}^{m_k} \sum_{j=0}^{n_l} B_{ij}^{kl} \binom{m_k}{i} \binom{n_l}{j} u^i (1-u)^{m_k - i} v^j (1-v)^{n_l - j} \tag{5}$$

This is possible since $p_{kl}(u, v)$ represents a tensor product patch. (There exist one-to-one transformations which map the a_i^k to the A_i^k, the b_{ij}^{kl} to the B_{ij}^{kl}, and vice versa (see [1].)

A problem which is inherent in the VDAFS definition is the fact that no explicit information is given on connectivity at the segment boundaries. A system

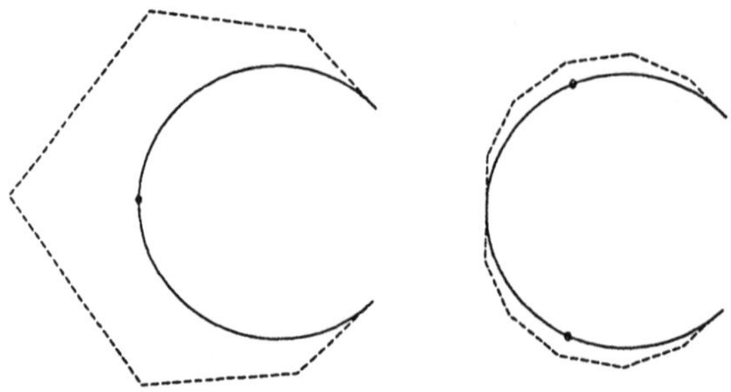

Fig. 4.3.6. Subdivision of a Bézier curve segment of degree 6

that used B-spline-curves and surfaces can transform these curves and surfaces into VDAFS format. In general, however, the opposite is not true since there exists no information within the VDA file about the differentiability of the curves and surfaces at segment boundaries. Using numerical methods to obtain this information from the representation used in the VDA file may sometimes not work due to numerical errors (see [2]). However, if it is known that, for instance, a curve consisting of cubic segments is a true c^2-curve, a (usually nonuniform) B-spline representation of this curve could be computed and passed on to the CAD/CAM-system based on B-spline curves and surfaces.

4.3.5 References

1. Bézier P: Numerical Control, John Wiley & Sons. (1972)
2. de Boor C: A Practical Guide to Splines, Springer Verlag (1978)
3. Forrest AR: Interactive interpolation and approximation by Bézier polynomials. Computer Journal, vol. 15, no 1 (1972)

4.4 Implementation of a VDA Interface in the CAD System STRIM 100

K.-D. de Marné

4.4.1 Abstract

Demand from the German CAD market has led to the implementation of a VDA (Verband der Automobilindustrie) interface in the CAD system STRIM 100. This product has been developed by the French company CISI (Compagnie Internationale de Service en Informatique). The VDA interface of STRIM 100 has been created by the German subsidiary of CISI, the LKS daten service AG in cooperation with the BMW AG in Munich. The mathematical representation of the STRIM 100 entities is a polynomial one using the well-known Bézier polynomials. The VDA interface is split into a VDA output and a VDA input module. The entities of STRIM 100: points, curves and patches, can be handled easily. Thc computer language used is FORTRAN IV. Preliminary experience with customer installations can be reported.

4.4.2 Introduction

The idea of exchanging information among different CAD systems is a very old one. But it was a big surprise that a few specialists of the German automobile industry were able to create within some months an interface that is now a standard for all CAD systems used in that part of German industry. The work initiated by the VDA (Verband der Automobilindustrie) has led to VDAFS, VDA Flächenschnittstelle [1], an interface that is able to exchange geometrical information as well as additional information in a special header or comments. Because a high percentage of the STRIM 100 users work in the automobile industry it was decided in 1984 to implement a VDA interface in the version 2.0 of STRIM 100. As will be shown in the following sections the simple mathematical structure of STRIM 100 allowed an implementation within only six man-weeks.

4.4.3 STRIM 100: the Product

STRIM 100 is a powerful and complete CAD/CAM system satisfying all mechanical construction requirements. It has been developed by the French company CISI (Compagnie Internationale de Services en Informatique). About 3000 persons work for CISI worldwide. The German subsidiary is LKS daten service AG.

The author is the leader of the LKS office in Munich and has implemented the VDA interface in cooperation with BMW AG.

There are three seperate modules communicating with each other via sequential or direct-access FORTRAN datasets:

- STRIM 100 C Construction in 2D, generation of complete drawings, 2 1/2 D NC machining preparation
- STRIM 100 T Construction and interactive NC machining preparation of complex freeform surfaces
- STRIM 100 M Generation and handling of meshings with interfaces to finite element calculation programs (CASTEM, NASTRAN, ...)

All modules run on the same hardware:

Computers	*Screens*
IBM 30xx	IBM 3250
IBM 43xx	IBM 5080
DEC VAX	TEKTRONIX 41xx

At the end of 1984 there were about 85 installations of STRIM 100 in Europe. To mention only some important STRIM 100 T customers:

- BMW AG, Munich, Germany
- VEGLA, Herzogenrath, Germany
- SAAB, Sweden

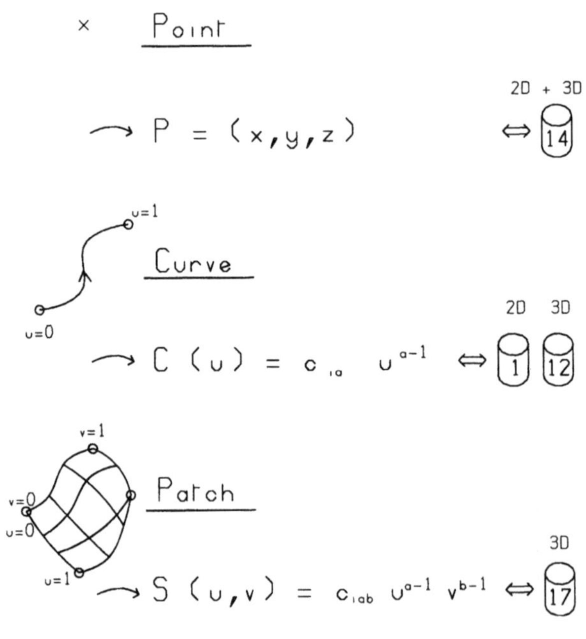

Fig. 4.4.1. The entities of STRIM 100 T and corresponding FORTRAN data sets

- F.B.M., Italy
- Aerospatiale, Marseille, France
- NEYPRIC, Grenoble, France

Because both the European and the U.S. market are being supplied, STRIM 100 is delivered in a French, English and German version (menus, texts and documentation).

The central module is STRIM 100 T. All 3 D information can easily be extracted, therefore the VDA interface was imbedded into that part of STRIM 100. Figure 4.4.1 shows the entities of STRIM 100 T. They can be stored in direct-access datasets with the indicated FORTRAN units.

A FORTRAN programmer refers to a dataset by its dataset reference number. In the statement specifying the type of input/output operation, the programmer must give the dataset reference number corresponding to the dataset on which he wishes to operate.

Points:

- "stand alone points" defined by their coordinates
- "points to be smoothed" (curve points) defined by x, y, z and a relation of spatial dependance R_1.
- "polygon points" defined by x, y, z and a Bézier polygon relation R_2.

Curve:

A parametrical polynomial representation defined as a vector:

$C(U) = C.U$

$C(u) = [C(i, j)]$

with:

$i = 1, 2$ or $i = 1, 3$

$j = 1, NU$

$NU \leqq 21$

$U = [u ** (j-1)]\ u\ 0, 1$

Patch:

A biparametrical polynomial representation defined by the matrix:

$S(U, V) = $ V.T.U.

$T = [T(i, j, k)]$

with:

$i = 1, 3$

$j = 1, NU$

$k = 1, NV$

$NU \leqq 21$

$NV \leqq 21$

$U = [u ** (j-1)]\ u\ 0, 1$

$V = [v ** (k-1)]\ v\ 0, 1$

A typical part constructed with STRIM 100 T is shown in Fig. 4.4.2.

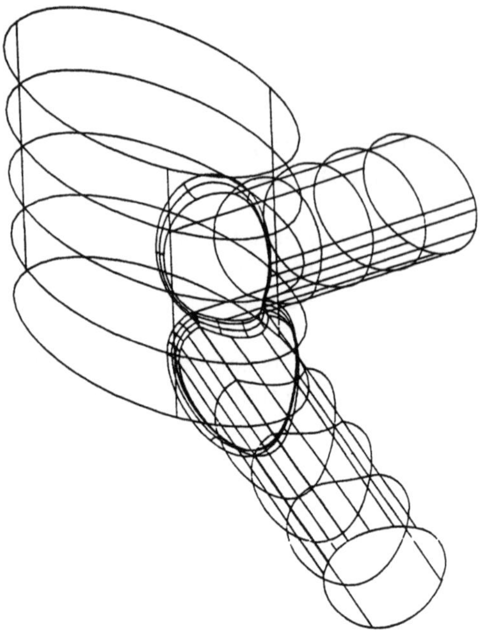

Fig. 4.4.2. Typical STRIM 100 design

4.4.4 Basic Concepts of the Interface

STRIM 100 is written in FORTRAN IV to be compatible with the operating systems supported in 1984 by the CISI team:

- IBM OS/MVS and VM/CMS
- DEC VAX VMS
- BULL GCOS
- APOLLO

Even though FORTRAN 77 will be the language standard for STRIM 100 in 1985 it was decided to implement the VDA interface in FORTRAN IV.

It was furthermore decided to use the graphic dataset 16 and 20, direct-access datasets which represent the current image on the screen. The datasets 1, 12, 14, 17 (see Fig. 4.4.1) are not used to extract or introduce VDA information (there is one exception, see Sect. 5.3).

Three new sequential datasets had to be introduced:

- unit 28: VDA output
- unit 29: VDA input
- unit 31: VDA protocol

These datasets may be dynamically allocated. The VDA protocol information is also written to the log dataset on unit 6. This log dataset is presented in the dialog area of the TEKTRONIX screen and is a shared dataset for the IBM screen version.

Due to the existing structure of the product these basic concepts allow the use of software engineering concepts (topdown, structured programming). For the

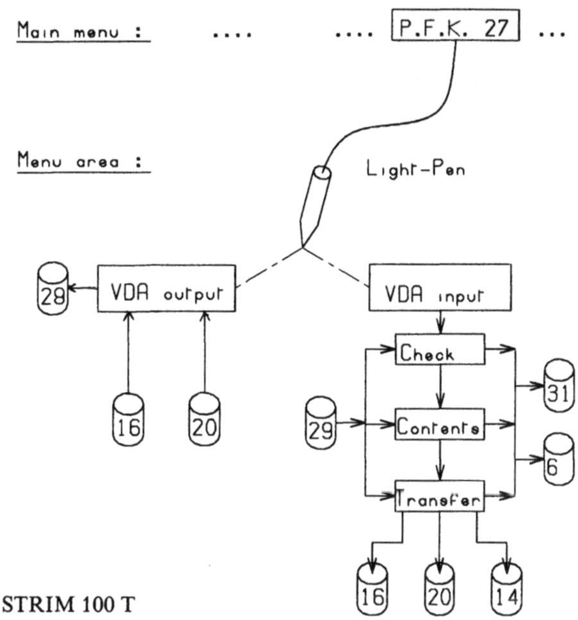

Fig. 4.4.3. The VDA interface of STRIM 100 T

15 VDA FORTRAN subroutines there exists internal documentation (cross reference, variables used, callercalled etc.) as well as external user documentation in French, English and German.

The system STRIM 100 T is menu driven. The main menu consists of 32 programmed function keys (P.F.K.). P.F.K. 27 is devoted to "Transfer". After pointing to this P.F.K. the user can select VDA output or VDA input (Fig. 4.4.3).

4.4.5 VDA Output

To use the VDA output module (writing on the sequential dataset 28) the user must prepare his work: he puts together on the screen all those entities he wants to transfer. This collects all actual points, curves and patches in the datasets 16 and 20. At the end of the action the coordinates, matrices and tensors are written in a D 23.15 format. The user can give names to the geometrical entities by overwriting the system defaults on the screen. After pointing to VDA output the following line appears on the menu area of the screen:

Point: PUNK0001 Curve: CURV0001 surf: SURF0001

As can be seen only the VDA entities POINT, CURVE and SURF are used, PSET and MDI have no analogy in STRIM 100. So the name of all points start with PUNK.... and are numbered beginning with 0001. The user can choose the first four alphabetic characters as well as the last four numerical values indicating the starting value of the VDA entity name. Syntax check is provided by the system.

The HEADER (following user specification), the file name and the name of the SET are automatically generated by STRIM 100 T. Only a single SET is created. The result of a VDA output action might look as follows:

```
STRIM1TC = HEADER/13        ...    10
++++++                      ...    20
...
+++++                       ...   140
STRIM100 = BEGINSET         ...   150
PUNK0001 = POINT/...        ...   160
...
PUNK0002 = POINT/...        ...   180
...
CURV0001 = CURVE/1, ...     ...   220
...
SURF0001 = SURF/...         ...   480
...
SURF0002 = SURF/...         ...   580
...
STRIM100 = ENDSET                1150
STRIM1TC = END                   1160
```

4.4.6 VDA Input

Experience shows that consistency of a VDA file with the specifications of VDAFS cannot be guaranteed, especially if files are generated or modified with an editor. The tool for reading VDA datasets must be more comfortable than that described for VDA writing. In STRIM 100 the user is provided with three functions which appear in the menu area of the screen after pointing to VDA input:

Check Contents Transfer

4.4.6.1 Check

This is a kind of "VDA-compiler" which checks the consistency of the information in the non-formatted VDA input file with VDAFS. There is a distinction between

- warnings and
- fatal errors

Warnings are inconsistencies which can be handled by STRIM 100 T (Sect. 4.4.5.3) without loss of geometrical information. For example: wrong line numbers, additional lines after ... = END.

Fatal errors are stated if there is obviously incorrect information in the input stream. For example: wrong number of coordinates, missing global parameters, integer values instead of floating values.

Both kinds of errors are written into a special VDA protocol (unit 31) and into the log file (unit 6). The error is described in detail with the line number of the input file and the paragraph of VDAFS which has been violated.

At the end of the action a message appears in the message area of the screen:

VDA input file correct, or VDA input file not correct

A REWIND is made automatically on the input unit and the system goes back to the menu of Sect. 4.4.6.

4.4.6.2 Contents

Obviously it must be possible for the user to have an overview of the information of the VDA dataset. The same output files are used as in Sect. 4.4.6.1. The subaction "contents" writes the name and type of every VDA entity found in the input stream. After each set a statistic of the VDA entities is created. The user can see the number of POINT, PSET, MDI, CURVE and SURF in every SET.

At the end of the action the message

Contents of VDA file generated

is written to the message area of the screen, a REWIND is done and the system goes back to the menu of Sect. 4.4.5.

4.4.6.3 Transfer

For this subaction the system assumes that the user knows the names of all VDA entities in the VDA dataset and that the syntax of this file is correct. The selected entities are written into the graphic datasets of STRIM 100 T and appear immediately on the screen.

Even though VDA output uses only POINT, CURVE and SURF this subaction can handle PSET and MDI as well. PSET is obviously treated like a number of POINTS. Each sextupel of an MDI is treated like a point plus a straight line, the starting point of the line being the point of the MDI, the direction and the length given by the vector of the MDI.

The selection submenu is as follows:

VDA Start: _________ VDA Stop: _________

The user has to give the name of the appropriate geometrical VDA entities. Four selection modes are possible:

VDA Start: blank VDA Stop: blank = The whole dataset is treated

VDA Start: name VDA Stop: blank = Only one entity is treated (This may be the name of a SET – this is the only case in which not only a geometrical entity may be given).

VDA Start: blank VDA Stop: name = All VDA entities from the beginning to the entity indicated in Stop are treated.

VDA Start: name VDA Stop: name = All entities from that named in start to that named in stop are treated.

After the user has done this selection he must indicate in the next submenu whether he wants to treat the points of the VDA input file as "stand alone points" or as "points to be smoothed". The submenu reads:

Point: ________ 0

If the value is set to zero, all points are interpreted as stand alone points and immediately drawn on the screen. If the user gives a number, this is interpreted as the starting address in the dataset with unit 14 where the points to be smoothed are stored. In this case the points are not represented on the screen but simply stored.

The process of reading is protocolled on the units 31 and 6. Curve segments and patch segments are treated as single curves or patches. The degree and global parameters, as well as the number of segments of CURVE and SURF, are written to the protocol.

At the end of the action a message appears on the screen to indicate whether the selected entity was found in the VDA dataset or not, a REWIND is made and the system goes back to the menu of Sect. 4.4.5:

VDA entity found or VDA entity not found

The user now has all selected entities on the screen. To store the information in the direct-access datasets 1, 12, 17 he can use the standard actions of STRIM 100.

4.4.7 Preliminary Experience

Initial deliveries of version 2.0 of STRIM 100 T have been made. The first was to the German company VEGLA (Vereinigte Glaswerke, Herzogenrath). They use STRIM 100 T and STRIM 100 C on a VAX 780 with one 4115 and two 4107 TEKTRONIX screens. The company produces windscreens for a lot of European automobile companies. The STRIM 100 T VDA Interface has been used effectively with different VDA datasets coming from VW, FORD and BMW.

BMW AG in Munich uses STRIM 100 T on an IBM 4381 with 15 IBM 3250 and 9 IBM 5080 screens. Because of BMW modifications of version 2.0 of STRIM the product is not currently used by the car-body design department; they still use version 1.0 with a VDA output option only. But all subroutines of the VDA interface of STRIM 100 are used in the BMW system GEORG, which is able to transfer geometrical data between the CAD systems STRIM 100 T, CD 2000 and CATIA. The absence of reported problems here too supports the use of the interface.

The final company to use version 2.0 of STRIM 100 T is SAAB in Sweden. They work with a VAX computer and TEKTRONIX screens. No problems are reported from this installation.

LKS/CISI has close contact with each customer installation. This constant contact, together with the STRIM user club which meets once a year will generate new demands arising from the normal daily work practice. This useful feedback from the customers will lead to a constant improvement not only in the VDA interface but in the whole CAD system STRIM 100, which is ready to meet the challenges of the coming years.

4.4.8 Conclusion

The CAD system STRIM 100 uses a VDA interface which is easy to handle in both input and output directions: The simplicity of the mathematical representation of the STRIM 100 entities allowed implementation within six man-weeks. Feedback from customer installations will lead to a continuous improvement in the VDA interface.

Acknowledgements. The author is indebted to Dr. Dankwort and his crew at BMW AG in Munich. He gratefully acknowledges their constant cooperation and many valuable discussions.

4.4.9 Reference

1. VDAFS: VDA-Flächenschnittstelle. Richtlinie des Verbandes der Automobilindustrie (1984)

4.5 The Implementation of the VDAFS Geometric Data Interface on Computervision's CDS 4000 CAD/CAM System

T. Phebey

4.5.1 Introduction

In co-operation with the Technical University of Munich's Department of Mechanical Design, Computervision has developed an interface with VDAFS format geometric data files. This interface has been developed on the series CDS 4000 computer systems running under CADDS 4X applications software. The aim of this article is to describe briefly the VDAFS format and then to discuss in more detail the methods used and the problems encountered during the implementation of the interface.

4.5.2 "What is the VDAFS Interface?"

4.5.2.1 Geometric Data Interfaces

The use of CAD/CAM systems enables product information to be captured and modified in the form of computer digital data. This information includes two- and three-dimensional geometric design data, manufacturing information (e.g. production drawings, NC machining information, etc.) and commercial data (part numbers, bills of materials, etc.). For reasons of functional capability, price, hardware base, etc., different CAD/CAM systems are installed in different companies and often large companies do not purchase from just one CAD/CAM supplier. In order to rationalise and reduce the likelihood of errors, it is often necessary to transfer the geometric data from one CAD/CAM system to another – for example the engineering division of a large company would provide the geometric model to the manufacturing division in order that the data could be used as a basis for the jig and tool design. Each CAD/CAM system uses a different format for its data and so there is a need for a program which will convert one CAD/CAM format into another. This program is known as a geometric data interface. There are two possible ways of handling the need for interfaces. These are shown in Fig. 4.5.1. The first method calls for the development of a special interface between each pair of CAD/CAM systems – for n CAD/CAM systems to interface with each other, $n\,(n-1)$ programs have to be developed (each interface requires two programs: one to output the data and the other to read the data). The second method involves transforming the data into a neutral format which is well-defined as a standard. This method requires $2\,n$ programs to be developed – an input and an output program for each CAD/CAM

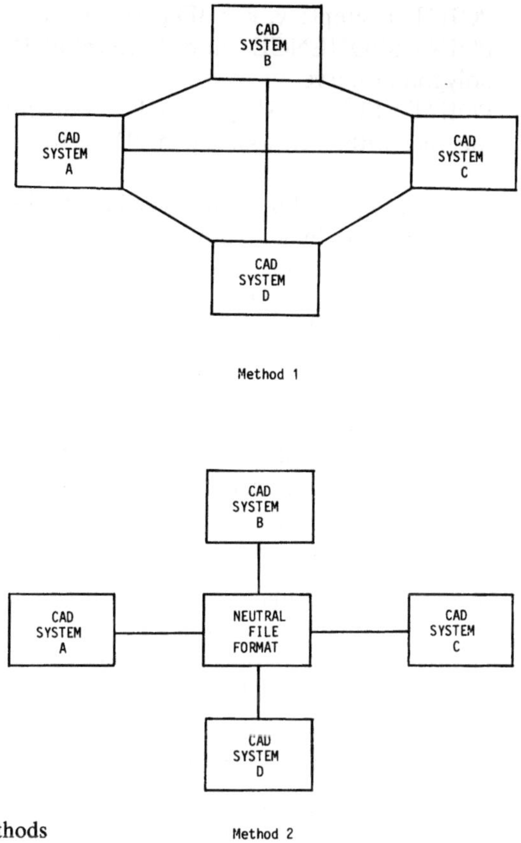

Fig. 4.5.1. Geometric data interface methods

system. From these figures, it is clear that the break-even point lies with three different CAD/CAM systems. When more than three systems have to be interfaced with each other, the second method involving the neutral file results in less programs having to be developed. It should be noted that the data interface is actually a file format specification. It is independant of the medium used to transfer the data. This medium could be magnetic tape, floppy disk, paper tape or even a direct communication link between the computer systems. The VDAFS interface is an example of this second method of solving the data interface problem, and the specification of the neutral file format has been released as a German Industrial Standard – DIN 66301.

4.5.2.2 General Description of VDAFS

VDAFS is limited to a subset of the geometric elements which are to be found in most CAD/CAM systems. The reasons for this are discussed below in Sect. 4.5.2.3. The graphic elements which are supported are:

- POINT: a simple x, y, z 3D cartesian co-ordinate location
- POINT SEQUENCE: an ordered set of 3D cartesian co-ordinates defining a polygon or curve
- POINT VECTOR SEQUENCE: an ordered set of 3D cartesian co-ordinates together with their associated 3D vector components for the transfer of NC data
- CURVE: a global parametrisized ordered set of curve segments, each segment being defined by polynomial co-efficients. The two ends of each segment correspond with the local parameter values zero and one.
- SURFACE: a set of surface patches, their definition range limits in the U, V directions and the co-efficients of each patch.

In addition to these geometric elements there are the records:

- HEADER: general information, e.g. system of origin, date of creation, etc.
- BEGINSET/ENDSET: used to structure the file by grouping geometric elements together into sets
- END: to terminate the file data and, of course, comment lines which may be freely inserted anywhere within the file.

The actual data format used is ASCII 80-column card image text. Records are free format containing both integer and real numbers (maximum 16 significant digits) with fields separated by commas.

Exact details of thc format are to be found in the DIN 66301 booklet.

4.5.2.3 Objectives of VDAFS

In 1982, the German organisation VDA (Verband der Automobilindustrie) whose members are companies within the automotive industry formed a CAD/CAM committee to promote and co-ordinate the introduction of CAD/CAM methods into the industry. One of the first projects which this commission tackled was the problem of transferring product definition data between the car manufacturers, tool manufacturers and parts manufacturers. In particular there was a pressing need for a method of exchanging car body data (free-form surfaces) between the various CAD/CAM systems in use within the industry, and the VDAFS specification was developed to fulfil this requirement. It was never intended that VDAFS should be a method of transferring complete design drawing data, instead emphasis was placed on simplicity and ease of implementation. At all times, the possibilities of merging the VDAFS format into future national or international standards for geometric data exchange were kept in mind.
These goals are reflected in the limited but sufficient geometric element set and the choice of the neutral file method.

4.5.2.4 Comparison with Other Geometric Data Interfaces

The IGES specification currently provides the only means of exchanging product data which has been implemented world-wide. One may wonder why, then, should other methods of data exchange be developed? A critical look at the status of IGES provides the answer immediately:

- The data format is unwieldy, difficult to read and long-winded.
- The element definitions are often unclear or not exact enough.
- The implementation of an IGES interface is a significant task which also assumes that a certain level of computer power is available, together with a relatively advanced CAD/CAM software package.
- There are no subsets of the specification based on the power of the CAD/CAM system on which it is to be implemented.
- Guidelines for the development and implementation of an IGES processor are not available.
- Guidelines for enhancements and changes to the specification have not been laid down.
- Many graphic elements existing in widely-installed CAD/CAM systems are not contained within the IGES specification.

The difficulties experienced by many CAD/CAM users in using IGES to transfer design drawing data are symptoms of the problems listed above. Of course, IGES as a specification is still under development and it is hoped that future revisions will resolve many of these problems.

There is a new format PDES (Product Data Exchange Standard) being developed by the National Bureau of Standards in USA. This is apparently a completely new specification, bearing no relation to IGES but it is not expected that installations will exist before 1990.

The French specification SET (Standard d'echange et de Transfert) from the French aerospace industry organisation (Societe Nationale Industrielle Aerospatiale, Division Avions) approaches the problem with a fresh and interesting methodology.

The software system GKS (Graphisches Kern-System) provides a practical way of transferring a physical drawing to a graphics output device (e.g. screen or plotter) via its Metafile. This file contains vectors and display control information only – the mathematical and logical definition has been discarded. For example, a circle would be represented by a set of interpolated line segments or vectors – the centre, radius and plane of definition is no longer stored.

VDAFS with its simple format, ease of implementation and focus on a user industry with a high and pressing need for exchange of CAD/CAM data has thus very quickly gained a wide acceptance, at least within Europe.

4.5.3 Implementation of the VDAFS Interface on the CDS 4000

The interface consists of two independant programs implemented under Computervision's CADDS 4X software package. The first program PUT VDAFS is used to create a VDAFS format text file from a CADDS 4X graphics database. The second program – GET VDAFS – reads a VDAFS file and creates a CADDS 4X part.

4.5.3.1 PUT VDAFS – Creation of the VDAFS File

Figure 4.5.2. shows the overall logic of the program. The user must first activate the part (file containing the geometric model data) to be converted and then enter

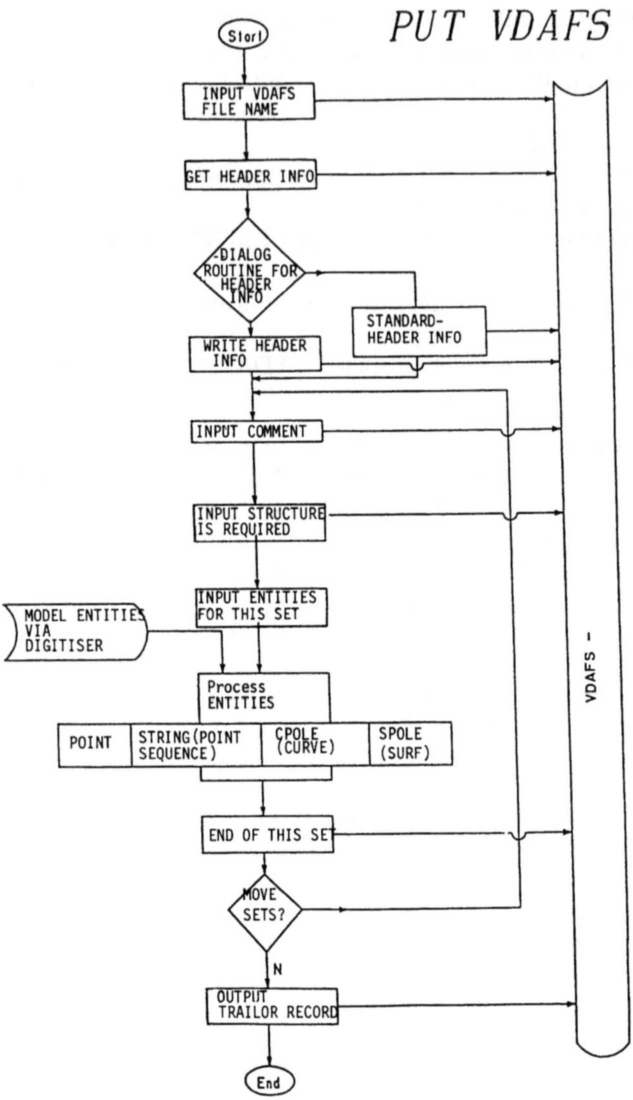

Fig. 4.5.2. PUT VDAFS Logic

the PUT VDAFS command. A dialogue routine then allows the entry of file name and header information before the main program loop which controls the definition of the sets of geometry to be output. This dialogue is table driven – i.e. the questions, legal responses and messages are defined in text tables enabling the program to be user language independant. By changing these text tables, the program will prompt for and accept input in any number of foreign languages.

It is possible to request that the program transfer all the visible data found in the part without further interaction, to the VDAFS file as one set, i.e. without structure. Alternatively, the user may build each set in the file interactively by

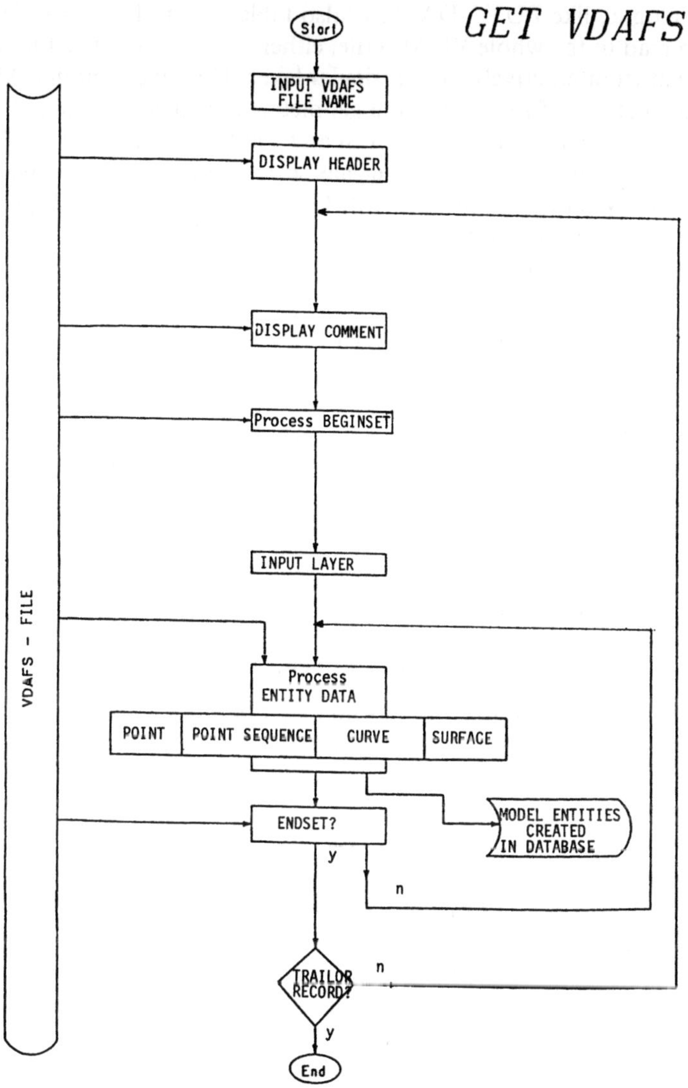

Fig. 4.5.3. GET VDAFS Logic

identifying at each point the geometric elements to be contained in the set. The program will loop building the sets until no more are requested.

4.5.3.2 GET VDAFS – Creation of the CADDS 4X Part from the VDAFS File

Figure 4.5.3. shows the logic of the program which reads the VDAFS file and creates geometric data in a CADDS 4X part. A part (not necessarily empty) must be activated prior to issuing the GET VDAFS command. Once again, a dialogue enables the user to select the VDAFS file to be read prior to the main loop. This dialogue, like PUT VDAFS, is also table driven. It is possible for the user then to read in the whole VDAFS file, either ignoring the structure (sets) or assigning each set interactively to a particular layer. This layer within CADDS 4X is simply the method of separating the geometry into logical groups. Layers may be displayed or blanked by the user in any combination. There are 254 possible layers available in a part. If the user has selected the interactive method of operation, then any comments prior to a BEGINSET record will be displayed on the screen. Data is then transferred into the CADDS 4X part set by set until the end of file record is encountered.

4.5.3.3 Correspondance Between CADDS 4X Entities and VDAFS Records

4.5.3.3.1 POINT

The VDAFS POINT record corresponds to the CADDS 4X POINT entity. The co-ordinates are CADDS 4X model (CPLANE TOP) space co-ordinates.

4.5.3.3.2 PSET (Point Sequence)

The VDAFS PSET record for a point sequence corresponds to a CADDS 4X STRING entity in 3D model space.

4.5.3.3.3 MDI (Point Vector Sequence)

The VDAFS MDI record has no direct parallel in the CADDS 4X database and has not been implemented in the first version of the interface – i.e. it will not be generated by PUT VDAFS and it will be ignored by GET VDAFS. See Sect. 4.5.4 below.

4.5.3.3.4 CURVE

The VDAFS CURVE record corresponds to a CADDS 4X CPOLE entity in model space. The CPOLE entity is a Bezier free form curve. CPOLE entities may have a maximum degree of seven and for the first version of the interface, CURVE records of higher degree appearing in the VDAFS file will be ignored by GET VDAFS. Furthermore, the GET VDAFS program currently only supports the CURVE segment between parameter values zero and one.

4.5.3.3.5 SURF (Surface)

The VDAFS SURF record corresponds to a CADDS 4X SPOLE entity in model space. The SPOLE entity consists of BEZIER surface patches up to and including order seven. GET VDAFS will ignore SURF records of higher order in the first version. Work is currently being done to define an algorithm which will approximate surfaces of higher order encountered in the VDAFS file.

4.5.3.4 Implementation Philosophy

The use of a language independant dialogue routine ensures that the VDAFS file structure created by PUT VDAFS is preserved by leading the user through the necessary steps. It is flexible enough to allow the user to check and correct his input at any stage.

The programs have been designed for use both in batch mode, resulting in minimal structuring of the data, and in interactive mode. It is hoped that this will cover most user needs but possible enhancements are being considered (see Sect. 4.5.4). Each VDAFS file produced by PUT VDAFS corresponds to the data contained in just one part. In this way, it is felt that it will be easier for the user to keep track of the transfers. Of course, if it is necessary to produce one VDAFS file based on geometric data contained in a series of CADDS 4X parts, then this may be accomplished by generating a series of VDAFS files (one for each part) which may then be merged together into one file using standard operating system and CADDS 4X text editing capabilities. Furthermore, several VDAFS files may be generated from one CADDS 4X part by running the PUT VDAFS program several times on that part, each time with a different geometry set selected. Also the data contained in several VDAFS files may be brought together in one CADDS 4X part through repeated use of the GET VDAFS program. In this way, maximum flexibility is provided for the organisation of the data.

4.5.4 Future Developments

As indicated in Sect. 4.5.3, there are a number of issues still to be resolved in order to meet fully the current VDAFS specification. The MDI record has no counterpart within CADDS 4X. Investigations are under way to see whether the same information can be obtained from the CADDS MABS and MPRO entities. These entities are generated by the CADDS 4X NCVISION application package and represent absolute and profile tool paths. It is intended to discuss possible implementations with existing CADDS 4X users in the automotive industry.

The high order surfaces which cannot currently be represented using the CADDS 4X SPOLE entity will have to be approximated in some way in order that they may be read in. It is hoped that current work taking place at the University of Berlin will provide a mathematical solution to this problem. Future development to the VDAFS specification (e.g. the inclusion of line and circle elements) will be closely followed by Computervision. When approved changes to the specification do appear, then these enhancements will be built in to the PUT VDAFS programs so far as is possible.

4.6 Experience with VDAFS

F. Elsässer

4.6.1 Introduction

One year after first test installations of the VDA-Surface Interface (VDAFS) it is still too early to write a comprehensive experience report. This contribution is based in part on discussions with members of the VDA-working groups "Geometrische Schnittstelle" and "Test" [3] but predominantly on the author's experience of data exchange with automobile sub-suppliers.

Meanwhile all automobile producers in Germany have either implemented their own VDA-interfaces and/or use vendor CAD/CAM-systems which have VDAFS already installed, e.g. CALMA, CATIA, EUCLID, STRIM. The situation of many sub-suppliers is similar, while others are implementing or planning implementation connected to available CAD/CAM-systems.

4.6.2 VDA-Working Group "Test"

After publication of the VDAFS-specification in July 1983 the working group "Test" was founded as a subgroup of the working group "CAD/CAM" of VDA (*V*erband *d*er *A*utomobilindustrie). The task [3] of this group was defined as follows:

Phase 1: Work out conditions and examples for the interface test and support first test runs.
Phase 2: Assist with utilization of the interface and anticipate expected problems.

Apart from the definition of an uniform diagnostic list as basis for processor implementations, the main task of this group was the preparation of an interface test. It consists of three test examples which are:

- Standard test surface (See Fig. 4.6.1)
- Outer surface (rear window) (See Fig. 4.6.2)
- High precision surface (front headlight) (See Fig. 4.6.3)

These examples can currently be requested from members of this group and will later be distributed by the VDA.

Currently the working group is dealing with a certificate for VDAFS-installations. It is planned to delegate the certification procedure to a test institute which has yet to be selected.

The minimum requirement for attainment of this certificate should be to undergo the standard test with an accuracy of 0.01 mm.

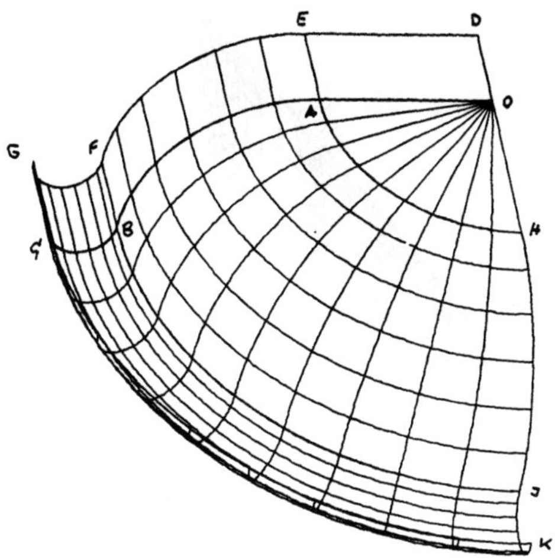

Fig. 4.6.1. Standard surface

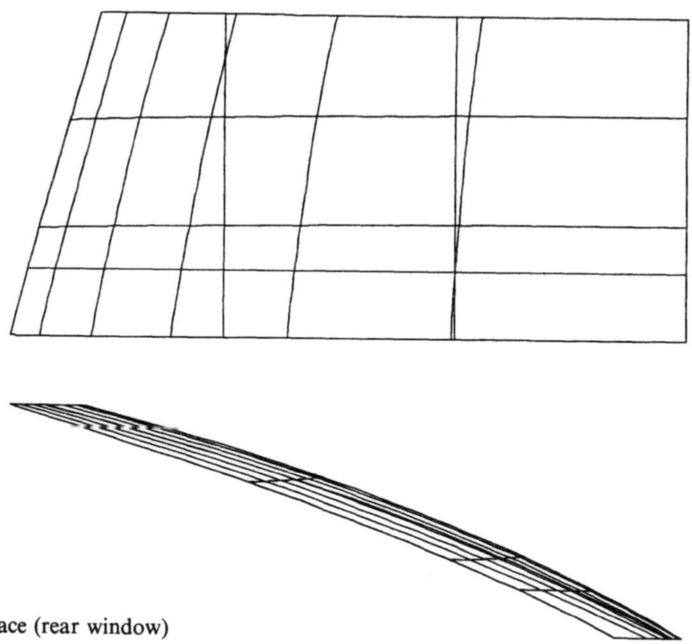

Fig. 4.6.2. Outer surface (rear window)

4.6.3 VDA-Interface Test

Besides the checking of pre- and postprocessors for functionality, the interface test serves as an initial precision test. Since the VDAFS does not specify precision limits, the working group "Test" has formulated the following requirement [3] as basic to all tests:

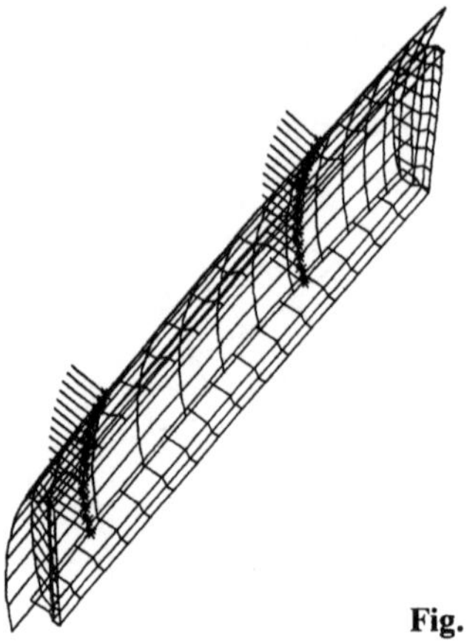

Fig. 4.6.3. High precision surface (front headlight)

- no loss of accuracy for data exchange,
- maximum deviation ± 0.01 mm in the direction of the surface normal,
- surface quality must be maintained (no waves).

The precision check is done by:

- numerical comparison: measure points and sections given by the data sender are compared to the generated data in the receiver system,
- visually checking by reviewing of single sections.

An additional check may be recommended:

- Send back the geometry built up in the receiver system and compare it with the original data of the sender system.

Standard Test

This is an example (Fig. 4.6.1) consisting of 6 tangential combined surfaces given as 1-patch-surfaces of higher order (max. 11) or as segmented surfaces with many patches of order (4, 4). The test datafile using all entities of VDAFS contains also control points and lines with and without normals.

All surfaces can be easily reproduced in the receiver CAD/CAM-system by a curve consisting of a straight line, a quarter circle and a semicircle with tangential transitions.

Outer Surface Test

This example shows a rear window of a passenger car (Fig. 4.6.2) represented by a 6 × 3-patch-surface of order (4, 4) or a 1-patch-surface of order (10, 6). The precision may be checked by 3 cross-sections.

High Precision Surface

Here we have a surface of a front headlight (Fig. 4.6.3) of a car consisting of 5 surfaces generated with high precision. The datafile contains points and 2 sections with normals for checking.

Up to now only members of the VDA-working groups have subjected to this test.

4.6.4 VDAFS-Interface Problems Resulting from CAD/CAM Systems

The quality of an interface specification is judged by how well the interface can handle restrictions of the CAD/CAM-systems resulting from different computers and different system concepts.

Since VDAFS [2] does not prescribe maximum numbers of certain parameters the data exchange of geometric data (PSET, MDI, CURVE, SURF) essentially depends on limits of the sender- and receiver-system. To reduce data exchange problems the sender should at least know the restrictions of the receiver system. Otherwise the receiver system has to handle all problems.

In the case of the entities PSET and MDI, exceeding of the point limit in the receiving system may not cause problems, because subdivision should be possible. But different limitations for CURVE and SURF create problems which cannot be solved by most of the processors or CAD/CAM-systems. Therefore the VDA-working group "CAD/CAM" has charged Professor Nowacki from TU Berlin with the development of a conversion and approximation algorithm [1], which should ultimately be made available to all VDA-members. The main task of the project is either to reduce the number of segments for CURVE or patches for SURF while simultaneously increasing the degree, or to reduce the degree while simultaneously increasing the number of segments or patches.

As the CAD-system of OPEL (FISHER GRAPHICS) has no surface entity – sculptured surfaces only exist temporarily – surface data are transferred as sections and flowlines. This procedure is less efficient, because surfaces have to be rebuilt in the receiver system with consequent loss of accuracy. Meanwhile 40% of about 18 OPEL-sub-suppliers who previously used an internal GM-interface (*D*ATA *E*XCHANGE *S*TANDARD) have already implemented VDAFS. Under these circumstances OPEL decided to develop an algorithm to approximate all temporary surfaces like straight element surface, Gordon surface and surface of revolution by a new type of surface, namely Bézier surface (order < 15). Without conceptual changes it was possible to introduce this entity into the system by using existing entities. Bézier points can be transformed easily into coefficients of the monomial surface representation of VDAFS and vice versa. First tests have been done successfully.

Minor problems are caused by the naming convention (2.2.3) of VDAFS. The limitation of element names to 8 characters forces systems with longer names to change names (automatic names) when sending data. This means loss of information which may be partly remedied if the original name is additionally written as comment.

Difficulties may occur when using the structuring element (4.3). Systems using multi-level sets will not be able to transfer such relations.

It should be mentioned that some of the enumerated data exchange problems are not VDAFS-specific and will appear in any CAD/CAM-interface.

4.6.5 VDAFS – Advantages

Current data exchange experience with sub-suppliers and test partners allows identification of the advantages at this stage:

- high data reliability
- capability of "free" format and usage comments.

By "free" format one understands the individual structuring of data respecting rule 2.3, i.e. applying commas as separators, blanks at any place and comments. Practice shows that preprocessors are using this possibility in manifold ways. Single firms even use the VDA-format as internal data bank format, where in this case compactness plays an important role.

The simplicity of VDAFS as an essential global property does not only reduce the implementation time of pre- and post-processors but affects the functionality and reliability too. Syntactical errors are very rare.

4.6.6 VDAFS – Extensions

As expected first amendment proposals came up soon after first implementations. The proposals may be grouped into three categories:

- standardization of the Header for automatic processing
- extensions by new entities (primitiva).
- limited surfaces – topology – relations.

These topics, especially the third, are currently being discussed by the "Geometrische Schnittstelle" group.

With the exception of Header standardization short-term extensions are not planned. But in the medium-term, as long as no equivalent international interface exists, an extension in the direction of topology is aimed at to improve data exchange with solid geometric modellers.

4.6.7 Outlook

After completion of the conversion and approximation algorithm by Professor Nowacki differing limitations of CAD/CAM-systems will no longer be obstacles to the exchange of surface data. The VDA-surface interface developed as an interim solution will then meet the expectations of the automotive and sub-supplier industries. So much is implied by the multitude of implementations in so short a time.

4.6.8 References

1. Dannenberg L: Spezifikation eines Approximations- und Konvertierungsprogramms für Flächendarstellungen (Teil 1, 2, 3). TU Berlin (1983/1984)
2. VDA-Flächenschnittstelle (VDAFS). VDA Frankfurt (1983)
3. Protokolle des VDA-Arbeitskresies „CAD/CAM“ und der VDA Arbeitsgruppen „Geometrische Schnittstelle“ und „Test“ (1983/1984)

Chapter 5

Specification and Validation

5.1 Specification of Interfaces: A Case Study of Data Exchange Languages

R. Gnatz

5.1.1 Introduction

There is a growing interest in the formal treatment of interfaces at the application level. The common property of all kinds of interfaces seems to be the exchange of data (i.e. some sort of representation of information), and as may be seen almost everywhere in the software business, the problems do not usually result from the syntactical aspects: the more serious problems result from the semantics of the data, when they are subjected to further automatic treatment.

Moreover, the syntactic and semantic aspects of data are very often mixed up with procedural details of the system architecture. For this reason emphasis is given to the following points:

- For the purpose of system specification (this includes in particular the specification of interfaces), the details of system architecture should be separated carefully from the details of data specification. It should be a matter of any further development to derive systematically from these specifications some efficient implementation which may finally merge very closely the procedural statements and the data constructs [1].
- A specification of the semantics of the data should be available before any discussion on syntactic matters takes place. The functions for the construction of the data objects define an abstract syntax, and the construction of some concrete syntax describing the "interface language" by means of a grammar remains as a minor problem.

Abstract (algebraic) data types [2] are given emphasis as an instrument for the specification of the semantics of data. Extensive experience of how to use abstract data types for the specification of syntax and semantics of (programming) languages is available from [3]. An introduction to basic notions like "abstract (data) type", "sort", "carrier set", "signature", "hierarchy (of types)", "model (of a type)", "program variable" can be found in [1] or [2].

This paper presents a case study which aims at a demonstration of the use of data types for the definition of interfaces of system components. In principle, the reader should be able to apply our specification methodology to data exchange files like IGES [4], VDAFS [5], or to the GKS-metafile [6].

5.1.2 The First Part of the Case Study

This case study is based on an example taken from the CAD area. As a first step, we assume that there are two system components which are part of the same program, and that a data transfer may occur within the main storage of that program. The second step modifies this situation in such a way that a file transfer may take place between the two system components. The file transfer needs, in particular, the coding of the data by some string of characters, i.e. a language representation.

We denote by CADA and CADE two components of a system denoted by CAD. CADA owns a storage area which is abstractly described by a program variable *vas*. This variable *vas* may contain structured objects ("values", "data") of some sort **go** (geometrical objects). The sort **go** will be defined by some abstract (data) type GO [1], this type can be a member of a hierarchy of types. CADE analogously owns a program variable *ves* which can contain structured objects of some sort **ls** (line set), and **ls** will be given as a carrier set of an abstract data type, too.

To transfer data from *vas* to *ves*, a transformation *T* is needed which maps **go**-objects onto **ls**-objects. To specify this transformation as a mathematical function is entirely a problem of the semantics of data. *T* may then be used to discuss semantic properties of the data transfer: if *T* is not an injective mapping, then two different **go**-objects are mapped onto the same **ls**-object, and, consequently, information is lost.

To be very concrete, we assume that the system CAD is a PASCAL program which contains the two procedures CADA and CADE, and that the data transfer is written simply as an assignment statement:

```
program CAD:
  type go = ...; ls = ...;
  var vas: go; ves: ls;
  procedure CADA; ...; procedure CADE; ..;
  function T(g: go): ls; ...;
  begin
  CADA; ves: = T(vas); CADE; ...
  ...
  end
```

Note that the type declaration of PASCAL should not be confused with the notion of abstract data types. The type declaration of PASCAL may serve, however, to implement abstract data types. The appendix (Sect. 5.1.11) exhibits the PASCAL implementation of some types.

---

[1] More precisely a "sort" is an identifier (a symbol) which designates a set of (structural) objects: The meaning of such a set – and, consequently, the meaning of the elements of this set – is specified by the laws (the axioms of the abstract type). The set is called a "carrier set" of the type.

5.1.3 The Types of CADE

Now, we start the discussion by specifying the data types of the systems CADA and CADE. These types are, in fact, hierarchies of data types which are based on primitive types. As primitive types we use:

BOOL: **bool,** *true, false, not, and, or,* ...
REAL: **real,** +, −, *, /, 0, 1, 2, ...
CHAR: **char,** 'a', 'b', ..., 'z', 'A', 'B', ...

These types should have the usual meaning. Note, that we use capital letters e.g. BOOL to designate a type as a whole (including the carrier sets, the signature, and the laws of the type) whereas **bool** designates only the carrier set of BOOL. The first type we specify explicitly formalizes the notion of points of the plane:

Type POINT based on REAL[2]:

---

carrier set: **point**

pt: **real** × **real** → **point**
A point is constructed from two real numbers: its coordinates.

xcrd: **point** → **real**
ycrd: **point** → **real**
The coordinates of a given point may be accessed again.

. + .: **point** × **point** → **point**
Two points may be added.

. * .: **real** × **point** → **point**
A point may be multiplied by a scalar.

$xcrd\ (pt\ (x, y)) = x$
$ycrd\ (pt\ (x, y)) = y$
$pt\ (x, y) + pt\ (u, v) = pt\ (x + u, y + v)$
$t * pt\ (x, y) = pt\ (t * x, t * y)$

A PASCAL implementation of this type is given in the appendix. The reader is invited to prove that the explicit function definitions satisfy the laws of the type POINT, i.e. to prove that the implementation is a "model" of the type (provided that there is no storage overflow).

The next type formalizes the notion of a line.

[2] The so-called signature of a type is given between the first two horizontal strokes. It contains the sort (e.g. **point**) which denotes the carrier set of the type, the function identifiers (e.g. *pt*) which denote functions, and the functionalities (e.g. **real** × **real** → **point**) which are associated with the function symbols. Between the second and the third line the laws (the axioms) of the type are given

Type LINE based on POINT and REAL:

---

carrier set: **line**

ln: **point** × **point** → **line**
A line may be constructed from two points.

val: **line** × **real** → **point**
defines the points on the line.

$val(ln(p, q), t) = (1 - t) * p + t * q$

Note that this type, in fact, defines oriented lines, because there is no law which states $ln\ (p, q) = ln\ (q, p)$. Of course, such a law could be added. This, however, would yield another type, the implementation of which would imply some additional effort. We decided not to include such a law.

Now we are ready to give the specification of the **ls**-objects which can be contained in the variable *ves* of the system CADE. The **ls**-objects are defined as finite sets of lines.

Type LS based on LINE and BOOL:

---

carrier set: **ls**

empty: → **ls**
This is the empty set specified as a nullary function, i.e. a constant.

include: **ls** × **line** → **ls**
Including a line into a finite set of lines yields again a finite set of lines.

isempty: **ls** → **bool**
tests whether a finite set of lines is empty or not.

contains: **ls** × **line** → **bool**
The element relation.

---

isempty (empty) = true
isempty (include (s, l)) = false

contains (empty, l) = false
contains (include(s, k), l) = **if** $k = l$ **then** *true* **else** *contains (s, l)* **fi**

include (include (s, l), l) = include(s, l)
include (include (s, k), l) = include (include(s, l), k)

The last two laws are most essential for the specification of sets: if an element l is contained in a set s an additional inclusion of this element yields the same set s; and a set does not depend on the sequence in which the elements are included.

The type hierarchy of CADE may be illustrated by the following diagram:

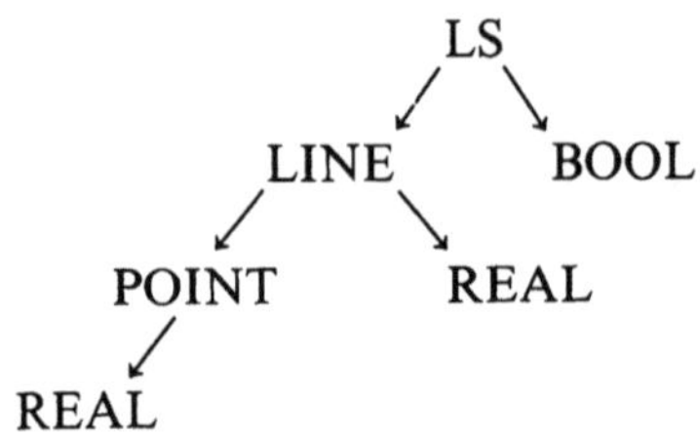

The triangle which has the vertices (13, 8), (4, 3), and (13, 3) for example, (or more precisely the set of three lines between these vertices) can be denoted by the following term

include (
include (
include (*empty*, *ln* (*pt* (4, 3), *pt* (13, 3))),
ln (*pt* (13, 3), *pt* (13, 8)),
ln (*pt* (13, 8), *pt* (4, 3)).

The above mentioned laws can be used to transform this term into another one representing the same triangle. Note, moreover, that such a term may be constructed during several steps of some program. Consequently, the laws may be used to justify some modification ("transformation") of that program.

It should be remarked, moreover, that each member of a carrier set of a type can be denoted by a term which is formed from a finite number of function identifiers of the type. The carrier set of a type cannot contain an element which cannot be denoted by such a term. We say that the elements are term-generated. This exhibits a very basic principle of informatics: A computer is able to deal only with those objects which have a finite representation and can be generated by a finite number of steps.

5.1.4 The Types of CADA

The data type of CATA will be somewhat more complicated. It is designed as a stack with components which are mixed from two sorts: line-objects again and Bezier curves.

We give a formalization of the notion of Bezier curves [7] first. These curves are defined by Bezier points in the usual manner. The algorithm of de Casteljau is used to compute from the Bezier points a point of the curve. The algorithm of de Casteljau is essentially a recursive linear interpolation algorithm. The auxiliary function h of the following type implements one linear interpolation step. Note that h is only partially defined in the carrier set of the type.

Type BEZIER based on POINT, LINE, REAL and BOOL:

---

carrier set: **bezier**

init: **point** → **bezier**
yields a Bezier curve built from one Bezier point.

append: **bezier** × **point** → **bezier**
appends an additional point to the sequence of Bezier points.

isinit: **bezier** → **bool**
tests whether a sequence of Bezier points of a curve contains only one point.

dc: **bezier** × **real** → **point**
the algorithm of de Casteljau. It computes a point of the curve.

h: {(*b*, *t*) **in bezier** × **real**: ¬ *isinit* (*b*)} → **bezier**
an auxiliary function which computes a linear interpolation step.

$isinit\,(init\,(p)) = true$
$isinit\,(append\,(b, p)) = false$
$dc\,(init\,(p), t) = p$
$\neg\ isinit\,(b) \Rightarrow dc\,(b, t) = dc\,(h\,(b, t), t)$
$h\,(append\,(init\,(p), q), t) = init\,(val\,(ln\,(p, q), t))$
$h\,(append\,(append\,(b, p), q), t) = append\,(h\,(append\,(b, p), t), val\,(ln\,(p, q), t))$

Now we are in a position to specify the type GO which belongs to the CADA system. Its variable *vas* can contain objects of the carrier set **go**.

Type GO based on BEZIER, LINE and BOOL:

---

carrier set: **go**

mpty: → **go**
yields the empty object.

inline: **go** × **line** → **go**
includes a **line**-object within a **go**-object.

inbezier: **go** × **bezier** → **go**
includes a Bezier curve within a **go**-object.

ismpty: **go** → **bool**
tests whether a **go**-object is empty.

isline: **go** → **bool**
tests whether the top element of the **go**-object is a **line**-object.

isbezier: **go** → **bool**
tests whether the top element of the **go**-object is a Bezier curve.

rest: {g **in go**: ¬ *ismpty* (g)} → **go**
deletes the top component if the **go**-object is not the empty object.

gtline: {g **in go**: *isline* (g)} → **line**
yields the top component if it is a **line**-object.

gtbezier: {g **in go:** *isbezier* (g)} → **bezier**
yields the top component if it is a Bezier curve.

---

ismpty (*mpty*) = *true*
ismpty (*inline* (*g*, *l*)) = *false*
ismpty (*inbezier* (*g*, *b*)) = *false*
isline (*mpty*) = *false*
isline (*inline* (*g*, *l*)) = *true*
isline (*inbezier* (*g*, *b*)) = *false*
isbezier (*mpty*) = *false*
isbezier (*inline* (*g*, *l*)) = *false*
isbezier (*inbezier* (*g*, *b*)) = *true*
rest (*inline* (*g*, *l*)) = *g*
rest (*inbezier* (*g*, *b*)) = *g*
gtline (*inline* (*g*, *l*)) = *l*
gtbezier (*inbezier* (*g*, *b*)) = *b*

Note that GO does not contain any law which would allow simplifications of **go**-terms. If, for example, an object is included twice then the **go**-object contains two instances of that object.

Hence, the term

inline (
inline (
inbezier (
inline (
inline (*mpty*, *l2*), *l3*), *b*), *l1*), *l2*)

which includes *l2* twice cannot be simplified by any law of the type GO. Nevertheless, a program may be written on top of GO to delete such superfluous instances. Note, however, that such a program maps the **go**-object generated by the above term onto quite another **go**-object.

The following diagram illustrates the complete hierarchy of types for the CADA system:

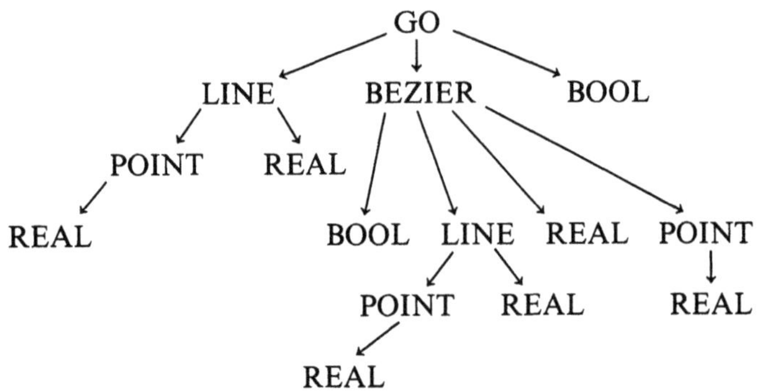

5.1.5 The Semantics of the Data Transfer

Now we are able to give a specification of the function T which maps **go**-objects onto **ls**-objects. Of course, it is fashionable to specify T by means of an abstract data type UE, too. This type UE belongs to the supersystem CAD which contains CADA and CADE as components. UE is based on both GO and LS hierarchies. It does not introduce a new carrier set.

Type UE based on GO, LS, LINE, BEZIER, POINT, REAL and BOOL:

T: **go** → **ls**
maps **go**-objects onto **ls**-objects. This function exhibits the semantics of the data transfer.

∪: **ls** × **ls** → **ls**
yields the union of two finite sets of line-objects.

bs: **bezier** × **real** × **real** → **ls**
Using a bisection principle, *bs* yields an approximation of a Bezier curve by a polygon.

d: **point** × **point** → **bool**
some termination criterion to be used by the bisection.

$$T(mpty) = empty$$
$$T(inline(g, l)) = include(T(g), l)$$
$$T(inbezier(g, b)) = include(T(g), \cup(bs(b, 0, 0.5), bs(b, 0.5, 1)))$$
$$\cup(s, empty) = s$$
$$\cup(s, include(r, l)) = include(\cup(s, r), l)$$
$$d(dc(b, u), dc(b, v)) \Rightarrow bs(b, u, v) = include(empty, ln(dc(b, u), dc(b, v)))$$
$$\neg d(dc(b, u), dc(b, v)) \Rightarrow$$
$$bs(b, u, v) = \cup(bs(b, u, (u + v)/2), (bs(b, (u + v)/2, v)))$$

The type UE does not contain any law specifying properties of the predicate d. Consequently, there is a wide variety of possible implementations for UE. Assume, for instance, that d is implemented by $|p - q| < epsilon$ then each real number $epsilon > 0$ yields an implementation. Note that d has to be implemented in such a way, that the bisection terminates for each **bezier**-object. If this bisection did not terminate for some **bezier**-object b the function *bs* would not yield a result for this object b, and *bs* would be implemented by a function which is only partially defined. Since, however, the functionality of *bs* which is specified in the signature of type UE is asking for a totally defined function a nonterminating bisection would be an insufficient implementation of *bs*.

Another remark should be added: The function T is obviously not injective. This means that information is lost when data are transferred from CADA to CADE.

5.1.6 The Second Part of the Case Study

Now we elaborate our case study by discussing a slightly modified situation. We assume that the data transfer is no longer done in a direct way but in an indirect way via a communication system COMM. Such a communication system could be, for example, a file system providing for character files, a component of a network, or a magnetic tape sent by mail. The essential point is that the communication system needs a character encoding of the data to be transferred. Such character encodings are strings of characters which we assume to be the elements of a carrier set **soc** of a type SOC. The single characters are taken from the primitive type CHAR. (In principle, CHAR can be assumed to be a parameter: If it is instantiated by a binary set we get a binary encoding: if we use an ASCII set we get an ASCII encoding.)

Type SOC based on CHAR and BOOL:

---

carrier set: **soc**

mty: → **soc**
the empty string.

mk: **char** → **soc**
makes a string which contains one character.

&: **soc** × **soc** → **soc**
concatenates strings.

ismty: **soc** → **bool**
tests whether a string is empty.

$ismty(mty) = true$
$ismty(mk(c)) = false$
$ismty(u \,\&\, v) = ismty(u)$ **and** $ismty(v)$
$mty \,\&\, u = u$
$u \,\&\, mty = u$
$(u \,\&\, v) \,\&\, w = u \,\&\, (v \,\&\, w)$

As usual, the following abbreviation may be used

$$"a \ldots z" \quad \leftrightarrow \quad mk('a') \,\&\, \ldots \,\&\, mk('z').$$

Now, the modified supersystem CAD has to provide for two functions *R* ("represent") and *P* ("parse") in such a way that *R*: **go** → **soc** generates a language representation for each **go**-object. *R* (**go**) being a subset of **soc** may be called the "interface language" which is defined by **go** with respect to *R*. The function *P* has to parse that language. *P* then yields **ls**-objects. Consequently, an obvious condition for *R* and *P* is that they should preserve the semantics of the date transfer, i.e.

$T(g) = P(R(g))$ for all g in **go**.

(Note that this condition stating the existence of such a function P, in particular, restricts considerably the class of possible implementations of the type SOC.)

Remember now that the data transfer needs an approximation of **go**-objects by **ls**-objects. This approximation can be done either by CADA or by CADE. Consequently, we immediately get two cases which can be characterized more formally in this way:

1) Approximation done by CADA:

The two auxillary functions
ra: **ls** → **soc**
pa: **soc** → **ls**
with
$pa(ra(l)) = l$ for all l in **ls**
lead to the equations
$T(g) = pa(ra(T(g)))$
$R(g) = ra(T(g))$
$P(s) = pa(s)$
The interface language has to represent only finits sets of **line**-objects. The receiving system CADE does not need to know anything about **go**-objects.

2) Approximation done by CADE:

The auxillary functions
re: **go** → **soc**
pe: **soc** → **go**
with
$pe(re(g)) = g$ for all g in **go**
lead to the following equations
$T(g) = T(pe(re(g)))$
$R(g) = re(g)$
$P(s) = T(pe(s))$.
In this case CADE has to know the type GO which describes the semantics of this interface language, R(**go**).

Note, however, that there is a third case which combines, at least to a certain extent, case 1 and case 2:

3) The interface language is defined independently from CADA and CADE.

This is the situation, for example, with IGES, VDAFS, or even with the graphics metafiles.
The independent definition of such an interface language is based, in particular, on a semantics which is introduced independently from GO and LS. Thus, associated with COMM there is an abstract data type CM which has to provide for two additional semantic mappings

Ta: **go** → **cm**
Te: **cm** → **ls**.

It may happen that on the roundabout way via CM information is lost, too. The specification of the file transfer via COMM now needs the auxiliary functions

ri: **cm** → **soc**
pi: **soc** → **cm**
such that
$pi(ri(z)) = z$ for all z in **cm**
holds. In this way, we get
$R(g) = ri(Ta(g))$
$P(s) = Te(pi(s))$.
The crucial point is whether the equation
$T(g) = Te(pi(ri(Ta(g))))$ for all g in **go**
holds. In principle a data exchange language (like IGES, VDAFS) has to be based on a data type which is general enough to maintain the above equation for any two systems exchanging CAD data. It has been stated that the semantics of IGES, for example, must be the semantics of a super-CAD-system.

5.1.7 A Concrete Interface Language

Now we give a specification of a concrete interface language for the first case. The method of defining this language should be easily applicable to the other cases as well.

The following type REPR does not introduce a new carrier set. Moreover, it should be mentioned that the parse functions P and pa are partial functions with respect to **soc**.

Type REPR based on UE, GO, LS, SOC, LINE, POINT, REAL, and BOOL:

R: **go** → **soc**
approximates **go**-objects and yields a language representation of the approximation.

ra: **ls** → **soc**
maps **ls**-objects onto strings.

pa: {*s* **in soc: exist** *l* **in ls:** $ra(l) = s$} → **ls**
parses a string of characters if it represents a **ls**-object.

P: {*s* **in soc: exist** *l* **in ls:** $ra(l) = s$} → **ls**
the same function as *pa*.

rl: **line** → **soc**
yields a character representation of a point.

rp: **point** → **soc**
yields a character representation of a point.

rr: **real** → **soc**
yields a character representation of a real.

$$R(g) = ra\,(T(g))$$
RA1: $ra\,(empty) = mk\,('EOT')$
RA2: $ra\,(include\,(t, l)) = rl\,(l)\ \&\ ";"\ \&\ ra\,(t)$
RL: $rl\,(ln\,(p, q)) = rp\,(p)\ \&\ ","\ \&\, rp\,(q)$
RP: $rp\,(pt\,(x, y)) = rr\,(x)\ \&\ ","\ \&\, rr\,(y)$
$$ra\,(l) = s \Rightarrow (pa\,(s) = l \textbf{ and } P\,(s) = pa\,(s))$$

The concrete interface language is defined by the four laws which are labeled by RA1, RA2, RL, and RP. By means of R, a triangle with the vertices $pt\,(3, 2)$, $pt\,(8, 2)$, and $pt\,(8, 6)$, for example, may be represented by

"3, 2, 8, 2; 8, 6, 8, 2; 3, 2, 8, 6;" & *mk* ('*EOT*').

Due to the laws of LS the string

"8, 6, 8, 2; 3, 2, 8, 2; 3, 2, 8, 6;" & *mk* ('*EOT*')

represents the same triangle. This example exhibits a problem: The signature of REPR asks *ra* to denote a function. On the other hand, the law $include\,(include\,(s, l), k) = include\,(include\,(s, k), l)$ of type LS, for example, immediately leads to the equality

$$ra\,(include\,(include\,(s, l), k)) = ra\,(include\,(include\,(s, k), l))$$

whereas

$$ra\,(include\,(include\,(s, l), k)) = rl\,(l)\ \&\ ";"\ \&\ rl\,(k)\ \&\ ";"\ \&\ ra\,(s)$$

and

$$ra\,(include\,(include\,(s, k), l)) = rl\,(k)\ \&\ ";"\ \&\ rl\,(l)\ \&\ ";"\ \&\ ra\,(s)$$

obviously represent two different strings of characters. This is a contradiction, and *ra* cannot be a function as specified in the signature of REPR.

To maintain the functionality of *ra*, there are two ways of proceeding:

1) In addition to the identity relation an equivalence relation can be introduced on **soc** in such a way that it reflects the laws of LS. Such a relation leads to a new type whose carrier set is formed by the associated equivalence classes of **soc**.
2) Axioms of LS which state that two different terms yield the same **ls**-object are (temporarily) ignored. Formally, this leads to a new type LSM, which is a modification of LS.

It is more convenient to adopt this second method without writing down explicitly the new type LSM. The idea is simply that any application of the laws takes place either before the process of data exchange has been started or after this process has been completed. Despite this demand, it is understood that the laws can be used to minimize the string of characters to be exchanged.

Introducing now the syntactic variables ⟨LS⟩, ⟨LI⟩, ⟨PT⟩, and ⟨RL⟩ we can derive from the labeled laws of REPR the BNF-grammar of the interface language by means of the following substitution [8].

$ra\,(\ldots) \quad \rightarrow \quad \langle \mathrm{LS} \rangle$
$rl\,(\ldots) \quad \rightarrow \quad \langle \mathrm{LI} \rangle$

$$
\begin{array}{lcl}
rp(\ldots) & \rightarrow & \langle \mathrm{PT} \rangle \\
rr(\ldots) & \rightarrow & \langle \mathrm{RL} \rangle \\
''a \ldots z'' & \rightarrow & a \ldots z \\
\& & \rightarrow & \\
mk\,('EOT') & \rightarrow & 'EOT' \\
= & \rightarrow & ::=
\end{array}
$$

Applying this substitution we get the grammar:

$$
\begin{array}{ll}
\langle \mathrm{LS} \rangle & ::= 'EOT' \\
\langle \mathrm{LS} \rangle & ::= \langle \mathrm{LI} \rangle ; \langle \mathrm{LS} \rangle \\
\langle \mathrm{LI} \rangle & ::= \langle \mathrm{PT} \rangle , \langle \mathrm{PT} \rangle \\
\langle \mathrm{PT} \rangle & ::= \langle \mathrm{RL} \rangle , \langle \mathrm{RL} \rangle
\end{array}
$$

Again we stress the point that the grammar of the concrete interface language is derived from the abstract syntax by means of the representation (or "encoding") functions. The abstract syntax is given by function symbols of the data types.

A remark should be added: If the functions for the construction of the elements of a carrier set are partial functions then the equations for the character encoding of these elements are subject to restrictions. The laws, then, are of the form

$$c \Rightarrow (a = b)$$

where the condition c characterizes the precise domain of the associated partial function. The BNF-grammar which we get by ignoring the left hand side of the implications does not express such restrictions. The grammar can only define a superset of the interface language.

5.1.8 A Glance at the Development of Programs

The paper should not conclude without a glance at a major advantage of our methodology: advantage is that we get a sound basis for further development using formal means. The laws of the types can be used to derive, for example, an efficient implementation of the function R which computes the character encoding of the **go**-objects without explicit use of the functions T and ra immediately. We get the derived laws

$$
\begin{array}{ll}
\mathrm{LE}: & R(mpty) = mk('EOT') \\
\mathrm{RI}: & R(inline(g, l)) = rl(l) \mathbin{\&} '';'' \mathbin{\&} R(g).
\end{array}
$$

By means of a new auxillary function

$$rbs: \mathbf{bezier} \times \mathbf{real} \times \mathbf{real} \rightarrow \mathbf{soc}$$

we get in addition for the approximating part:

RB: $R(inbezier(g, b)) = rbs(b, 0.5, 1)$ & $rbs(b, 0, 0.5)$ & $R(g)$

$d(dc(b, u), dc(b, v)) \Rightarrow$

$rbs(b, u, v) = rp(dc(b, u))$ & ";" & $rp(dc(b, v))$ & ";"

$\neg d(dc(b, u), dc(b, v)) \Rightarrow$

$rbs(b, u, v) = rbs(b, (u+v)/2, v)$ & $rbs(b, u, (u+v)/2)$

The derivation of LE and RI is done simply by substitution. The proof of AB needs induction, and, of course, the use of LSM instead of LS is understood.

Acknowledgement. The author appreciates very much some valuable remarks by E. G. Schlechtendahl.

5.1.9 References

1. Bauer FL, Woessner H: Algorithmic language and program development. Springer, Berlin Heidelberg New York (1982)
2. Wirsing M et al.: On hierarchies of abstract data types. Acts Informatica 20: 1–33 (1983)
3. The CIP language group: The Munich Project CIP. Volume I: The wide spectrum language CIP-L. Lecture Notes in Computer Science, vol 183. Springer, Berlin Heidelberg New York (1985)
4. The American Society of Mechanical Engineers: Digital Representation for Communication of Product Definition Data (IGES). ANSI Y14.26M-1981 American Standard Institute, Engineering Drawing and Related Documentation Practices, New York (1981)
5. VDA-Arbeitskreis 'CAD/CAM': VDA Flächenschnittstelle. Version 1.0, Verband der Automobilindustrie, Frankfurt (1983)
6. Graphical Kernel System (GKS): Functional Description. ISO/IS 7942. Information Processing 1985
7. Boehm W, Kahmann J: Grundlagen kurven- und flächenorientierter Modellierung. In: Informatik-Fachberichte 65. Springer, Berlin Heidelberg New York Tokyo (1983) 173–210
8. Bauer FL, Goos G: Informatik, eine einführende Übersicht. Band 2, 3. Auflage. Springer, Berlin Heidelberg New York Tokyo (1984)

5.1.10 Appendix: Pascal Implementations

(* Type POINT based on REAL *)

```
type point = @pr;
      pr = record x, y: real end;

function pt(u, v: real): point;
   var h: point;
   begin
      alloc(h);
      h@.x := u;
      h@.y := v;
         pt := h
   end;
```

```
function xcrd (p: point) : real;
    begin xcrd : = p@.x end;
function ycrd (p: point) : real;
    begin ycrd : = p@.y end;
function plus (p, q: point) : point;
    begin plus : = pt (xcrd (p) + xcrd (q), ycrd (p) + ycrd (q)) end;
function mult (t: real; p: point) : point;
    begin mult : = pt (t * xcrd (p), t * ycrd (p)) end;
(* End of type POINT *)
```

```
(* Type LINE based on POINT and REAL *)

type line = @lr;
       lr = record a, e: point end;
function ln (p, q: point): line;
    var h: line
    begin
      alloc (h);
      h@.a : = p;
      h@.e : = q;
      ln :    = h
    end;
function val (l: line; t: real) : point;
    begin
      val : = plus (mult (1 − t, l@.a), mult (t, l@.e))
    end;
(* End of type LINE *)
```

```
(* Type LS based on LINE and BOOL *)
(* Auxiliary functions for ordering *)
function pk (p, q: point): boolean;
    begin
      pk : = (xcrd (p) < xcrd (q)) or ((xcrd (p) = xcrd (q)) and (ycrd (p) <= ycrd (q)))
    end;
function pg (p, q: point): boolean;
    begin pg : = pk (p, q) and pk (q, p) end;
function lk (g, h: line): boolean;
    begin
      lk : = (pk (g@.a, h@.a) and ¬ pg (g@.a, h@.a)) or
             (pg (g@.a, h@.a) and pk (g@.e, h@.e))
    end;
function lg (g, h: line): boolean;
    begin lg : = lk (g, h) and lk (h, g)
end
```

```
(* The main part of LS:                      *)
(* LS is implemented by means of sorted lists. *)

type ls = @rls;
     rls = record li: line; rs: ls end;

function empty: ls;
    begin empty := nil end;

function include (s: ls; l: line);
    var h: ls;
    begin
      if isempty (s) then
      begin
        alloc (h);
        h@.li := l;
        h@.ls := s;
        include := h
      end
      else
      if lg (l, s@.li) then
        include := s
      else
      if lk (l, s@.li) then
      begin
        alloc (h);
        h@.li := l;
        h@.rs := s;
        include := h
      end
      else
      begin
        alloc (h);
        h@.li := s@.li;
        h@.rs := include (s@.rs, l);
        include := h
      end
    end

function isempty (s: ls): boolean;
    begin isempty := (s = nil) end;

function contains (s: ls; l: line): boolean;
    begin
      if isempty (s)
        then contains := false
        else if lg (l, s@.li)
          then contains := true
          else contains := contains (s@.rs, l)
    end;

(* End of type LS *)
```

5.2 Validation of Graphics Systems

W. Hübner

5.2.1 Introduction

In a computer-aided design process the user must present and manipulate data by means of a computer graphics system. These tasks are handled by a communication subsystem which should be separate from other components of the CAD system. The communication subsystem consists of modules for dialogue, for input and output of data and for graphical information processing.

The requirements of separation, uniformity and standardization in the graphics software in CAD systems are satisfied by standards like GKS, the Graphical Kernel System [1]. It was developed by the DIN-NI UA 5.9 and by the ISO TC97/SC5/WG2 and has now reached the stage of being an international graphics standard for 2D applications.

The Graphical Kernel System defines a functional interface between an application program and a configuration of graphics devices. This interface has to be implemented on different system configurations embedded in a particular programming language.

The major goals of the standardization efforts were to guarantee

- the portability of programs
- the independance from particular devices
- the independance from application programs
- the unification of graphics software
- the promotion of good user interfaces
- the adaptability of system interfaces

To maintain the integrity of the standard it is essential to provide a means of examining the conformity of existing GKS implementations. Therefore in 1981, while experts were developing the standard, a special subgroup 'Methodology of Certification of Graphics Systems' was formed within the ISO group with the aim of defining a certification scheme to guarantee, verify and certify GKS implementations that are offered on the market.

5.2.2 Goals of Certification

The standard lays down a functional specification of a system of procedures for graphics programming. It is not determined in which way and by which algorithms the services of the system have to be realized. The document consists of a semi-formal specification of the functions, and an informal description of the philosophy and the effects of the functions within a natural language. Implementors interpret the document from their point of view and set up a mental model of the standard which they will realize in terms of computer programs. Some design rules are left free to the implementors, but in other aspects they are restricted by strict rules.

With the rapid emergence of GKS implementations [2] the dangerous situation arises that realizations which are announced to be GKS implementations do not conform to the standard and, moreover, 'GKS-like' packages are offered that are based on the global philosophy but do not adhere to the standard in detail. Therefore the major goal of certification is to check the conformity of GKS realizations to the standard by validation means.

Another task is the improvement of the more or less informal specification of GKS, with the final aim of developing a formal specification. A special group within the ISO certification group is working out a general philosophy and methodology to support formal specifications of graphics standards [3].

Moreover, a very pedantic analysis of the document was necessary for the implementation of validation tools. A number of inaccuracies and inconsistencies were outlined. In those cases 'requests for clarification' were sent to the GKS-Control-Board within ISO.

Both implementors and customers will be supported by certification centres. Programmers may be assisted by the test centre in the debugging-phase. This could be done either by making test software available or by providing information on request.

For vendors of graphics packages a certificate or a test report will give additional criteria for deciding which implementation they prefer. Validation tools will help users to run selftests in cases where an implementation is suspect. The functionality, capability and quality of graphics devices can be examined in detail.

Finally the reliability and credibility of GKS will improve especially in areas of critical applications.

5.2.3 Software Validation Techniques

In the area of software validation two countercurrent strategies have been established, the verification and the falsification approach.

Program Verification is the attempt to prove the correctness of an implementation. For this technique a formal specification of the standard is needed. The verification process is based on formal methods for program construction and on correctness proofs. Starting with the specification, an implementation should be derived by a series of transformation steps. Proving the correctness of each transformation step and presuming the correctness and completeness of the specification, the correctness of the generated implementation is demonstrated.

Several problems arise by following this approach:

- A complete formal specification of GKS does not exist at present.

- Up to now techniques of correctness proofs and program generation are applicable only to small software packages. Even at its simplest level GKS provides a great number of (partly) complex functions.
- Some functional aspects should not be exactly specified by mathematical methods. Their realization is deliberately left up to the implementor. Features like representation of attributes (e.g. the occurrence of linetypes) can only be checked visually. Human perception and judgement are the criteria of correctness of those attribute realizations.

The falsification model, on the other hand, is a more practical strategy. It is the attempt to prove that an implementation is incorrect. This test-orientated approach is used for compiler validation and is well-known in the area of computer graphics (pictorial testing). A set of test programs examines several features of an implementation. The results are compared against correct reference results to discover errors. This model for checking the functional correctness based on carefully designed test-strategies at several interfaces where data can be made accessible was preferred.

The key problem of falsification approaches in graphics systems is the generation of correct reference results. Some reference data can be derived from the GKS document by hand because they are specified exactly.

Other reference data should be produced automatically. Especially at the internal device interface reference results are configured from a specification to simulate the data exchange with the devices at the same logical level to ensure correct comparisons. In this area concepts of verification, especially formal specification and program generation methods, are used to construct reference systems.

If the sets of candidate and reference results are not identical, the candidate implementation is assumed to be incorrect. If no errors are detected it is not guaranteed that the implementation is correct. But with a well-defined test suite, which is progressively strengthened by experience, a very large number of potential error situations can be checked. Therefore some degree of confidence is inspired in any implementation surviving the rigours of the test procedures.

5.2.4 The Interfaces for Testing

At this point the question arises which features of a graphics system can be tested and which data can be made accessible. An implementation can be seen as a black box. Black box testing is always a data check at some interface. As shown in Fig. 5.2.1, three interfaces can be identified.

The most obvious interface is the application interface between the graphics system and the application program. It consists of all functions defined by the standard.

In contrast to compiler-implementations, a huge amount of data is not available at the interface with the application program. Results are provided in terms of graphical output and input and interaction mechanisms. Consequently two further interfaces were identified.

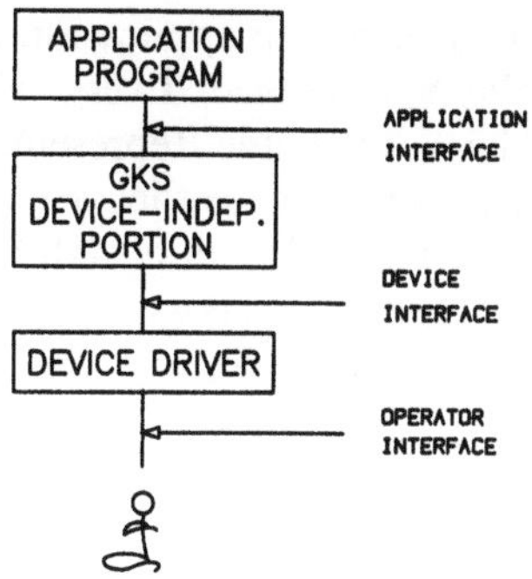

Fig. 5.2.1. The interfaces for testing GKS implementations

At the so-called operator interface between the graphics devices and an operator, visual output and user input is tested at a pictorial level.

Nearly every implementation provides an internal device interface that separates the device-independent part from the devices. This interface is not fixed for each implementation. Therefore the functionality of the device interface has to be configured for each realization. Then the candidate's results will be compared with the configured reference results.

The following sections present the strategies of testing at these interfaces in detail.

5.2.4.1 Testing at the Application Interface

The interface between the application program and the GKS realization is the appropriate point to check the conformity of the following features:

- The language-specific binding,
- the GKS data structures,
- the error behaviour,
- the input functions,
- the utility functions.

The Graphical Kernel System provides a set of graphics functions in a language-independant way. An implementation integrates this nucleus in a higher programming language by subroutines or procedures. The application programmer uses those functions provided by standardized language-dependant layers. For several higher programming languages like FORTRAN or PASCAL those language bindings for GKS (i.e. function names, parameters, data types, etc.) have the status of international standards. The certification centre will check those language layers.

The application interface consists not only of the function set defined by the standard. GKS defines a number of internal state lists, providing a detailed record of the current state of a program using GKS. Changes in the state variables are effected by graphics functions. Additionally GKS contains description tables with static values that cannot be modified by the application program. Every entry of those data structures (state lists and description tables) can be interrogated by the application using inquiry functions like 'Inquire Maximum Display Surface Size'. Every value of the state lists can be changed with set functions like 'Set Polyline Representation'. The data structures are part of the application interface because they are directly accessible by the programmer.

About 70% of all GKS functions are set or inquiry functions. The effect of those functions is exactly specified by the document. The following state lists are present in GKS:

- GKS State List
- Segment State List
- Workstation State List
- Error State List
- Input Queue

The description tables contains constants that are implementation or workstation dependant:

- GKS Description Table
- Workstation Description Table

The following model for data structure validation was established (see Fig. 5.2.2).

1) The current state lists are inquired and stored.
2) The function to be tested is called.
3) The data from the state lists after the function call are inquired and compared with the stored state lists.
4) The changes are reported.

The test results have to be compared against correct reference results which are derived from the document according to the called function:

5) It is checked that the expected changes are executed and no unexpected changes occur.

Consider the function 'Set Window' for instance. It is important to verify that the specified normalization transformation is modified in the GKS state list – and equally important to verify that the current transformation is not modified (unless of course it is the current transformation that is being changed).

That procedure can be extended for testing groups of GKS functions to check the interdependence and interaction between the functions.

The same automatism can be applied to the error handling tests. The error behaviour is specified for each function in the standard. Error situations are generated and the system reactions are reported. They are checked by the expected error numbers. In those cases where every expected error occurs but no unexpected error appears the error behaviour is said to be correct.

The test of input functions at the application interface is limited to the data returned by an input call. A function call at the application interface orders an input which an operator generates at the operator interface. The result can be checked automatically by a test program or visually by human judgement. Therefore testing of the input facilities is a combined task of application and operator interface and is discussed in the following section.

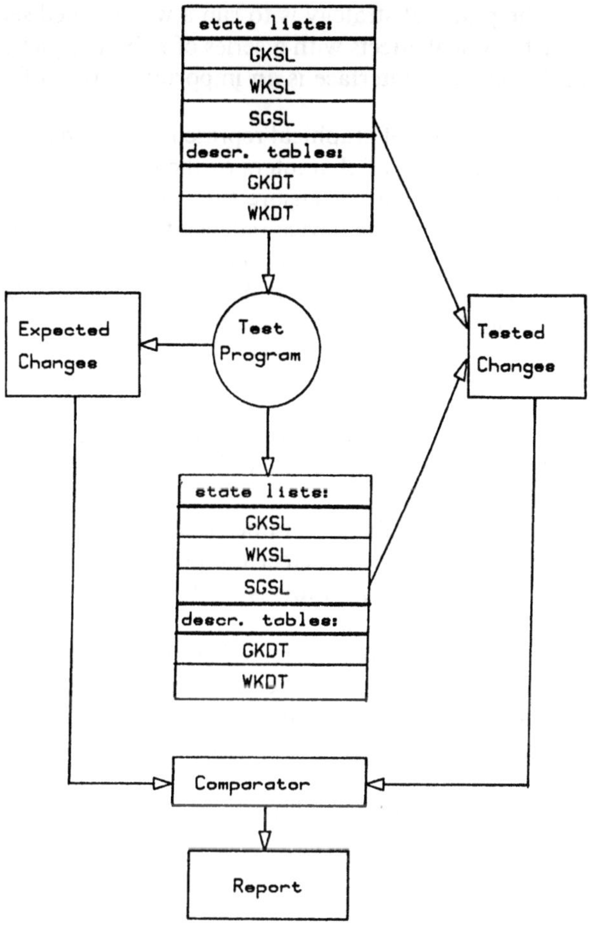

Fig. 5.2.2. Data structure test

Another short test examines the GKS utility functions construction of transformation matrices. The utility functions are called with some predefined fixed points, shift vectors, rotation angles and scale factors. The resulting matrices are verified.

5.2.4.2 Testing at the Operator Interface

This human interface exchanges information on a pictorial level between graphical devices and operators. It consists of output checked visually by an observer, operator action on input devices and system reactions like prompting, echo or acknowledgement.

The operator interface test is a manual process and cannot be automated like those at the application or device interface. It is conceivable that this test may perhaps in future be automated by image processing techniques.

The practical strategy is to run a well-defined set of test programs and compare the visual effects with a series of reference pictures created by hand. Testing at the operator interface is an important aspect of certification because

- the suitability of graphical representation can only be checked visually, e.g. the recognizability of characters or the echoing of operator actions,
- it is the only way to ensure that the whole graphics system works correctly, including both the device-independent part and the device drivers,
- the general purpose of computer graphics is to generate pictures and therefore the credibility of any certification scheme will be enhanced if the graphical end-product is seen to be correct.

However, a number of problems arise in visual testing at the operator interface.

1) Visual checking is a subjective task because it involves human judgement. One operator can accept a test which another rejects. Moreover human errors are not excluded.
2) The design of the test frames is a sophisticated task because they have to be simple in nature to detect the possible errors in an easy way. Although the number of test programs is limited, a maximum number of error possibilities should be checked.
3) Because of the great variety of graphical devices with distinctive characteristics the results of the test suites differ in their implications. The tests must take the allowable difference into account. A full description of the allowable differences is given in Annex D of the GKS document.

A test suite was developed to check the facilities of level 0a. The following aspects are tested:

1) Control functions
2) Output primitives
3) Colour
4) Output primitive attributes
5) Transformation
6) Clipping
7) Metafiles

At first the mandatory capabilities all implementations have to provide are tested. For instance all workstations must support linetypes 1–5, marker types 1–5, 'string' and 'char' precision and interior style 'hollow' at level 0a. Then the non-mandatory features supported by the devices are tested according to the entries in the Workstation Description Table.

For testing input facilities a combined strategy of automated and visual testing is chosen. The operator produces input of specified values. In a 'request locator' frame, for instance, he is asked to input within outlined squares. The application program knows the expected values and can execute a suitable comparison. In the case of an error the operator is asked whether he wants to repeat his input to eliminate operator errors.

5.2.4.3 Testing at the Device Interface

The testing of pictorial output and input cannot be limited to visual checking at the graphics devices. It was recognized that an additional automated test is necessary. The graphics data at the operator's disposal are exchanged at an internal interface between the device-independent body and the device drivers. This device interface exists for nearly every implementation (the exception will be workstations providing the whole GKS functionality in hardware or firmware).

The interface consists of a set of functions defining a possible logical capability of a device driver. Testing at this interface provides criteria for identifying whether an occured error is attributed to the GKS implementation or to the device drivers.

The problem is that the logical level differs for each implementation. The functionality and the data format depend on implementor's decisions, the capabilities of the physical devices and the programmer's use of them.

Permitted differences at the device interface are, for instance, the availability of output primitives at the device such as 'Cell Array' or 'Fill Area', or the capability to support certain primitive attributes. The capability of polyline attributes, for instance, can be divided into the four categories 'not available', 'static', 'bundled' or 'aspect source flag evaluation'.

Beyond the quality of attributes that a device supports, quantitative aspects of attributes are also important, i.e. how many linetypes are available at the dcvicc.

Furthermore the representation can differ because linewidths can be described with integer data types (indices) or with reals (scale factor from a standard width).

Other implementation dependencies are transformation (whether NDC or DC coordinated are passed to the device) or clipping (not available, static or dynamic).

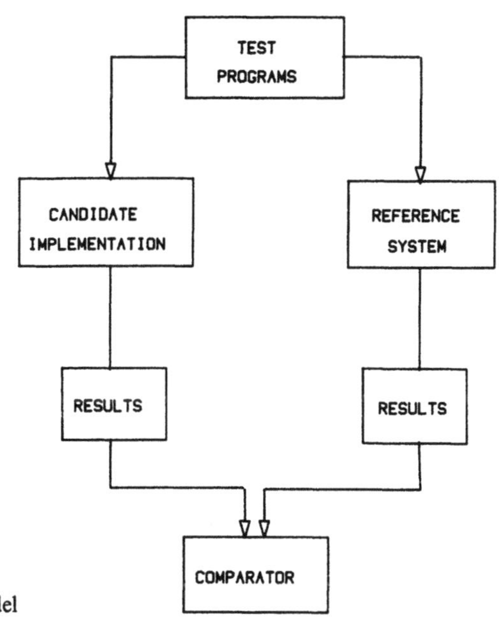

Fig. 5.2.3. The reference model

For all those different eventualities an equivalent reference system must be configured. The comparator can be fixed because exactly the same device interface is matched for both candidate and reference. Figure 5.2.3 illustrates the testing model.

Attempts are being made to define a superset of device driver functions with the capacity to connect most of the common graphics devices. The result will be a Computer Graphics Interface (CGI), defined by ANSI X3H3 [5], which is expected to be integrated in many GKS implementations. Nevertheless it will be some time until this standard is established and no implementor will be forced to use it.

The implementation of the falsification approach at the device interface is a sophisticated task. The following problems have to be solved:

- how to identify and describe the internal interface where data generating a picture can be collected and assessed;
- how to configure correct reference data at the appropriate logical level to be compared with the candidate data.

5.2.4.4 Configuring a Reference System

The process of generating a reference system which simulates the functionality of the candidate at the device interface is now described in detail. The configuration process is divided into five phases (see Fig. 5.2.4).

In an initial step a suitable specification of GKS is first defined. It describes the effect of the GKS functions at the device interface in more detail than the GKS document. This generic device-independant reference specification includes all possible implementation decisions (e.g. type of transformation modules and their possible sequences) and device facilities. It is a prerequisite for the configuration phase.

For this reference specification of GKS a special formal language was developed. The transformation of the GKS functions is described by sequencies of

No	Phase	Tool	Result
0	Specification	Specification language	Reference specification
1	Description	Editor	—
2	Configuration	Configurator	—
3	Generation	Interpreter	Reference implementation
4	Testing	Comparator	Certification

Fig. 5.2.4. The phase model

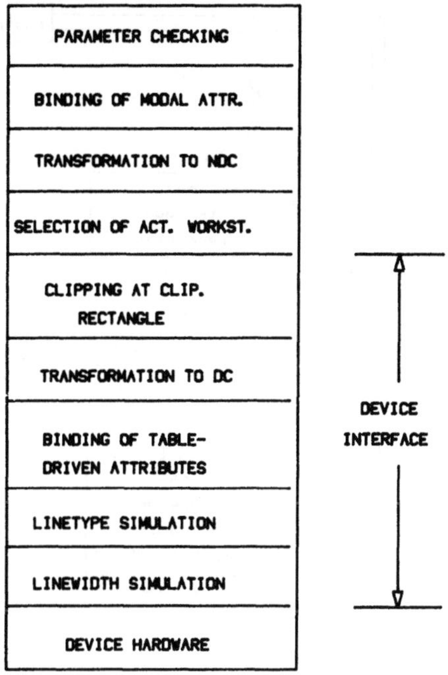

Fig. 5.2.5. Polyline pipeline

methods which can be seen as abstract data types. These methods are understood as black boxes communicating via their parameters. The methods are defined by their effect on the current picture element description and represent the transformation steps.

This configurable specification divides the transformation beginning with the call of the subroutine at the application interface and ending with a picture description sent to the respective device interface into single steps. For each step which can be seen as an entity, a function is defined describing the effect on the picture element description. Every functional module which can occur in any implementation is described. The transformation steps are gathered in pipelines as shown in Fig. 5.2.5.

When the polyline function is called, the parameter checking, the binding of the modal attributes, the normalization transformation and the selection of all active workstations are executed. Those steps are device-independent. The following steps convert the picture element description to a form closer to that at a device. The process stops when the picture description contains exactly the information used at the particular device interface.

Consider a device taking over polylines with normalized device coordinates. The clipping rectangle and the polyline bundle index are evaluated by the device driver. For this device no further modules are configured.

A second device takes over a vector set in clipped device coordinates. All table driven attributes are bound to the output primitive. In this case the clipping, DC-transformation and the table-driven attribute binding are executed within the

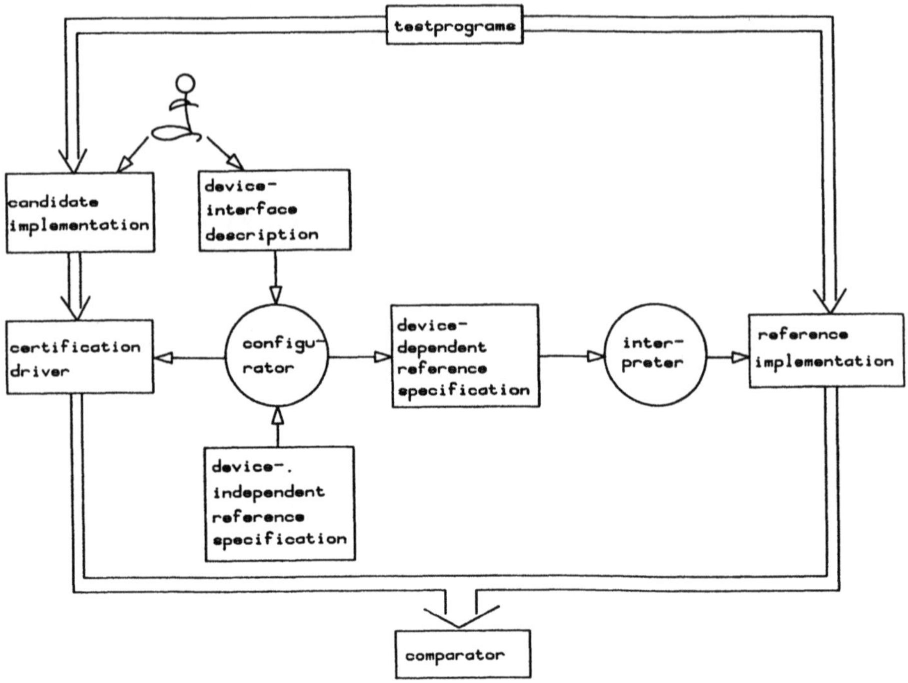

Fig. 5.2.6. The configuration process

GKS implementation before mapping the picture element description to the device.

A third very low intelligence device expects solid lines after attribute simulation is performed within GKS. Then all transformation steps are configured to the reference specification.

In phase 1 to 3 a reference implementation is created for each candidate implementation so that in the last phase (4) test programs can run on both sides (see Fig. 5.2.6).

In the description phase the device interface is specified by the implementor of the candidate. He describes among others the facilities of the device, the functionality of his device interface and the data types he uses at the interface. A specification editor has been developed to support the implementor in describing his device interface.

With the device interface description and the device-independent reference specification a reference system is configured containing only the necessary functions in the right order and the correct data types (phase 2). The configurator is controlled by derivation instructions describing all possible device interface structures and the rules generating the specific interface. At each node one device description element (generated by the editor in phase 1) selects the following path. The resulting reference is an abstract description of the program's effect (but not of its implementation) in the specification language.

Furthermore the configurator has another aim. It derives a virtual certification driver from the description of the candidate. This special driver takes the place of the device driver. The data accessible at the device interface are converted by the certification driver to a format dechipherable by the comparator. Some information, like polyline bundle tables etc., which can be held in the device driver by some devices must in this case be controlled by the certification driver.

The description medium of the device dependant reference specification is the abstract specification language. For running test programs a program system in the same language as the candidate is needed. For this reason an interpreter has been developed which generates code in a higher programming language (phase 3).

Besides syntactical and semantic analysis the interpreter converts the specification constructs into programming language constructs, complex data structures into data types of the programming language and links the procedures belonging to the methods used in the specification. A module library contains all procedures according to the specification methods. Those programs were developed in an earlier phase and are available for running test programs.

An implementation of a first interpreter generating FORTRAN source code is complete, others will certainly follow.

In the final test phase (4) programs run on both candidate plus certification driver and configured reference, producing results in the same format. A comparator checks whether the function names, data types and data are identical. The comparator is fixed for all candidates and has a standard format. It produces a formatted report of the conformity of the results.

A more detailed description of the certification process is given in [6, 7].

5.2.5 Conclusions and Further Planning

The methodology of testing graphics standards described so far is implemented within several software packages. By late 1984 the data structure tests had been completed up to level 2b. Error tests are available for all level 0a functions. Visual testing has been concluded for level 0a and is being extended to level 1b facilities in 1985. In the area of device interface testing most work had to be undertaken to set up the generating process for the reference implementation. We are now able to configure 0a references and compare their output to the candidate output at the device interface.

As the work of implementing test procedures for GKS is nearly finished (at least for FORTRAN environments) emphasis has to be shifted to organizing the running of tests and the delivery of certificates.

An organizational framework for the certification process in practice was developed by the ISO [8].

The accreditation of a testing laboratory at the 'Gesellschaft für Mathematik und Datenverarbeitung (GMD)' in the Federal Republic of Germany is in process. The institute is testing the test software itself with several implementations and developing further test software.

A subset of test software is offered at the moment to help programmers in testing their implementation. When the test software is reasonably stable, GMD will run a full testing service. This is expected at the end of 1985. The institute is willing to submit its intended GKS testing service to a European or worldwide certification system at CEN/CENTER or ISO/CERTIO.

Other testing laboratories outside the Federal Republic of Germany will be established: The 'Bureau d'orientation de la Normalisation en Informatique (BNI)' in France and the 'National Computing Center (NCC)' in the United Kingdom accredit a GKS testing service. First contacts with the 'National Bureau of Standards (NCS)' in the USA are being made.

So the goal of establishing certification centers at the same time as GKS became an international standard (early 1985) was nearly achieved.

Acknowledgements. I would like to express my gratitude to the many experts involved in the design and realization of the certification model for GKS. Particular thanks are due to Ken Brodlie, Martin Göbel, Günther Pfaff and Jose Encarnacao.

5.2.6 References

1. ISO: Graphical Kernel System (GKS); Functional Description. Draft International Standard. ISO/DIS 7942 (1984)
2. Enderly G: GKS Implementations Overview, 2nd edition. Computer Graphics Forum 3, 181–189 (1984)
3. Carson S: A Formal Specification of the Programmers Minimal Interface to Graphics, X3H3/82-43 (1982).
4. Maguire MC: Visual testing of GKS at the human interface. Comput. Graphics 8, 19–27 (1984)
5. Computer Graphics Interface, Working Draft. ANSI Document number X3H33/84-10R1 (Dec. 1984).
6. Pfaff GE: Functional conformance testing of graphics software. Comput. Graphics 8, 29–37 (1984)
7. Göbel M, Hübner W: Configuring Reference Systems for Certifying GKS Implementations. Submitted to Eurographics 1985, Nice (Sep. 1985).
8. Certification of GKS Implementations. ISO/TC97/SC5/WG2/N192, Gananoque/Canada (Sep. 1983)

5.3 Testing and Validation of IGES Processors

H. Grabowski and R. Glatz

5.3.1 Introduction

The exchange of product definition data between different CAD/CAM systems within one or more companies is of increasing importance. Such an integrated data exchange on the basis of coupled systems yields advantages relating to the economical and expanded use of CAD/CAM technology [1]. However, because of great differences in handling and storing of product definition data within the CAD/CAM systems, the exchange of this data was in earlier times nearly impossible or very expensive.

The Initial Graphics Exchange Specification (IGES) [2, 3] was the first attempt to provide a general and useful solution to this problem. It was developed to serve as a standardized interface for the data exchange of current CAD/CAM systems.

The realization of the IGES concept requires the implementation of special software programs, the so-called IGES pre- and postprocessors (Fig. 5.3.1). These processors handle the access, analysis, mapping and storage of product definition data in the CAD/CAM data base and/or the IGES file.

IGES processors are often very complex and expensive software systems. Because so much depends on the CAD/CAM product models and data bases used, these processors have to be implemented seperately for each CAD/CAM system. The general basis for the implementation is the IGES specification which gives information about the representation of product definition data. However, for the design and implementation of algorithms and programs only minimal information is included in the specification. Therefore the capability and quality

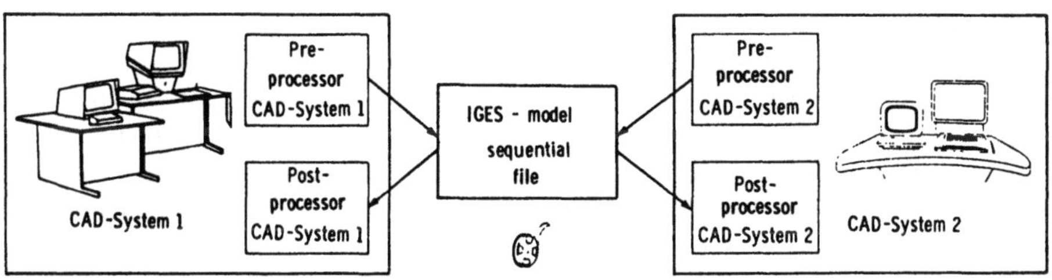

IGES • Initial Graphics Exchange Specification

Fig. 5.3.1. Data exchange via IGES

of the implemented IGES processors often differ considerably from one system to the other.

The main condition for a frictionless data exchange in industry is the guarantee, that the product definition data is processed completely and correctly by the sending as well as the receiving system. This overall condition is not fulfilled by todays IGES pre- and postprocessors. On one hand the IGES specification limits the amount of exchangable data, on the other hand the exchange is restricted by errors or incompatibilities within the communicating processors. For all these reasons, it is necessary to gain detailed knowledge about the applicability of supplied IGES processors in industrial environment.

The achievement of this aim is expensive and manifold. Thus IGES processors are not only tested by the IGES implementors but also by CAD/CAM users as well as by independent working groups and institutions. In the U.S. basic work in the area of testing and validation was done by the IGES Test, Evaluation and Support (T, E & S) Committee and Booz, Allen & Hamilton Inc. In Germany the Working Group 20 (AG 20) of the CEFE (CAD/CAM-Entwicklungsgesellschaft) and the RPK (Institut für Rechneranwendung in Planung und Konstruktion) are working on these problems.

In these groups a lot of experience has been amassed concerning the problems arising and possible solutions in the field of processor testing. Based on this experience, the methods and tools actually used for the testing and validation of IGES pre- and postprocessors will be discussed in detail in the following sections. Additionally, some new aspects and approches with respect to systematic and overall testing and validation will be shown. First of all a short overview of the basic concepts of IGES is given.

5.3.2 Basic IGES Concepts

The Initial Graphics Exchange Specification was developed at the end of 1979 and first published as Version 1.0 in January 1980. This version became part of the ANSI Y14.26M standard [3]. Among the IGES committee Version 1.0 was reviewed and published in February 1983 as Version 2.0 [4].

The development of IGES was centred around the possibilities of CAD/CAM systems, which were developed in the mid seventies in the U.S. Therefore, withing IGES the exchange of product definition data is mainly performed on the basis of drawings, wireframe and simple surface models.

The basic information unit in IGES is the entity. In IGES all product definition data are expressed as a list of predefined entities, which can be logically related to each other. Therefore in Version 1.0 37 different entity types with partly distinct subforms were defined in the IGES-Specification. (In Version 2.0 this was raised to 46.) For every entity-/subformtype a prefixed set of defining parameters is given.

The available entities can be subdivided into three categories:

- geometry entities: for the description of the shape of a product (e.g. point, line, arc, plane, ruled surface)

- annotation entities: for the description of dimensions and technological informations of a product within a drawing (e.g. angular dimension, general label, centerline)
- structure entities: for the description of logical relationships within a product definition (e.g. associativity, property, view, subfigure, MACRO instance).

For the physical exchange of data between different systems an IGES file is used. An IGES file is written on 80 column records, using the ASCII character set. The 80 character records were chosen as being a universal medium for the transfer of information between different computer systems. In Version 2.0 an alternative binary format was defined but never implemented.

An IGES file is logically seperated into five sections:

- START SECTION: provides a man-readable prologue to the file
- GLOBAL SECTION: contains information describing the pre-processor and information for the post-processor (e.g. date, units, names, number of bits)
- DIRECTORY ENTRY SECTION: contains all cntitics and thcir cntity-independent information (e.g. level, line font, view) in a fixed format
- PARAMETER DATA SECTION: contains for all entities the entity-dependent information (e.g. coordinates, radius, pointer) in a free format
- TERMINATE SECTION: indictates the end of an IGES file and contains the sum of records for each section.

Each record is marked with a unique letter which identifies the section to which it belongs. Additionally a sequence number indicates the position of a record within a section. These sequence numbers are not only used for the ordering of record entries but also for the addressing of entities. Thus the values of pointer

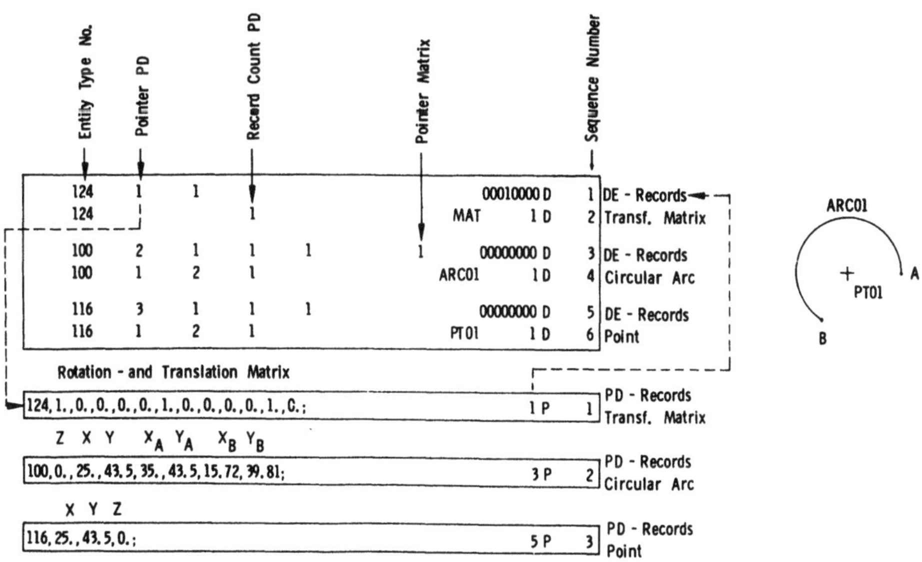

Fig. 5.3.2. DE- and PD-Entries in IGES for a simple example

parameters of an entity are dependent on the physical position of related entities within the file.

All product definition data are stored in the DIRECTORY ENTRY (DE) and PARAMETER DATA (PD) SECTION. For each entity there are two DE-Entries and at least one PD-Entry necessary (see example in Fig. 5.3.2). Because of the fixed DE- and record formats IGES files are very storage intensive. Another problem often mentioned is the strong physical pointer structure within an IGES file [4].

5.3.3 General Test Criteria

The application of IGES pre- and postprocessors in industry has shown, that the exchange of product definition data via IGES is possible and useful. However, problems often appear in conjunction with the data exchange like loss of information, incompatible entities or wrong data.

In order to develop and execute tests of IGES processors it is first necessary to discover the basic problem, which may arise in using IGES. Together with practical experience of the application of IGES processors this leads to a set of important test criteria. In the following sections problems and test criteria will be explained in more detail.

5.3.3.1 Entity Set

In todays IGES pre- and postprocessors only subsets of the whole entity set of IGES have so far been implemented [5]. Even if the continual development of processors is taken into account it is expected that in future too only subsets of the IGES entities will be supported. The supported entity set is determined by the range of processible product definition data in the CAD/CAM system. In particular some geometric entities (e.g. rational B-Spline) or application-oriented entities (e.g. FEM, Electric) are of limited use. The supported entity set within the IGES processors of a test system is therefore one of the main important criteria in practical IGES testing.

Entity sets can be determined either in terms of the IGES specification (specification-oriented) or in terms of a desired CAD/CAM application (application-oriented). In the first case the complete entity set of IGES is used as a reference, in the second case only those entities are considered which are neccessary for a desired application. Beneath predefined entities IGES also allows the use of user-defined entities. The supported user-defined entities must also be taken into consideration.

For efficient and comparable testing different test levels should be defined. Specification-oriented levels could be defined by functional sets of entities or information in IGES (e.g. 2D-wireframes, dimensions, DE-attributes, associativities); application-oriented levels by special applications or products (e.g. Autofact-V-part, sheet metal part, FEM-model).

5.3.3.2 Exchangeability

The processing of IGES entities in one CAD/CAM system does not guarantee that all the supported entities can be completely and correctly exchanged with other CAD/CAM system. The first restriction is caused by different supported entity sets within the CAD/CAM systems. The exchange of entities between two systems is therefore limited to the common set of supported IGES entities.

Another restriction of exchangeable entities results from errors in the communicating processors, so that even common supported IGES entities can not be interpreted, or are wrongly interpreted. These errors often result from different entity mappings (see Section 5.3.3.3) or from wrong or different interpretations of the IGES specification.

In practice not only the exchangeability of entities between two test systems is important, but also the exchangeability within a chain, ring or network of CAD/CAM systems.

5.3.3.3 Functionality

CAD/CAM systems often differ fundamentally in the selection, definition and storing of product definition data. Even for commonly used entities in the CAD/CAM systems, like wireframe geometry, different definitions are possible.

In Fig. 5.3.3 seven partly equivalent definitions for the entity type circular arc are shown. This set of definitions could be further expanded by consideration of constructive definitions e.g. as intersection of surfaces. The choice of a certain entity definition within a CAD/CAM system depends on the underlying model philosophy and the desired application functions.

In the IGES specification for every entity-/subform type there exists one fixed definition. In many cases therefore it is neccessary to map the CAD internal entity

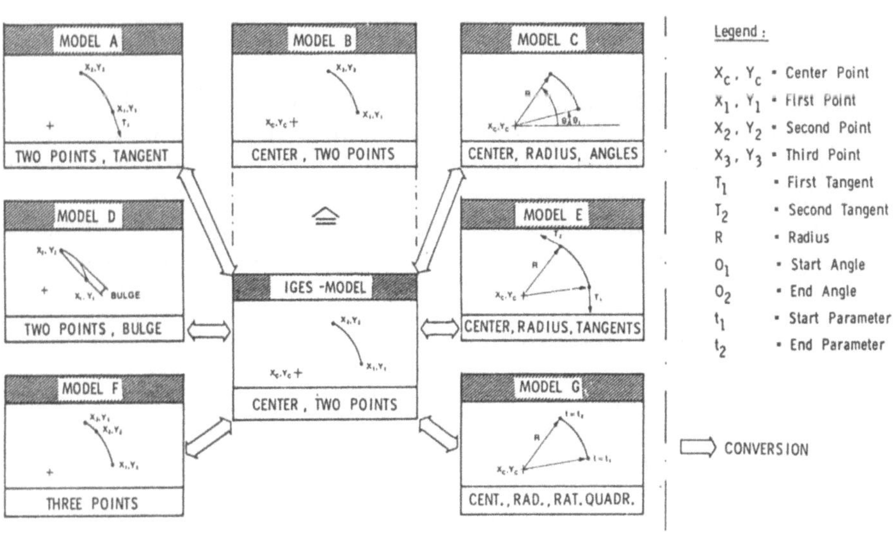

Fig. 5.3.3. Different definitions of a circular arc

definition on one or more IGES entity definitions or vice versa. The performance of entity mappings is one of the main problems during processor development.

In principle one can distinguish between the following kinds of mapping:

- 1:1 mapping: one entity is mapped on an identical or equivalent entity
- 1:N mapping: one entity is mapped on several entities
- N:1 mapping: several entities are mapped on one entity
- Approximation: one entity is approximated by one or several entities
- O-mapping: no entity mapping is possible

The mapping of entities often leads to a loss of information and therefore to a reduction of functionality. In many cases only 1:1 mappings preserve the full functionality.

When testing IGES processors it must first be checked, which entities can be exchanged without any loss of functionality. For the remainder the degree of loss of functionality has to be determined.

5.3.3.4 Graphical Representation

The IGES interface is strongly centred on the exchange of drawings. For this reason many IGES entities and parameters refer to the graphical representation of product definition data (e.g. drawing entity, annotation entities, DE-parameter).

Drawings are still important for the description of products in industry. Therefore the correctness of graphical representations of exchanged data is often used as an independent criterion during IGES processor testing. This criterion is especially applicable if modifications of the graphical representation are not required, so that full functionality of the represented entities is not absolutely necessary.

5.3.3.5 Accuracy

An IGES file is a simple text file. All numerical data which are usually stored in binary format within the CAD/CAM systems have to be converted for the data exchange into a decimal number representation. Within this conversion a slight loss of accuracy is possible.

Greater loss of accuracy sometimes arises from rounding errors during the mapping of entities. These errors can in high risk cases lead to a complete misin-

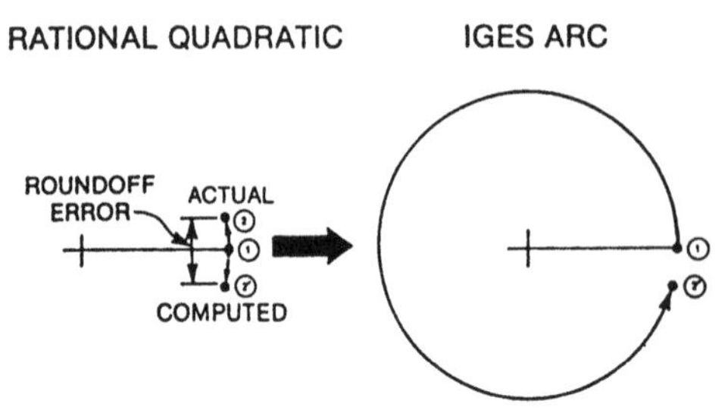

Fig. 5.3.4. Catastrophic rounding error (source [6])

terpretation of entities. An often used example is shown in Fig. 5.3.4 where a short arc is changed into a nearly full circle because of rounding errors.

Because of the requirement that all data have to be correct after the data exchange, the determination of the accuracy and numerical stability for all IGES entities is of great importance.

5.3.3.6 Syntactical Correctness

The medium for data exchange is the IGES file. All logical data have to be mapped onto the physical structures and data formats of the file. For successful processing and interpreting of generated IGES entities the IGES file must at least be syntactically correct. Experience has shown that exchange problems encountered were often based on syntax errors. Especially in the case of errors the syntactical correctness of generated IGES files must be validated.

5.3.3.7 Software Quality

The criterion of software quality can be considered as a separate part of processor testing. The IGES specification itself gives no direction for the implementation of IGES, so that processor implementors have full freedom in the design of their processors.

With respect to software quality some of the following criteria are usually taken into account:

- control of entity mappings by the user
- correction of fatal error
- complete syntax check by the postprocessor
- messages about processed and unprocessed entities
- detailed error messages
- modularity and expansibility of the processors
- adequate performance
- stability of the processors etc.

Criteria for software quality will not be considered in the following.

5.3.4 Test of IGES Processors

Assessment in accordance with the established criteria requires appropriate tests. According to the results desired the following test methods and test data are usually applied or discussed.

5.3.4.1 Test Methods

For testing IGES processors the test methods shown in Fig. 5.3.5 can in principle be distinguished:

The easiest method is the cycle-test. In this method the generation of test data, the conversion into IGES format as well as the reconversion into CAD/CAM

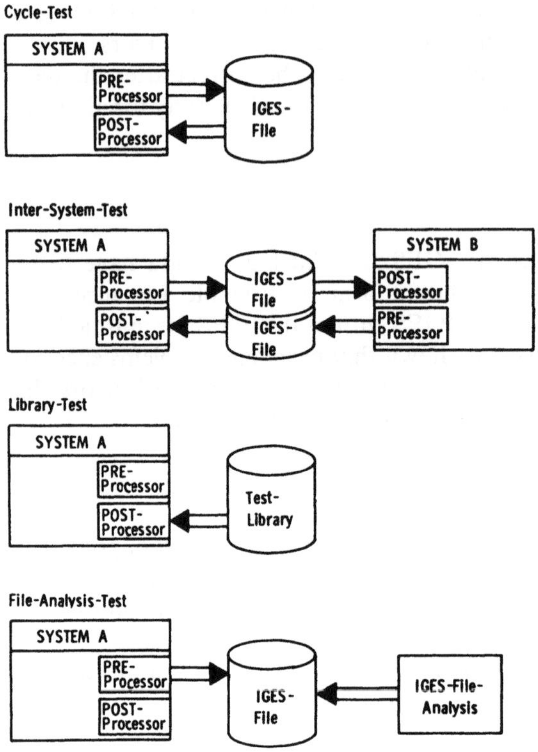

Fig. 5.3.5. Test methods for IGES processors

data base is performed on the same CAD/CAM test system. The advantage of simplicity is offset by the fact that if an error occurs during the data exchange it could be influenced by either the preprocessor or the postprocessor. A decision about the error location is not possible. Another problem consists in the possibility that errors in the preprocessor could be compensated by analogous errors in the postprocessor. Despite these problems this test method is very useful for a fast and explicit investigation of the entity set of a test system.

In the case of the inter-system-tests test data is exchanged between two or more different systems; this means that a real data exchange is performed. Thus this test method is suitable for a fast examination of the exchangeability of entities between communicating test systems. However, the problem of error location also exists with this test method. This problem can be handled if one of the systems is a so-called "jury system". For a jury system the IGES processors must be ascertained to be correct for the applied test data in the inter-system-test.

The library-test concentrates on an explicit test of IGES postprocessors. In this method proofed IGES files are read into the test system. Then the results of the postprocessor are validated. This test method is used mainly in conjunction with the IGES-Test-Library Version 1.3 (see Sect. 5.3.4.2). The basic problem with this test method lies in the guarantee that the IGES files used are correct.

A possible variation of this test method aims at the flexibility of the IGES postprocessor in the case of errors. Therefore errors are inserted in the IGES file on purpose to analyse the reaction of the postprocessor.

The opposite of the library-test is the file-analysis-test. Here an IGES file is created from test data in the test system. This file is then analysed manually or by special programs. This method aims to constitute an explicit test of IGES preprocessors. The problem with this method also lies in the analysis of the IGES file.

To eliminate errors during testing the described test methods are often used in parallel or in combination. In the study of Booz, Allen & Hamilton [5] for example three test methods were used to test IGES preprocessors.

5.3.4.2 IGES Test Library

Within the IGES committee T, E & S (Test, Evaluation and Support) the IGES Test Library Version 1.3 [7] was developed. This library is based on IGES Version 1.0 and consists of 36 test cases for simple and often used entities in IGES format on a tape. This test tape is read and processed by the IGES postprocessor. For the validation of the test results additional graphical representations of the entities are available.

Although a lot of time was spent in the development of this library only a small portion of the possible IGES entities are considered.

Table 5.3.1. Range and Status of tested entities in the IGES Test Library 1.3 (Source [8])

ENTITIES CLASS	total number	complete tested	incomplete tested	not tested
GEOMETRY-Entities	20	6	3	11
ANNOTATION-Entities	13	8	1	4
STRUCTURE-Entities	13	0	1	12

5.3.4.3 Test Data

The ability and validity of tests is directly influenced by the applied test data. Within a test it is therefore important to determine which criteria should be fulfilled by which test data.

Tests of IGES processors are mostly performed on the basis of so-called benchmarks. Benchmarks are existing and representative test data of selected products within CAD/CAM systems in the form of drawings, wireframe and/or surface models of the product.

The use of existing data has the advantage that there is no additional work necessary for the generation of test data. Another advantage lies in the fact that benchmarks are representative of real CAD/CAM applications. For this reason they are suitable as test data for application oriented inter-system and cycle-testing.

For the complete and systematic testing of IGES processors benchmarks are mostly insufficient because of redundant or missing test cases. Thus the development of special specification-oriented test data is discussed.

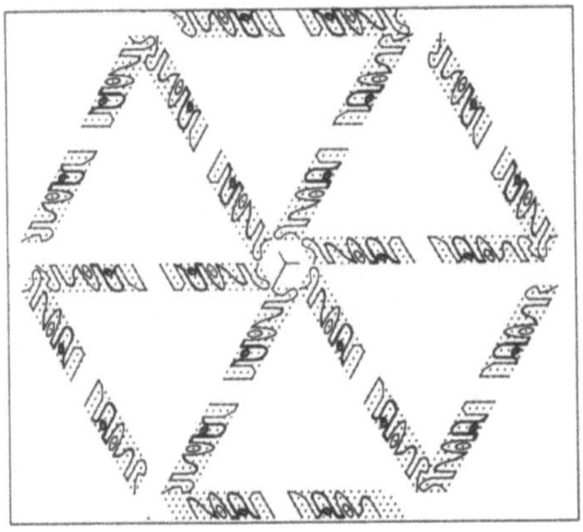

Fig. 5.3.6. Synthetic test cube

One possibility lies in defining test data in the form of independant entity tests. An entity test consists of a collection of different test cases for one entity type with a view to a complete test of functionality and accuracy. This means that within systematic parameter variations especially critical and abnormal test cases are taken into consideration. The IGES Test Library is, for example, based on the definition of entity tests.

Another approach which is applied more to the systematic and complete testing of logical sets of entities leads to the development of synthetic test parts. A synthetic test part results from a test oriented combination of different entity types. The combination can be made with a view to completeness, nonredundancy and/or structuring. Synthetic test parts are especially suitable for the examination of defined implementation levels or entity structures.

An example of a synthetic test part is the test cube shown in Fig. 5.3.6. This test part is used to verify the existence of the basic wireframe entities and the possibilities for their orientation in the model space.

5.3.5 Validation of Test Results

After the execution of tests it is necessary to validate the received test results. Depending on the test criteria and the test results available different validation methods are applicable.

5.3.5.1 Comparing Pictures

The validation of test results is generally based on a comparison of the graphical representation of the original and exchanged test data. Therefore a graphical representation of the test data is generated via drawing programs before as well as after the test. The comparison is especially easy if one plots the graphic output on transparent paper with different colours. The testresults can then be easily compared by laying one sheet on top of the other on a light table.

The disadvantage of this graphical validation results from the fact that the graphical representation or the interpretation of the graphical representation does not necessarily correspond with the content of the CAD/CAM database. One test showed, for example, that a correctly represented graphical annotation was built up of line entities although IGES offers special annotation entities for this purpose. This shows that the functionality of entities as well as the logical relationships between entities (e.g. grouping) can not be checked by comparison of pictures. Because of the inaccuracy of graphical representations it is also difficult to recognize small differences in numerical data (e.g. equality of coordinates).

5.3.5.2 Comparing Data Bases

The original as well as the exchanged data are stored in the CAD/CAM databases of the test systems. The equivalence of the content of these databases could therefore be checked by special functions of the database managers of the CAD/CAM system.

However, because of the great differences in the product models and database managers of CAD/CAM systems the comparison of two distinct databases is nearly impossible.

5.3.5.3 Comparing Operations

The contents of databases of distinct CAD/CAM systems and hence the functionality of exchanged entities in particular can be compared indirectly via the results of CAD/CAM operations. The test data of the sending as well as receiving system are used as input for identical operations. To allow a graphical comparison those operations are selected which produce different graphical outputs or error messages in the case of wrong data. These are in particular operations for the modification or joining of entities like stretch, trim, delete, translate, intersect etc.

The comparison of operations is especially useful for the validation of logical data (e.g. entity type), structured entities (e.g. views, drawings) and relationships. With the application of a stretch operation for example (see Fig. 5.3.7) the loss of an associativity between geometry and annotation can easily be detected. Operations are also useful in determining the accuracy of numerical data.

With the specification of fixed sequences of operations and suitable test parts it is possible to define extensive and standardized validation procedures.

5.3.5.4 Handchecking

Testing IGES processors also requires the analysis of IGES files. This can be done by checking the IGES files manually either against the IGES specification or against a correct IGES file.

In the first case all data in the IGES file are compared with the IGES specification at least in terms of their syntactical correctness. Because of the huge amount of data and the many pointers within an IGES file handchecking is expensive and faulty.

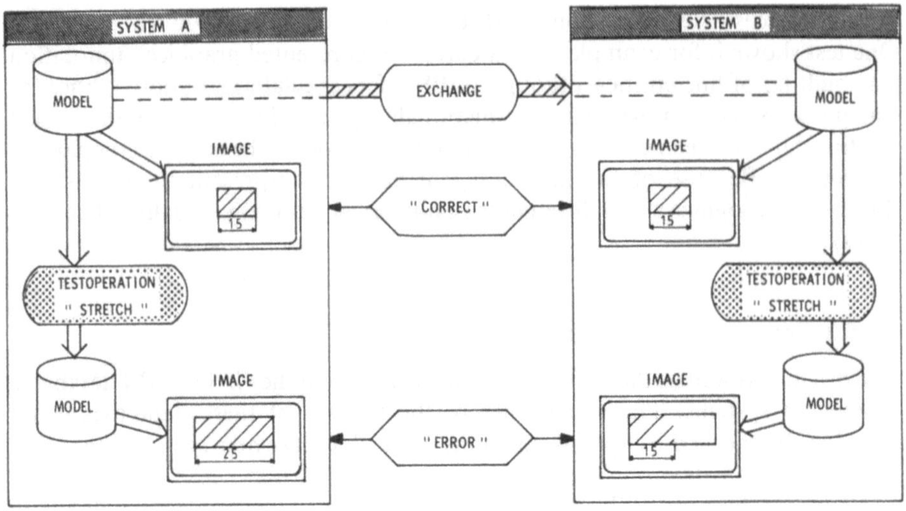

Fig. 5.3.7. Comparing operations

Additional problems arise in the case of the comparison of two files by handchecking. The ordering of entities within an IGES file is not fixed. Therefore a sequential record by record comparison of 'identical' IGES files is mostly not possible. Furthermore entities are pointered by use of their sequence number (position in the section). This means that even identical entities differ in the value of pointers from one IGES file to another.

For this reasons handchecking is only used for special purposes (e.g. validation of selected entities) or in conjunction with other test and validation methods.

5.3.5.5 Software Tools

The analysis of IGES files is best done with the aid of special software tools [9]. Software tools can be applied system independently for the processing of IGES files for the purposes of:

- syntax checking
- sorting of entities
- comparison of files
- selection of entity sets etc.

The first experiences with implemented software tools have shown that they are useful and necessary for fast and economic validation of IGES files.

5.3.6 IGES File Analysis System

The IGES-File-Analysis-System (IFAS) is an example of a system-independent software tool. It was developed at the Institut für Rechneranwendung in Planung und Konstruktion (RPK). IFAS is intented to support:

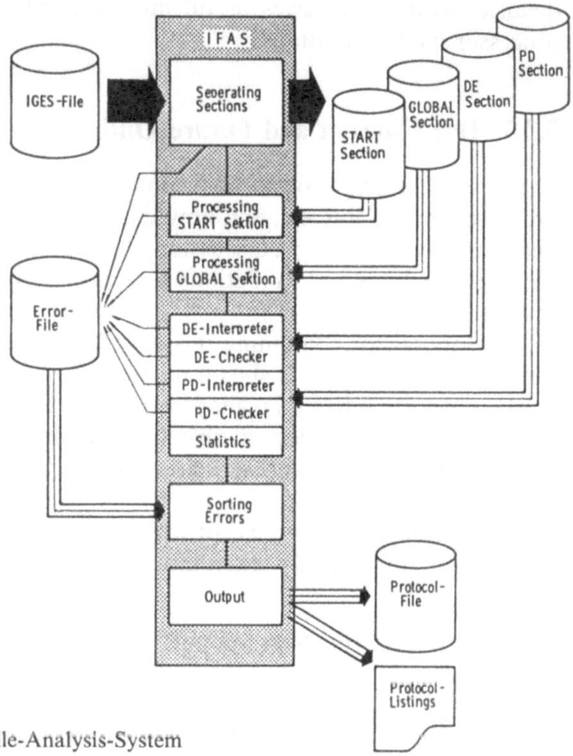

Fig. 5.3.8. Concept of the IGES-File-Analysis-System

- the syntactical analysis of an IGES file (i.e. file format, sections, data formats, physical pointers etc.),
- the semantic analysis of data within an IGES file (i.e. data contents, logical pointer) and
- the output of a detailed error listing and a statistical record of the entities in the IGES file.

The concept of IFAS is shown in Fig. 5.3.8.

The IGES file is sequentially read into IFAS and stored in direct access files in order to allow faster processing. During this process the correctness of the file and sections are validated. Subsequently the syntactic and semantic analysis of the single entities is carried out. On discovery of an error the error type and the error location is stored. This information is used after the analysis to generate a detailed error listing. In parallel to the error analysis a statistical record of the entities within the file is also created.

This software tool is very useful for various purposes. It primarily allows thc fast examination of file-analysis-tests but can also be used together with the other test methods. In the case of library-tests it supports the checking of developed test cases or synthetic test parts. During inter-system-testing it is used to determine the supported and exchanged entity set on the basis of the entity statistics. Finally the detailed error listing gives useful informations for necessary modifications in processor implementations.

5.3.7 Test Concept and Future Outlook

To assess the testing procedures it should be clear which information about IGES processors are of interest, and how this information can be received completely and correctly. Therefore a discussion of a suitable choice and combination of test data, test methods and validations is necessary. This leads to the definition of an overall test concept.

A proposal for combining the described methods to yield a structured and systematic test concept is shown in Fig. 5.3.9.

This concept is based on a separation into four distinct test levels. These levels are based on classes of logical objects within an IGES file. For every level the test criteria, test data, test and validation methods which should be applied are described.

If one compares this concept with the practical test assessment only parts of the concept are generally taken into consideration. For this several reasons can be mentioned:

- todays IGES processors support only a limited set of entities, so that some entities need not to be tested in detail (e.g. structured entities, application entities),
- the necessary resources and tools for the described methods are not fully developed (e.g. libraries, synthetic parts, software tools, validation procedures),

TEST LEVEL	OBJECTS	CRITERIA	TEST DATA	TEST METHOD	VALIDATION
FILE LEVEL	FILE - RECORD AND DATATYPES	- SYNTACTICAL CORRECTNESS	- BENCHMARKS - FILES WITH SYNTAX ERRORS	- FILE ANALYSIS - LIBRARY TEST	- SYNTAX CHECKER - HANDCHECKING - ERRORCODES OF POST - PROCESSOR
ENTITY LEVEL	INDEPENDANT BASIC AND COMPLEX ENTITIES	- ENTITY SET - GRAPH. REPRES. - FUNCTIONALITY - ACCURANCY	- IGES - TEST - LIBRARY - DIFFERENT TEST - CASES OF ENTITIES - SPECIAL HIGH - RISK - TESTCASES	- CYCLE TEST - LIBRARY TEST - FILE ANALYSIS	- COMPARING PICTURES - COMPARING FILES
STRUCTURE LEVEL	ASSOCIATIVITIES AND STRUCTURES OF ENTITIES	- ENTITY SET - GRAPH. REPRES. - EXCHANGEABILITY - USER - DEFINED STRUCTURES	- SYNTETIC TEST PARTS - DIFFERENT TEST - CASES FOR STRUCTURES	- LIBRARY TEST - FILE ANALYSIS - INTER - SYSTEM TEST	- COMPARING FILES - COMPARING OPERATIONS
APPLICATION LEVEL	APPLICATION - ORIENTED ENTITY SETS	- ENTITY SET - GRAPH. REPRES. - EXCHANGEABILITY - USER - DEFINED ENTITIES	- BENCHMARKS FOR SPECIFIC APPLICATIONS	- INTER - SYSTEM TEST	- COMPARING PICTURES - COMPARING OPERATIONS

Fig. 5.3.9. Test concept

- the examination of tests is time-consuming and expensive and
- the IGES specification is inexact so that the distinction between correct and incorrect data is often very critical.

However, the application and development of IGES processors is still increasing. Permanent tests for the determination of the capabilities of supplied IGES processors are therefore required. When considering the solution of the above mentioned problems new strategies for the complete and economic testing of IGES processors have to be considered.

First of all, testing IGES processors should be more systematized. The whole processor test should be logically structured in separate test areas, test levels and test cases. Beginning with global tests, e.g. for all entities, the test should become more and more detailed in considering special entities or detected errors. Additionally, subsequent tests of new processor versions should be limited to those test areas/levels which previously lead to significant problems.

Secondly the assessment of test should be more centralized. This means that tests should be examined by established test bodies. This would yield the following advantages:

- all IGES processors are tested in the same way,
- IGES processors (actual versions) are only tested once,
- frequent usage allows the development of expensive test tools,
- the costs of the development and assessment of tests could be borne by the sale of test results.

Altogether, because of the great difficulties and the costs that arise with the testing and validation of IGES processors an international and independent certification body is required.

5.3.8 References

1. Schuster R, Trippner D: Anforderungen an eine Schnittstelle zur Übertragung produktdefinierender Daten zwischen verschiedenen CAD/CAM-Systemen. In: Fachgespräche auf der 14. GI-Jahrestagung, vol 89. Springer, Berlin Heidelberg New York (1984)
2. ANSI: Digital Representation of Product Definition Data (Y14.26M) (1981)
3. NBS: Initial Graphics Exchange Specification Version 2.0 (NSIR 82-2631) (1983)
4. DIN IGES Review and Proposed Extensions. DIN-Dokument NAM 96.4/2-84 (1984)
5. Cotter SL, Gutmann KA, Stoehr AA: Information Transfer between Computer-Aided Design Systems: An Assessment of IGES. Fachgespräche auf der 14. GI-Jahrestagung, vol 89. Springer, Berlin Heidelberg New York Tokyo (1984)
6. Lewis JW: Specifiying and Verifying IGES Processors. General Electric, USA (1981)
7. IGES Test, Evaluate and Support Committee Initial Graphics Exchange Specification, Test Library Version 1.3 (1983)
8. Gibbons AJ: Initial Graphics Exchange Specification (IGES) Update: Prospects for an international Standard Corporate Systems Integration, Report 84-DW401-R1 (1984)
9. Grabowski H, Glatz R: Werkzeuge zum Test und zur Verifikation systemneutraler Produktdefinitionsdaten. In: Fachgespräche auf der 14. GI-Jahrestagung, vol 89. Springer, Berlin Heidelberg New York (1984)

Chapter 6

Outlook

6.1 Progress in the Development of CAD/CAM Interfaces for Transfer of Product Definition Data

R. Schuster

6.1.1 Transfer of Product Definition Data

6.1.1.1 The Necessity for Transfer of Product Definition Data

CAD/CAM systems are currently used in virtually all sectors of technical product development. This has improved the product's quality, lowered its price and shortended the development time.

A considerable increase in productivity results from the integrated use of CAD/CAM if chaining of design steps allows multiple access to design data once it has been created. A prerequisite for an integrated design and production process is, however, the exchange of product definition data in the information flow between:

- different technical sectors of design (bodywork design, engine design),
- design, production preparation, and production,
- manufacturers and suppliers or branch factories,
- time-sequential development of models,
- different CAD/CAM systems, and
- different versions of CAD/CAM system ("Versionitis").

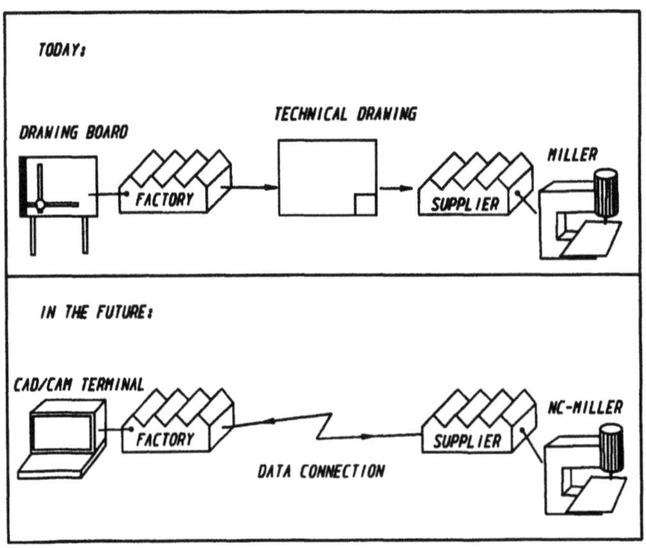

Fig. 6.1.1. Change in technical communication

Today, the conventional exchange of product data primarily makes use of technical drawings, parts lists and models. The time and costs involved in handling these conventional data media make the use of EDP aids necessary for more efficient transfer and more rapid access (Fig. 6.1.1.).

The advantages expected from product data exchanged using EDP facilities can be summarized as follows:

- reduction of throughput times,
- minimization of errors,
- clarity due to improved quality,
- improved access to information,
- reduction of repetitive work,
- reduction of administrative costs,
- availability of standardized and purchased parts.

6.1.1.2 Product Definition Data as an Internal Computer Model

Product definition data are those data which contain information about an object – or parts of an object – and which permit its subsequent manufacture on the basis of an internal computer model (Fig. 6.1.2):

- *Representation data* contain information indicating how an object is to be represented graphically, i.e. colour, line thickness, line type, or angle at which a model is viewed.
- *Geometrical data* determine the shape and dimensions of a product model.

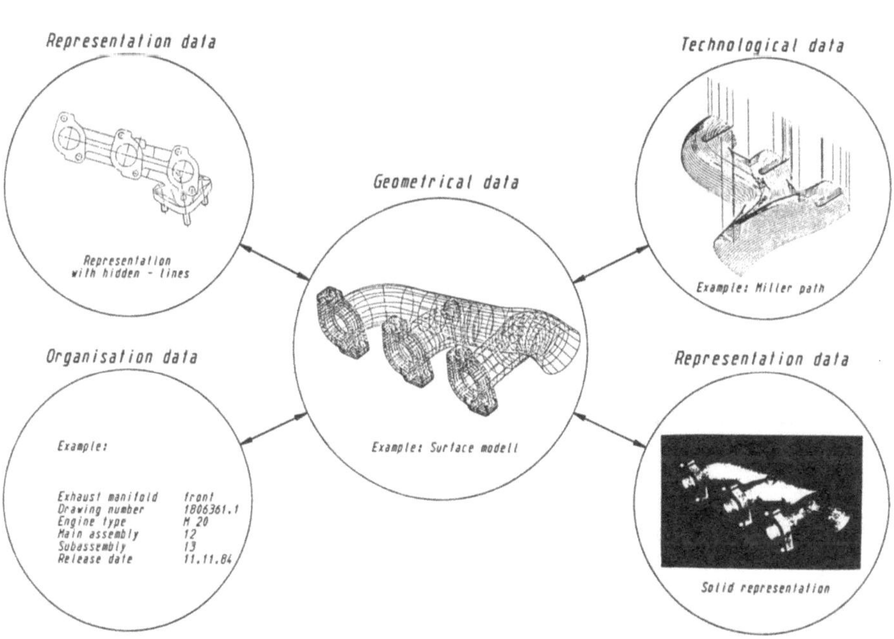

Fig. 6.1.2. Different internal computer models based on Product definition data

Model	Product data	Application excample	Interfaces
Product-model	Technological, organizational, geometrical, representation data -Parts list -Assembly -Material data -Tolerances - . - .		?
Geometrical model	Geometrical and representation data -Circles -Ellipses -Regular polygons - . - .	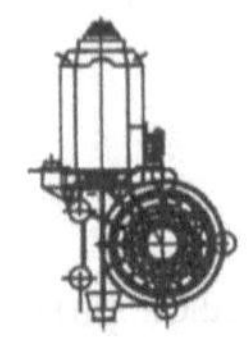	IGES VDAFS
Represen-tation data	Representation data -Line type -Line thickness -Color - . - .	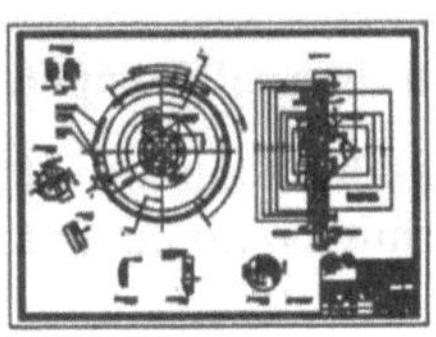	GKS

Fig. 6.1.3. Levels of product definition data

- *Organizational data* are necessary in order to identify an object or parts of an object during the production process and to permit assignment of planning data to the object. These include data of the master parts record such as part number, name, release status or name of person who created the data.
- *Technological data* contain information used to specify the object more accurately, or to permit its further use within the overall production process. Typical data are material data, production data, or calculation information.

The description of an internal computer model consists of a subset of all product definition data, the particular subset being a function of the emphasis of the application and the performance range of the CAD/CAM system.

Regardless of the application sector, internal computer models can be divided into three levels (Fig. 6.1.3):

- a product model, consisting of technological, organizational, geometrical, and representational data,
- a geometrical model consisting of geometrical and representational data,
- a representational model consisting solely of representational data.

6.1.1.3 Principle of Operation and Status of Implementation of CAD/CAM Interfaces

The CAD/CAM systems currently available on the market differ not only in their different application aims and performance levels, but also in data structures and data formats on which each internal "CAD/CAM model" is based. Differences in the data format, resulting from the use of different computer types or operating systems, determine the day-to-day operations. Further problems result from the different quantities of data elements (entities) which are defined in each CAD/CAM system. Only entities which can be handled in both systems can be interchanged between two CAD/CAM systems without further manipulation. Until now, there have been two common solutions to the problem of transferring data from system A to system B:

- To extract and convert data from system A by means of a processor such that they can be processed in system B. The functional scope and the principle of operation of the processor is matched to system A and system B. Two processors are required for transfer of data in both directions. However, this method has the major disadvantage that connections between N different systems require 2 * (N − 1) additional processors for each further connection to another system. This results in high costs for program creation and maintenance (Fig. 6.1.4).
- Data from one internal representation in a CAD/CAM system are not converted directly into another representation, but first into a common, system-independent data format. Conversion into any other format is done in two steps. This method requires a standardized data interface which is the basis for all processing operations. Only two further processors are required for each new connection between N different systems (Fig. 6.1.5).

With the exception of special applications, the exchange of data via a standardized interface is certainly the only economical and sensible alternative in the long run. Various national and international committees are working on solutions.

The first standardized interface in this sector was defined in 1981 in the USA with ANSI standard Y14.26M. A major component of this standard is IGES Version 1.0 (Initial Graphics Exchange Specification), which was developed by the NBS (National Bureau of Standards) (Fig. 6.1.6).

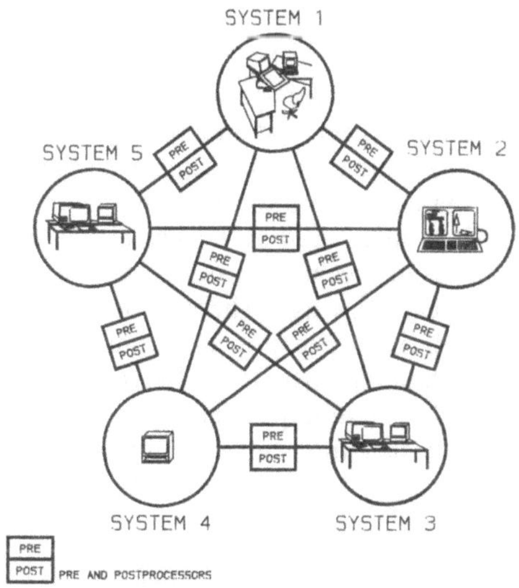

Fig. 6.1.4. Direct system-to-system transfer

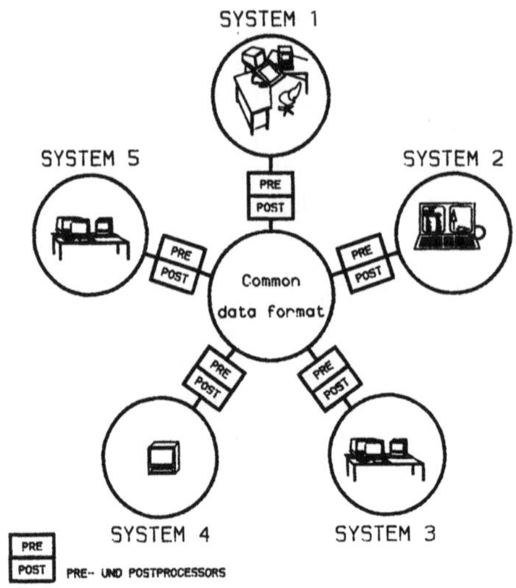

Fig. 6.1.5. System-to-system transfer via common data format

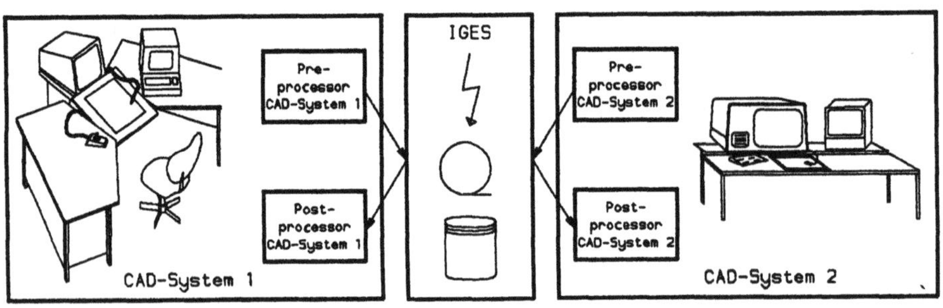

Fig. 6.1.6. Principle of data exchange via IGES

IGES is based mainly on the characteristics of CAD/CAM systems which have been developed and sold by American vendors since the 1970's. The initiative for standardization came from the American Department of Defence in order to create a method for handling the transfer of data between the large number of CAD systems used in the aircraft industry. The emphasis of the application was placed on mechanical design and was restricted primarily to the exchange of technical drawings. These options characterize the basic concept of IGES, although the application spectrum has been increased in subsequent versions. The basic data unit in an IGES file is the entity. There are 34 different entity types with 41 different subtypes defined in the standard (IGES VERSION 1.0). IGES divides basic entities into the three entity classes:

- geometry entities,
- annotation entities,
- structure entities.

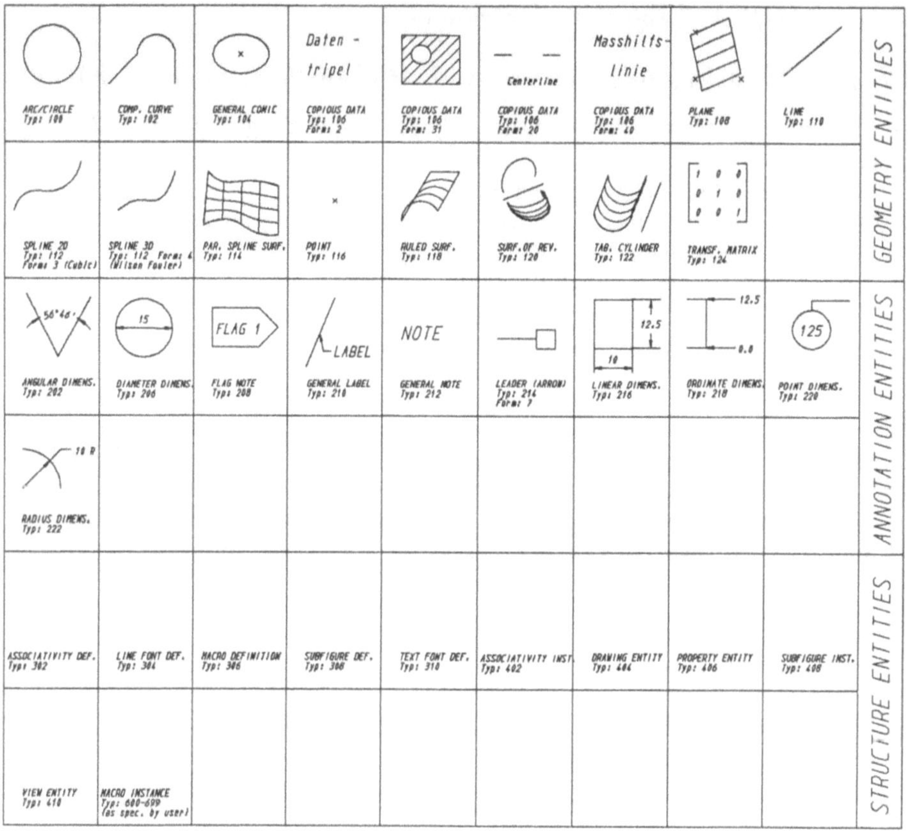

Fig. 6.1.7. IGES entities (version 1.0)

However, this assignment to classes was not strictly followed in the definition of the elements (Fig. 6.1.7).

An IGES file consists of 5 sections:

- The START SECTION contains a readable text which can be transferred together with the model.
- The GLOBAL SECTION contains information for the postprocessor. This section defines, for example, which delimiters are used and how many bits are used for the representation of a real number.
- The DIRECTORY ENTRY SECTION contains two records in fixed format for each entity; these contain data which are independant of the element type, such as version identification, attributes, or pointers.
- The PARAMETER DATA SECTION contains all parameters of each entity in free format.
- The TERMINATE SECTION consists of one record which contains the number of records of each section.

6.1.2 CAD/CAM Interface Development

The following statements can be made with respect to the performance of IGES:

- The exchange format can be used only for a specific group of CAD/CAM systems
- There is no subset or level structure
- Definitions are not precise and element classes are intermixed
- There is no recognizable element hierarchy
- There is no concept for possible future extentions
- There are no clear guidelines for implementation
- The data formats are complex and complicated.

Because of these shortcomings, further interfaces have been defined, or the definition of such interfaces started, on the basis of the IGES development. An example here is the VDA surface interface, which became the German standard DIN 66301; this is the result of cooperation between the German Car Manufactures Association (Verband der Automobilindustrie, VDA) and the DIN working committee DIN NAM-96.4. VDAFS handles special applications in the sector of free form geometry. The following elements are defined in the VDAFS:

- Point
- Point sequence
- Point-vector sequence
- Curve (polynominal of any order)
- Surface (bipolynominal of any order).

In addition to pure geometric data, comments in the transfer file can be assigned and transferred. Additionally, geometrical elements can be combined into groups.

6.1.2.1 Requirements for a CAD/CAM interface from the Application Viewpoint

The different performance capabilities and application aims of the various CAD/CAM systems define the characteristics of a transfer interface. Problems arise, for example, when trying to receive volume elements in a system which is designed for the creation of two-dimensional drawings.

For this reason, requirements must be specified for the definition of an interface.

- Each CAD/CAM system should be able to create and receive all data of its elements in the transfer format to be defined.
- The data in the transfer file must be prepared so that each system can extract maximum information. Example: If, in the transmitting CAD system A, the line L1 is defined as the intersection between the planes E1 and E2, then CAD system B, which does not have the intersection function, should still be capable of receiving line L1 with its starting point P1 and end point P2 (Fig. 6.1.8).
- The user must be able to control processing during generation or interpretation of transferred data.

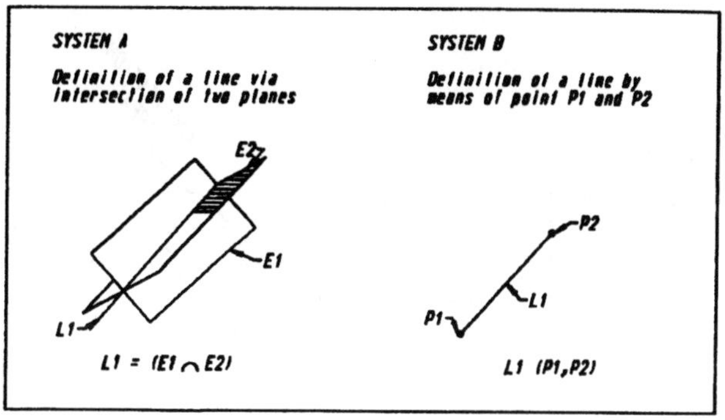

Fig. 6.1.8. Example of line data transfer

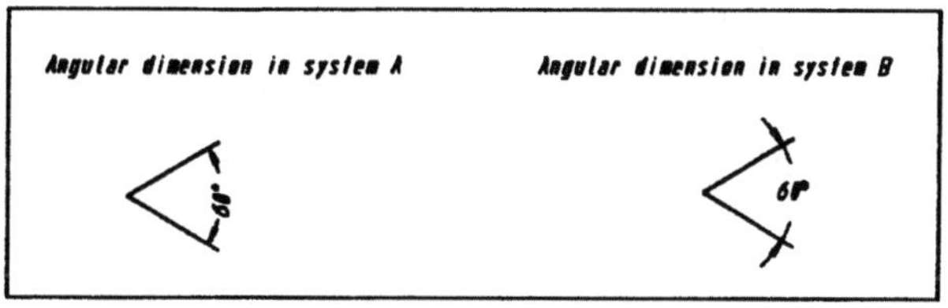

Fig. 6.1.9. Example of annotation data transfer

Example: (Fig. 6.1.9). During transfer of angular dimensions, either the functionality of the dimensions or only the representation of the dimensions may be more important, depending on the requirements. If the angular dimensions created in system A (DIN standard) are to be transferred via an exchange format to system B (ANSI standard), then the user should be able to select how the dimensions are to be stored in system B. If the user selects functionality, then he can continue to handle the dimensions as angular dimensions, although the representation no longer complies with the DIN standard. If he decides to select standard representation then the system loses the semantic of the angular dimensions.

- It is necessary to ensure that the user receives specific information from the processor indicating not only the data contents, but also possible errors in the transfer file.
- When using processors which are available today, the non-specified scope of performance of the interface leads to problems. In practical applications, the performance of pre- and postprocessors of CAD/CAM software manufacturers deviates greatly from the standard, as only a small subset of the elements defined in the standard is normally covered.

In order to avoid this problem, the possible reduction must be taken into account during definition of the interface. A level structure similar to that defined in the GKS again appears advisable.

The principle of the level concept would consist in relating entities as defined in the standard to certain application areas, product life cycle phases, model types and degree richnesses, thereby defining performance levels (Fig. 6.1.10).

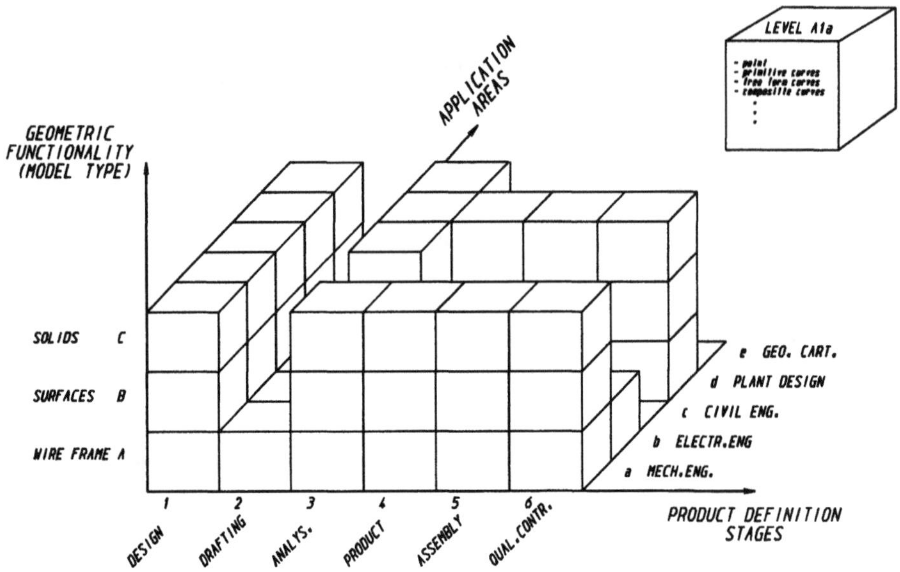

Fig. 6.1.10. Level concept for product definition data

6.1.2.2 General Requirements for a CAD/CAM Interface Concept

A basic prerequisite for successful implementation of processors is a clear, structured concept of the interface and a precise formal description of the interface. In addition, an expansion strategy should already be defined during the creation of the concept in order to permit technical innovations to be included in the interface without the necessity of constantly modifying existing definitions. The points to be taken into account during interface definition can be summarized as follows:

- Selection of elements which are free from redundancy,
- clear element classification,
- unambiguous conversion algorithms,
- file structure,
- formal description as a basis,
- implementation, verification, and documentation.

Element selection, element classification and creation of the conversion algorithm must be based on the CAD/CAM systems which are in common use today and also on foreseeable CAD/CAM developments.

The concept of the standard itself must be based on a principle, which allows the product definition data to be viewed from different viewpoints in the process hierarchy.

Thereby three different layers (stages) can be recognized (Fig. 6.1.11).

- The application-oriented layer
- the basic logical layer and
- the physical layer.

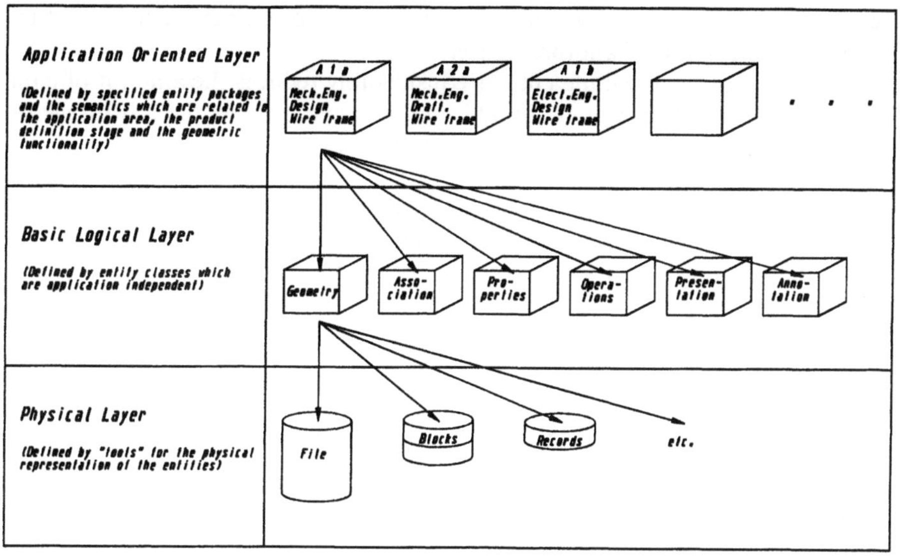

Fig. 6.1.11. Layer concept

Application-Oriented Layer

The viewpoint is application-dependent. In this layer entity packages are specified which define processor performance levels related to the application area, the product stage and the model type. The entities may therefore be independent or composite. All application-oriented entities must be mappable into entities of the basic locical layer.

Basic Logical Layer

The viewpoint is application-independent. In this layer entity classes are specified which consist of application independent entities.

An entity is, in this relationship, the smallest identifiable data unit in a transfer file. Due to the wide range of product data to be transferred, different entity types must be defined, whereby each entity type consists of a specified number and sequence of numerical or alphanumeric data.

Entity types can be divided into the following classes on the basis of standard criteria:

- The classes of independently descriptive entities
  - The class of *geometric elements* consists of entities of zero to three-dimensions which are described by purely metric values.
  - The class of *annotation elements* consists of entities such as text and graphical symbols required in the dimensioning, tolerancing, labelling and identifying of product models in drawing type documents. The annotation entity can be independent of or associated with others.
- The classes of entities which provide further information about the descriptive entities or which affect the descriptive entities:

- *Attribute entities* describe characteristics which do not belong to the actual basis information of another entity.
  Definition of the attribute entities considerably reduces the amount of data contained in other entities. In addition, this concept has the advantage of being flexible with respect to future expansions.
- *Structures/relations*
  This class contains entities which can establish relationships between entities in the form of an m:m relationship. Relation entities contain only the relationship identification and the pointers to other elements.
  Examples:
  - Construction of solid bodies from a hierarchy of basic geometrical elements
  - Attribute assignment
  - Assignment of operations
- *Representation entities* contain elements which clearly define the representation rules of other entities in a drawing.
  These include:
  - Arrangement of the drawing
  - Clipping
  - Perspectives
  - Sections
  - Explosion drawings
- *Operation entities* generate result data from the input data. The result of an operation on an entity is again an entity. A distinction can be made between the following operations:
  - Generating operations
  - Modifying operations.

The Physical Layer

The viewpoint is storage-structure, data base oriented in a logical sense. The basic concepts in this layer are

file, record, block, sub-block or the like

In order to minimize the software development effort for each system, system independent software modules such as

- CALL Interface,
- Approximation algorithms and
- Conversion methods

can be separately developed and implemented.

In particular, with the requirement that the data transfer and entity translation into the receiving system must be possible without extending the functional capabilities of the receiving system, system independent software must be developed which provides the function of transforming data stored at one functional level to a lower level, in case the receiving system does not support the original functional level of the data in the transfer file.

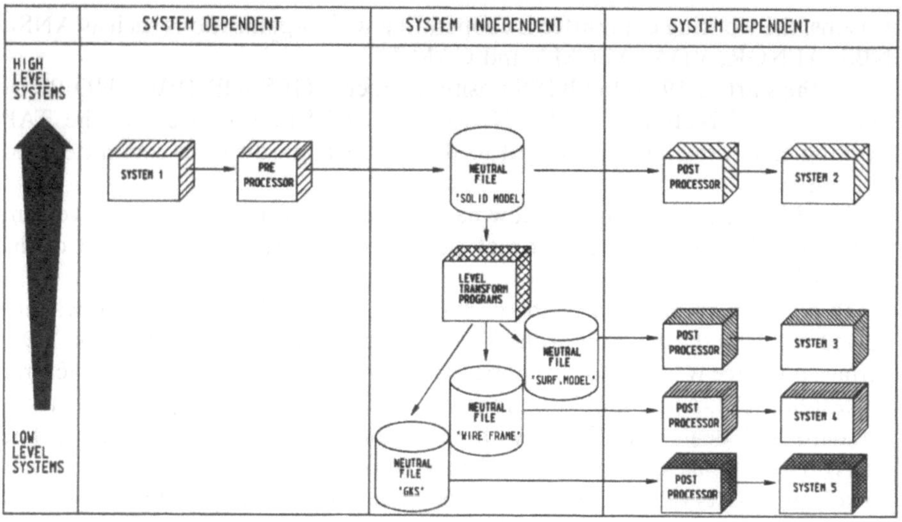

Fig. 6.1.12. Examples of the Level Concept for CAD/CAM data transfer

For that reason "Level Transform Programs" (Level Adapter) must be independently developed and made generally available. The functional capabilities must be defined by the standard. At the moment such a adaption appears between levels of different model type and perhaps entity richness.

For example representations can be reduced to lower levels in the following level hierarchy (Fig. 6.1.12):

- Volume model
- Surface model
- Wireframe model.

6.1.3 Status of Standartization of an Interface for Transfer of Product Definition Data in Germany

The DIN working committee DIN NAM 96.4, with the title "Transfer and archiving of product definition data" (TAP), has been working since 1983 on standardization of an interface for transfer of product data between CAD/CAM systems.

The work in the TAP working committee concentrated primarily on the analysis of existing standards in this sector and on examination of their utility as a German standard.

In addition to IGES, whose concept was the main emphasis of this analysis, the interface definitions ANSI Y.14.26M CHAPTER V, XBF, STRAWMAN, PDES, PDDI and SET were examined.

As a result of this analysis, it is possible to say that none of these standards are suitable as a German standard in their existing form without modification.

Since development of CAD/CAM can only be regarded from an international point of view, national solutions in this area should not be attempted. For these reasons, the working committee is cooperating with organizations such as ANSI, NBS, AFNOR, VDA, AECMA and CAM-I.

At the start of 1984, the IGES position paper "IGES REVIEW AND PROPOSED EXTENSIONS" (DIN NAM AA 96.4/2-84), produced by the TAP working committee, was presented to the NBS standardization committee and discussed.

The IGES position paper is now part of the basis for concrete improvement of IGES and also for the creation of guidelines for further development of the standard.

In addition to creation of these guidelines, the working committee was involved with standardization of the VDA surface interface (VDAFS). This VDA surface interface was created in cooperation with the German Car Manufacturer Association (VDA); it should be regarded as the first part of a comprehensive standard and deals specifically with the subject of free form geometry. The VDAFS, which has already been implemented by many CAD/CAM vendors, has already proved its value in practical applications and was adopted by the German Standards Institute under DIN 66301.

The TAP activities are presently centered on determining guidelines for specification of product definition data. These guidelines refer the definition of clearly structured and extensive CAD/CAM transfer to the following sets of tasks:

- Determining a basic model concept
  - model structuring
  - level and subset formation
  - element classification
  - element hierarchies
  - redundancy-free selection of elements
  - extensions and modification strategy
  - conversion algorithms
- Determining model contents to be transferred
  - Determining geometric contents
  - Determining technological and organisational contents
  - Compatibility with graphics standard
  - Element functionality (dimensioning, tolerances)
  - Element parametrization (norm and standard parts)
- Determining transfer format
  - logical and physical data file structure
  - logical and physical element structure
  - efficient memory modes
- Documentation and verification
  - formal description
  - implementation instructions
  - error protocol
  - test procedures

6.1.4 References

1. ANSI (American National Standards Institute): Digital Representation of Product Definition Data (Y14.26M) (September 1981)
2. Initial Graphics Exchange Specification (IGES): Version 2.0 (February 1983). U.S. Department of Commerce, National Bureau of Standards
3. VDAFS Format zum Austausch geometrischer Informationen; Normentwurf für DIN Norm 66301. DIN NAM 96.4/25-84 (Juli 1984)
4. SET Specifications Rev. 1.1 (Standard d'Echange et de Transfert); Aerospatiale Direction Technique (March 1984)
5. Anderl R, Glatz R, Nowacki H, Schuster R, Trippner D, Tröndle K: IGES Review and proposed Extensions. DIN NAM AA 96.4//Z-84
6. Glatz R, Schuster R, Trippner D: National Activity Report of the DIN working committee NAM 96.4 (TAP). DIN NAM 96.4-84 (August 1984)
7. DIN NAM/SC 96.4 – WG1-Sub-Group 1: Logical Definition and Classification of Entities DIN NAM 96.4/4–85
8. Schuster R, Trippner D: Anforderungen an eine Schnittstelle zur Übertragung produktdefinierender Daten zwischen verschiedenen CAD/CAM-Systemen. GI Jahrestagung, Braunschweig (1984)

Contributors

Jörg Bechlars
Zentraleinrichtung
für Datenverarbeitung
Freie Universität Berlin
D-1000 Berlin 33

Dr. N. Cullmann
GTS-GRAL
Alsfelder Strasse 7
D-6100 Darmstadt

Dipl.-Ing. Lothar Dannenberg
EDS Electronic Data Systems GmbH
Eisenstrasse 56
D-6090 Rüsselsheim

Friedrich Elsässer
EDS Electronic Data Systems GmbH
Eisenstrasse 56
D-6090 Rüsselsheim

Prof. Dr.-Ing. José Encarnação
Technische Hochschule Darmstadt
Institut für Informationsverwaltung
und Interaktive Systeme
Alexanderstrasse 24
D-6100 Darmstadt

Dr. Günter Enderle
Standard Elektrik Lorenz AG (SEL)
Lorenzstrasse 10
D-7000 Stuttgart 40

Dipl.-Inform. Rainer Glatz
Institut für Rechneranwendung in
Planung und Konstruktion
Universität Karlsruhe/TH
Kaiserstrasse 12
D-7500 Karlsruhe 1

Dr. Rupert Gnatz
Technische Universität München
Institut für Informatik
Postfach 20 24 20
D-8000 München 2

Prof. Dr. Hans Grabowski
Institut für Rechneranwendung in
Planung und Konstruktion
Universität Karlsruhe/TH
Kaiserstrasse 12
D-7500 Karlsruhe 1

D. Hopert
Control Data GmbH
Tiergartenstrasse 95
D-3000 Hannover 71

Dipl.-Inform. Wolfgang Hübner
Zentrum für Graphische
Datenverarbeitung (ZGDV)
Bleichstrasse 10–12
D-6100 Darmstadt

N. Kastner
S.E.P.P. GmbH
Lohmühlweg 4
D-8551 Röttenbach

G. Klebes
S.E.P.P. GmbH
Lohmühlweg 4
D-8551 Röttenbach

Dr. K.-D. de Marné
Cisigraph GmbH
Seidlstrasse 30
D-8000 München 2

Prof. Dr. Horst Nowacki
Technische Universität Berlin
Sekr. SG 10 – Geb. 12
Salzufer 17/19
D-1000 Berlin 10

Klaus Pasemann
c/o Volkswagen AG
Postfach
D-3180 Wolfsburg 1

Dr. Günther Pfaff
GTS-GRAL
Alsfelder Strasse 7
D-6100 Darmstadt

Terry Phebey
Computervision GmbH
Berg-am-Laim-Strasse 47
D-8000 München 80

Dipl.-Ing. Rainer Putensen
Tektronix GmbH
Sedanstrasse 13–17
D-5000 Köln 1

Dr. W. Renz
Daimler-Benz AG
Postfach 226
D-7032 Sindelfingen 1

Dr.-Ing. Richard Schuster
BMW AG
Postfach 400240
D-8000 München 40

Dr. Horst Seeland
Daimler-Benz AG
Technische Datenverarbeitung E7D
Postfach 202
D-7000 Stuttgart 60

Dietmar Trippner
BMW AG
Postfach 400240
D-8000 München 40

Dr.-Ing. Ernst Vöge
BMW AG
EW 4
Postfach 400240
D-8000 München 40

T. Weissbarth
Control Data GmbH
Tiergartenstrasse 95
D-3000 Hannover 71

Uwe Weissflog
IBM Deutschland GmbH
VU Industriesysteme
Maulbronner Strasse 25
D-7032 Sindelfingen

Dipl.-Ing. H. G. Wilfert
Daimler-Benz AG
Technische Datenverarbeitung E7D
Postfach 202
D-7000 Stuttgart 60

MIX
Papier aus verantwortungsvollen Quellen
Paper from responsible sources
FSC® C105338

If you have any concerns about our products,
you can contact us on
ProductSafety@springernature.com

In case Publisher is established outside the EU,
the EU authorized representative is:
Springer Nature Customer Service Center GmbH
Europaplatz 3, 69115 Heidelberg, Germany

Printed by Libri Plureos GmbH
in Hamburg, Germany